M000202327

More Praise for Said Dawlabani's
The Light of Ishtar

"I remember our first meeting. Elza brought radiant sunshine into the lives of those fortunate enough to have met her. As time reaps its toll on her being, Said helps us remember the outstanding service and wisdom that his beloved soulmate gave to the world. She is clearly a very special person, fulfilling her promise to help transform the Middle East where she was born. Said's story of her succumbing to the ravages of dementia and of his response to the devastating loss is so compelling that I read the book in one sitting. Highly recommended."

—Nancy Roof
Founder, *Kosmos Journal*

"As a psychologist, I was mesmerized by Said's attempt to make sense of Elza's powerful and sensitive voice being silenced in its prime. He tells the story of the tragedy with love and compassion in a lyrical and beautiful style, weaving through it Ishtar's timeless myth. The honesty and intimacy of the writing in an effort to understand that which cannot be understood makes this a book well worth reading. It is a love story. I could not put it down."

—Marjorie Coburn, PhD

"Not since Ken Wilber's *Grace and Grit* has a brilliant, sensitive man's memoir about his love for his ailing wife moved and taught me so much. If possible, Said Dawlabani's *The Light of Ishtar* is even more accessible. His strength and acceptance in the face of tragedy is profound."

—Sharron Brown Dorr
Retired publishing manager, Quest Books

"This book is an extraordinary testament to the full spectrum of the agony and ecstasy of the human experience. Said's and Elza's ecstatic and utterly delightful romance promises an experience of human and spiritual love in mythic dimensions. We hold our breath as we travel with them on a journey to the very heights of the possible. Through them we experience the rare fruition of our human potential in all its unreasonable joy. Then suddenly and equally without apparent reason, fate coldly steals it all away in the form of Elza's incurable illness. Said's irreconcilable grief at the loss of all he held dear—and with it the loss of access to higher meaning and purpose—catalyzes a profound inner reckoning to come to terms with the ultimate mystery of existence. This is a passionate love story that breaks our hearts and compels us to wrestle with life's deepest existential questions."

—Andrew Cohen
Teacher of enlightenment

"Rumi once said, 'Love is the bridge between you and everything.' *The Light of Ishtar* reaches to the very depths of one's soul by inviting the heart into a poignant journey of loss and recalibration. The transcendent love of Elza and Said bridges the impermanence of being with the extraordinary eternal nature of our essence and its connection to everything in existence."

—Diane Williams
Founder, the Source of Synergy Foundation; co-initiator, the Evolutionary Leaders Circle

"Elza Maalouf is a towering figure among the greatest of the world's peacemakers, and nothing is more important than making and keeping peace as humanity faces its critical opportunity to abandon hostilities in favor of global harmony. Bless Said for bringing her story and his to light in time to serve this human species' metamorphosis!"

—Elisabet Sahtouris, PhD
Evolution biologist and futurist; author,
Gaia's Dance: The Story of Earth and Us

"I was fascinated with the details of Elza's early life in Lebanon, drawn from her unpublished memoir – quite amazing! Her fight against patriarchy began early on, and rightly so. Eventually the beautiful, brilliant, and vivacious Elza meets Said, beginning their touching love story and dynamic, purposeful life together. Elza's work with Don Beck and Spiral Dynamics in the Middle East achieved so much, with Elza always advocating for the cause and equality of women. That the voice of this magical dynamo of a higher vision has been silenced is truly heartbreaking, while the courage of Said's love to bring the best for Elza is truly inspiring. It is a mythic story that indeed captures one's heart and mind—and it is a remarkable book."

—Olivia Hansen Founder, the Synthesis Foundation
and The Spiritual Life TV Channel

"Said's poignant memoir reminds us that the soul's essence lies beyond identity. As his love for his twin flame, Elza, transcends tragedy and self-interest, he finds that inner core where sorrow is tempered by the sacred ecstasy of feeling connected to the universal source and the cosmos."

—Deepak Chopra, MD
New York Times bestselling author

"*The Light of Ishtar* is a wondrous, true story of conscious partnership to cocreate Heaven on Earth. The lovers Elza and Said are driven by bliss, passion, and a heartfelt commitment to serve humanity. Transcending time, space, and even disease, their experience of a perpetual "honeymoon effect" offers us an opportunity to move beyond misperceived limitations and write new empowering stories for ourselves, our children, and the world. This book will inspire your spirit as you comprehend the enormous potential of applying its insights and wisdom to your life."

—Bruce H. Lipton, PhD
Bestselling author of *The Biology of Belief* and *The Honeymoon Effect*;
coauthor (with Steve Bhaerman) of *Spontaneous Evolution*

October 29, 2021

Dear Jamie,

Thank you for choosing to read our journey through life.

May your path always be filled with LIGHT!

Gus

Elza Maalouf, 2006

THE LIGHT OF ISHTAR

A Story of Love, Loss, and the Search for Meaning

SAID ELIAS DAWLABANI

Waterside Productions

Printed in the United States of America

First Printing, 2021

ISBN-13: 978-1-954968-18-9 print edition
ISBN-13: 978-1-954968-19-6 ebook edition

Waterside Productions
2055 Oxford Ave
Cardiff, CA 92007
www.waterside.com

To those who dispel the darkness with their light,
to my guru and teacher Kirpal Singh, who taught me to live the life
of soul, and to my friend and mentor, Dr. Don Edward Beck,
who taught me how to fight like hell for a better humanity

Mythology is not a lie, mythology is poetry, it is metaphorical. It has been well said that mythology is the penultimate truth—penultimate because the ultimate cannot be put into words. It is beyond words. Beyond images, beyond that bounding rim of the Buddhist Wheel of Becoming. Mythology pitches the mind beyond that rim, to what can be known but not told.

—Joseph Campbell, *The Power of Myth*

CONTENTS

ILLUSTRATIONS

FOREWORD

This story of my friend Elza Maalouf and her husband, Said Dawlabani, as he so eloquently relates it, takes you on a harrowing passage through life and myth, and I'd like to tell you why the journey is worth making. Aside from growing to admire and cherish them both, in the course of the book we become aware of the importance of aligning ourselves with our mythic dimensions in order to respond to even the cruelest of circumstances at the highest level we can achieve.

Myth, according to my late friend Joseph Campbell, provides a bridge between one's local consciousness and the universe, "the sheer vast, overwhelming environment of Being. It reconciles local, historical space-time with the transcendent realms and the eternal forms." Most importantly, myth fosters "the centering and the unfolding of the individual in integrity" with him – or herself, the culture, the universe, and ultimately with the creative Mystery that is "both beyond and within" the individual and "all things."[1]

We rarely believe that we live in mythic times and often forget our origin, the vast, untapped possibilities of mind, body, and spirit that reside in each of us. When an individual or a society is in a state of collapse and renewal—as we are today in dealing with a global pandemic—a new order is often required that only myth can provide. Myth, at the levels of the personal and the collective, the physical and the metaphysical, tells the compelling story of the possible human. It is full of horrible, beautiful, and awesome living patterns that can hasten, devastate, or transform the human endeavor at any time and at any place along life's turning.

Elza's and Said's story is a powerful example of how myth reflects and shapes our human experience. It is a reminder of those deep patterns that have repeated since time immemorial. Like many of us who answer the call to a transcendent adventure, the two of them emerge as the hero and the heroine on that journey. Their story awes us with how life follows myth and how, in the archetype of partnership, one can find his or her soulmate on their journey to communing with the archetypal union of the soul.

I would like to share with you the impression Elza left on me when I first met her almost two decade ago. A mutual friend wanted to introduce me to this young Arab American woman so that she could take part in one of my mentoring programs. The subject line of the email he sent about her read, "Watch out! She's a tornado." What followed in the body of his email was a cautionary tale: "She's serious about changing the Middle East and she needs your help."

Well, that outspoken woman didn't much need my help. She was an Athena in the making. From our first meeting, Elza dazzled those around her with her knowledge and her captivating presence. She was far wiser than her years as she spoke in words of ancient feminine wisdom. In a flash she could quote from the Bhagavad Gita or the wisdom of Avicenna or the philosophies of Al-Farabi. Her knowledge spanned a wide spectrum, from Jungian spiritual psychology and the archetypes to the mystical poetry of Rumi and Kabir. But nothing animated her more than when she spoke of ancient myth—particularly feminine myth and the urgency for us to reawaken Gaia, the goddess of the earth and the ancestral mother of all life.

For a decade and half, I witnessed Elza transform many powerful woman and men throughout the Middle East and elsewhere through her work. She became the embodiment of that force which empowers the feminine and a fierce and tireless advocate for the rights of women. Said perceptively recognizes Elza's mythic counterpart as the Mesopotamian goddess Ishtar, who, like Inanna and Aphrodite, is a goddess of fertility, love, and war. The story of Ishtar's love for her husband, Tammuz, is that of Isis and Osiris and of many other gods and goddesses, and we can find the thread of it in the moving romance of Elza and Said.

But this story is not to be taken lightly. Mythic journeys should not be perceived as interesting esoteric diversions. They are transformational experiences that include not only the search for the divine Beloved but the immensely potent themes of wounding, suffering, and loss. The story this book tells is one that repeats in every myth from every epoch. Ishtar's descent to the Underworld is the same as that of Inanna and Persephone; the lesson is one. In myth, it symbolizes the painful detachment from the material world, and in Jungian psychology, it is the recognition of the repressed and the disavowed aspects of the self. While the goddess's eventual emergence from the Underworld symbolizes immortality, it also serves to balance shadow and light in individuals and in culture. Or so the pattern goes.

The wounding can seem catastrophic beyond measure, a paradigm shift that nihilates our former sense of self, just as in the myth Ishtar is stripped of all her apparel as she passes through the seven gates of the Underworld. In Elza's life, on a mythic level that shift could be seen as the retaliation of the patriarchy against which Elza had fought so hard. Said relates that Michel, Elza's brother, has speculated that the gods don't want the Middle East to change. In any case, the cosmic blow that she suffered took the form of a debilitating brain disorder in the prime of her life. It was a devastating condition that progressively robbed her of her ability to think, to communicate, and to relate. Tragically, over a period of seven years she was transformed from a keynote actor on the world stage to an invalid who needs hourly care. The reader feels Said's torment as Elza is struck down by forces beyond their ability to comprehend, much less control, and they embark on a tortuous journey through the American medical system—which seemed like a descent to the Underworld in itself.

In 2015, during one of my visits to San Diego, Elza, Said, and I got together, as we often do when I visit the city. That's when I first noticed that something was amiss with Elza. The lioness who lived a mythic life, and always spoke of how she was transforming parts of the Middle East, sat silently. There was no talk about confronting the male ego or empowering the feminine in that region of the world. The year before, she had helped one of her clients make it to Forbes's list of the most powerful businesswomen in the Middle East. But instead of speaking about that, and her ongoing work, she sat somber and quiet.

Elza had lost her courage, and, although her medical symptoms were not fully known, the decline that I observed spoke volumes to the mythic forces she was battling. I had thought that, as in the myth of Ishtar, the heavy weight of the world Elza was battling was forcing her into the darker side of the psyche and that she would emerge from the shadow a much stronger person. But, alas, that was the last time I saw my friend. Over the next two years, she declined several invitations to share her wisdom with my students and her own colleagues. She avoided meeting me on my visits to San Diego, and by late 2017 she wasn't responding to any calls or emails.

Myth is full of tragedy, and Elza's and Said's story is no exception. It wasn't until 2018 that I heard from Said about the valiant battle they were both fighting, he with the medical establishment to restore her to health and she with the thief in the night—the disease that was robbing her of her essence and her beauty.

When disaster of such mythic dimensions strikes, this book asks, what is the highest response we can make? To submit, yes. To endure, yes. But beyond that, and as Said and Elza both demonstrate with extraordinary dignity, we can respond with courage, authenticity, and compassion. We can live at the level of one soul recognizing another despite all the finery having been stripped away. We can live at the level of two souls simply loving each other.

As Said probes the tragic dimensions of his and Elza's wounding, he shows us how to do the same regarding ourselves. He shows us how to discover the mythic dimensions of our own story in order to heal those aspects of our lives that have us trapped in a kind of frozen despair. In reading this book, align yourself with the mindfulness that places you at the heart of the story. It is in that place that you approach the soul and quicken your own journey and deepen your own path.

The problems we face today have been with us for centuries. Since the beginning of the Industrial Age, we have increasingly turned to the material realm and away from the mystery of life. Communication between the conscious and unconscious zones of the human psyche has been badly eroded by our concentration on external and superficial realities and by our denial of the deeper, inward world of spirit. Through all this, the soul has suffered most. It has either been abandoned as nonexistent or considered so ephemeral as to be unworthy of notice. Today, the estrangement has reached its limits, yet curiously there is new hope, for the void that estrangement creates commands us to become aware and conscious of our actions and seek deeper solutions to renew our lives. This book is a superb guide for how to do it.

The extraordinary life that Elza and Said live is an example of the soul unfolding, the rise of Ishtar and Tammuz. It is through the immanent image of our soul directed living that we discover ourselves as characters in the drama of the world soul, the *anima mundi*. The marriage of Elza and Said, like the marriage of Ishtar and Tammuz, is a marriage to the soul. While the union of gods and goddesses is associated with the marriage of Heaven and Earth, they also represent the merging of the souls of men and women who find a transcendent love in each other on their shared quest. It is this mythic journey so profoundly told on the pages of this book that gives the reader a glimpse of higher possibility, the possibility of living a mythic life.

Said Dawlabani makes a compelling and compassionate case for why very little else matters outside the realms of living a transcendent life. His telling of love, success, pain, and loss elevates experience to a much larger context in space and time—the home region of soul and spirit and of higher existence. It is there where we communicate with mythic beings of all kinds who tell the tale of our times. It is there where we try to come together again in a form that allows for larger and more soulful living, for a new order of partnership among men and women, different cultures, and the many varieties of conscious experience. The experiences that color the pages of this book, like the ones that life throws our way, should serve as the gateway to the reader's higher self. I encourage you to come on this harrowing journey. It is one of many that awakens the deeper inward world and raises the soul and brings it to the court of renewal, the place of light where we reconcile with our disavowed selves and heal our humanity.

In the archetypal hero's journey, the protagonist answers the call to adventure, journeys to the Underworld where he or she fends off demons, and then returns with a gift of wisdom that enhances the lives of everyone in the community. Elza Malouf's terrible disease might seem to have left her stranded in the Underworld, doomed to a sort of death in life, plundered of all her efficacy in the world. And so on one level it has done. But through the love of her soul partner, her larger-than-life personality and sparkling brilliance is restored to us. In this book, Said includes long passages of Elza's unpublished memoir in which we are able to hear her voice again in all its power and clarity before her illness stole it from her. This book itself—in its searing honesty, unfailing commitment to the beloved, and transforming acceptance of a fate that can be gently ameliorated but not changed—is indeed the gift of wisdom the hero has brought back to our entire human community. Read it and rejoice in the beauty and truth of these two souls even as, at the end of the day, Elza and Said can still dance to Rumi's tambourines in their garden by the sea.

—Jean Houston
Ashland, Oregon

ACKNOWLEDGMENTS

This book came as a result of a deep inward journey borne out of a consuming fire. Whom do I acknowledge when all meaning in life disappears and human frailty comes into greater focus? As I began to write this book, long-forgotten teachers reappeared with hands extended to remind me of what matters. It is in our darkest hour that we get to know who comes to our rescue and guides us back to the world with tenderness and profound consciousness.

I am eternally thankful to Jean Houston, who always sees the extraordinary and the mythic in us all. This book started as a collection of personal journals I kept as a record of my journey into the dark night. It was Jean's unwavering love, encouragement, and support that helped me expand them into what became this book. I am forever thankful to my friend and mentor, Don Beck. With a heart the size of Texas, he is the guardian angel without whom Elza and I would not have come this far. I also want to take a deep bow to Ken Wilber for his profound influence and courage in sharing his extraordinary journey with his wife Treya in his book *Grace and Grit*. Rereading that book fifteen years after I had read it for the first time became the inspiration that helped me explore the darkness and set my creative spirit free. I also want to thank Elza's and my friend Richard Dance, who appeared in our lives as a guide and a helper around the time Elza and I met. It was at his philosophical salons that Joseph Campbell came alive and awakened us to an extraordinary call to adventure. My soulful thanks also to our friend Graham Mummery, for his poetry and his love and compassion.

I want to thank my family for their boundless and unrelenting love. To my older brother Nassif, for his selflessness and for always being there to help us navigate the minefield of American medicine, and to Nickolas, my younger brother, for being the medical researcher who left no stone unturned in his ceaseless efforts to ease our burden. To my sister, Nuha, who offered to take care of us and cook our favorite meals, and to my mom who prays to the Virgin Mary every night for a miracle to ease our pain. To my late dad, Elias "Abu Nassif," who passed away at age ninety-five while I was in the middle of writing this book. "All you can do is love her" he said when he heard about Elza's illness. That was in 2016, and no therapist, doctor, or philosopher since has uttered more comforting words. May your rebel soul rest in eternal peace, Abu Nassif.

I want to thank my publisher, Waterside Productions, for believing in the power and the significance of my message. And, finally, I would be remiss if I didn't thank my editor and my most critical reader, Sharron Dorr, who fanned the flames of my fire and made it into a beacon of light. Without her tough patience, persistent hope, and gentle nudging, this book would have not been possible.

—Said E. Dawlabani
La Jolla, California
June 2020

I am Ishtar

For Elza and Said

I am Ishtar,
Goddess of love and war.
Heaven and Earth, I knew, were not enough.
I had to know the ways of the Underworld.

Alone I put on my bridal robes with lapis lazuli.
Alone I headed for the gatehouse to the Underworld.
The gatekeeper told me of seven gates I had to pass.
At each I was to surrender an item of my apparel.

At the first gate, he demanded the crown of my realm.
"Surely not that," I cried.
"It's the Law of the Underworld. It
must be obeyed," he replied.

At the second gate, he demanded my sceptre.
"Surely not that," I cried.
"It's the Law of the Underworld. It
must be obeyed," he replied.

At the third gate he demanded my choker from my neck.
"Surely not that," I cried.
"It's the Law of the Underworld. It
must be obeyed," he replied.

At the fourth gate he demanded my neck-
lace its gems, ripe fruit on my breasts.
"Surely not that," I cried.
"It's the Law of the Underworld. It
must be obeyed," he replied.

At the fifth door he demanded my ring with the seal on it.
"Surely not that," I cried.
"It's the Law of the Underworld. It
must be obeyed," he replied.

At the sixth door he demanded the
golden girdle above my hips.
"Surely not that," I cried.
"It's the Law of the Underworld. It
must be obeyed," he replied.

At the seventh door he demanded I surrender my robe and stand unadorned.
"Surely not that," I cried.
"It's the Law of the Underworld. It
must be obeyed," he replied.

Naked I went through the last door and stood before
The seven judges of the Underworld
And my sister Ereshkigal, its queen.
"You are guilty of hubris" they pronounced. "Death!
Your corpse will be hung out to the vultures."

On these words I shrivel into a death.
The vultures peck. … The worms chew. …
My sister gloats over my impaled body.
I barely remember my name.

I AM ISHTAR *For Elza and Said*

I no longer go out to war; I am a spoil of war.
I no longer make love.
Who would want to make love to a putrefying corpse?

In the worlds I knew before there is little light.
Lovers walk and sleep alone.
Flowers do not pollinate.
Grain does not grow.
From my father Anu's court,
I hear him say: "Ishtar sought to know
The ways of the Underworld from which nobody returns."

But Enki, god of wisdom and creation, is moved:
"No goddess should be reduced to this."
He sends two emissaries to take
Water of Life to salve my wounds,
Food of Life to feed my emptiness
So now I rise again to Earth and Heaven
Who rejoice at my return:
The lilies can bloom in gladness,
Hearts of lovers meet again.

I am Ishtar,
Goddess of love and war,
Who knows the ways of Heaven, Earth,
And the Underworld,
The star that sets in the evening
To rise each morning between dark and light.

—Graham Mummery
12 May 2020

INTRODUCTION

Ishtar was an ancient Mesopotamian goddess of love, fertility, and war. As the story goes, she decides to visit her sister, Ereshkigal, who is Queen of the Underworld. To enter the Underworld, as the preceding poem by poet and transpersonal psychotherapist Graham Mummery eloquently describes, the proud Ishtar must be stripped of all her clothing and accoutrements—divested of all the trappings that symbolize her identity—and proceed naked and completely vulnerable.

When she gets to the Underworld, Ereshkigal immediately kills her for her hubris, and all fertility on Earth dries up. Eventually Enki, the wily god of crafts, wisdom, and creation, contrives to restore Ishtar to the upper world, but the deal is that someone must take her place in the Underworld. She instructs the demons to substitute her husband, the agricultural god Tammuz, enraged as she is to find him sitting on her throne and not grieving her absence. Eventually Tammuz's sister, the goddess Geshtinanna, negotiates with the forces that be that she herself will spend six months in the Underworld so that Tammuz can return to Earth for the other half a year. In some versions of the myth, Ishtar and Tammuz reunite.

Like the story of Persephone in Greek mythology, the tale of Ishtar and Tammuz is one of cyclical death and rebirth linked to seasonal decline and abundance as well as to spiritual withdrawal and reemergence. I see it as the guiding metaphor for the story of my wife, Elza Maalouf, and me in our own journeys to the Underworld: Like Ishtar, Elza has been a renowned warrior. A lawyer by training, she has spent most of her professional career focusing on cultural and political reform in Palestine, Kuwait, Dubai, and Syria and especially on strengthening the rights of women in the Middle East. And with her inspiration and overwhelming influence in expanding my intellectual focus and spiritual vision, she has certainly been the goddess of love in my life. Where our story departs appreciably from the myth is that I, unlike Tammuz when he lost his wife to the darkness, did not fail to mourn. To the contrary, I have spent almost a decade—granted, just a blip in mythic time—wrestling with my own grief and demons as well as the medical profession to rescue her from fate and restore her to health.

This book is the story of that loss, of the struggle to reclaim the loss, and of the love that has endured despite all losses. It is about my personal account of the power of love. It's about the union of the self with the Higher Self that gives my life meaning and purpose. It's also an account of my personal challenge to cope with difficult change outside the traditional realms of comfort and modern-day therapy. It's about finding inner peace in the midst of an existential storm. It's about my own understanding of the universal laws of existence and identifying with our soul's brief journey in this world. It's about meeting the other and coming to the realization that serving a higher purpose is the ultimate goal of a union that goes beyond physical, emotional, and intellectual attraction. It is about transcending a personal reality defined by identity and impermanence to embrace a universal truth that is eternal and immutable.

Most essentially, this book is about my life with a passionate and powerful soul who was sent to this earth to fight injustice. Elza had laid out much of her vision for her rare calling in life in an unpublished manuscript she tentatively entitled *Lifting the Veil*. Throughout this book, I will share some of what she had written to shed light on the type of transcendent beliefs and values that drive an extraordinary person like her to find true meaning. Her purpose was to reject the complacency brought about by the material comforts that shroud our true purpose behind layers of silken veils. Her journey has been strewn with the obstacles of life and death and unexpected twists and turns that challenge those of us who sail the high seas and are never satisfied in the harbors of ordinary existence. Her battle has been with the patriarchal forces that have ruled over humanity since the dawn of the Abrahamic religions, the patriarchy of mythology and of men who have repressed the feminine aspects of the collective psyche. Along the way, the heavens have sent her helpers who have made her stand strong in a modern-day heroine's journey like no other. But the mythic life she led ended up exhausting her far before her time. Her unimaginable presence that unfolded before she reached the age of fifty awakened the patriarchal wrath and presented us with our *greatest* unintended life experience: a slow journey into the dark night of the soul that continues to shake us to the core to this very day.

But that is not the end of the story. It is true that the struggle remains amid the overseeing of Elza's health care and caregivers and the painful witnessing of her decline. There isn't a day that passes without me mourning the loss of what we once had amid the reluctant return to the ordinary with its a thousand-and-one other details of our daily existence. Today, the stillness of the ordinary and the routine has reappeared as a virtue. Today, underneath my pain and grief that began in 2014, there seems to be leavening of sorts—a return to the belief in eternal truth and divinity. Oftentimes we forget our transcendent nature and get lost in the physical world that consumes us. Yet in that physical existence, I see a light shimmering in the distance. It is what we have managed to find on our hard-fought journey through a long and dark night. At times it feels fragile and fleeting, yet the light remains ours.

1

A LIFE UPROOTED

Yesterday I was clever, so I wanted to change the world.
Today I am wise, so I am changing myself.
—Rumi

Not in a million years did I think this would be my next book. Not in a thousand lifetimes would I have thought that my writings would take on such an esoteric and ethereal form. Never have I thought that a return to faith and the embrace of myth would become a necessary passage that gave meaning to my new and unintended reality. Rarely have I thought that believing in mythical gods and psychological archetypes would again become a needed path for what has become my life's new journey. Stories from the great masters of the East to the perennial philosophers of the West that lent soulful meaning to my life in the past had until recently all been sidelined. Although that wisdom has had a big influence on my personal growth and helped shape who I am today, I hadn't felt the urge to revisit it in depth again. Until recently, this form of psychospiritual profundity had become confined to the myriad of books that belonged on forgotten shelves crowding the rooms and hallways of our home. Whenever I reached for answers within their pages, it was always to confirm my journey toward success and a fulfilling and rewarding life. Today, I spend my days devouring these same books looking for comfort among the faded lines and in notes made in margins that could provide relief from the darkness in which I find myself.

The direction my life has taken recently was not a part of a script my partner and I had crafted, nor did we have contingency plans to deal with an unpleasant reality of this magnitude. We had life and everything in it all figured out. We had all our bases covered, our "I"s dotted and our "T"s crossed. We were the masters of our own destiny, and together we had successfully charted an impossible journey. The world was our oyster, and the pearl within it was ours for the taking. We were young and foolish and blindly committed to solve the ills of humanity no matter their magnitude, no matter the geography. Nothing was going to stop us from pursuing our dreams and our commitment to make the world a better place.

Our egos soared with our newly found stature as published authors and when people familiar with our work conferred upon us the term *global change agents*. Our rise to prominence in our chosen field of work was meteoric as we were being exemplified as the modern-day power couple. I was working in the field of evolutionary economics, and my partner was working on bringing peace to the Middle East by helping its people and leaders understand the fundamental aspects of human and cultural change. We were both using a human-development framework that at one point was called the theory that explains everything. Known as Spiral Dynamics, its cocreator was Donald E. Beck, PhD, with whom we had worked closely for most of the last two decades. Dr. Beck in many circles is considered the master architect behind South Africa's transition from the apartheid system of institutionalized racism. After the events of 9/11, he sought to apply the same principles of evolutionary change to the Middle East. Under his genius guidance, my partner and I had become masters of the framework and its field applications. We were destined to become the rightful inheritors of this magnificent legacy. The oyster of our world was breaking its shell, ready to reveal its prized pearl.

Then the universe chuckled, as if it wanted to remind us of who's in charge. It is in that chuckling, in that uncontrollable power that exposes us to unpleasant life experiences, that today I am reminded of the frailty of human existence. In our carefully orchestrated life, there was rarely a need to dwell on the deeper meaning of such unintended experiences, falling as they did outside our positive and optimistic view of the world. Today, understanding them has become my soul's yearning. These types of passages that shake us to our core are known in spiritual circles as the passage of the soul through the dark night. This realm is where all perceived meaning collapses. It is where a violent and an unexpected intrusion comes into one's life and shreds it into meaningless, unrecognizable slivers of a once joyous existence. Suddenly, nothing we have known makes sense anymore, and everything we experience defies explanation. The perfect life we had created for ourselves seems to be in a perpetual collapse that prevents us from holding on to even the smallest fragment of meaning we had before. Ours was a life we had fashioned with great conscious awareness that gave deep significance to our activities and achievements. Today, all the things that gave us purpose and joy and set the parameters to what we considered important seem to collapse into one black hole from which there doesn't seem to be an easy escape.

These journeys of the dark night of the soul have visited me twice in my lifetime now. The first transpired about twenty-three years ago. It deeply shook my belief system to the core and sent me on a journey of self-discovery. As I emerged from that experience, I realized that very few things in my old world still made sense. Through my passage through the darkness, I found myself embracing new beginnings. Unbeknown to me, this was the start of an unpredictable journey, one that would eventually lead to deeper meaning and higher consciousness. It was toward the end of that journey that I met my partner and soul mate, Elza Maalouf.

To use a cliché, meeting her was like a match made in heaven. The gods had sent me a gift that was far bigger than I deserved. Suddenly, my life had new purpose that transcended everything I'd known before. From the day we met, I knew our lives would never be the same again. I knew that together we could be a force for good in the world. We could do our small part to help humanity, and for fifteen years we tried to do just that. All that would have not been possible without my first journey into the dark night that forced me to seek higher purpose and deeper meaning. For me to gain a deeper understanding of the transformative nature of such a journey, I had to understand the cost and the consequences of living an ordinary life when the life force within me, my karmic destiny and my calling, was commanding me to be extraordinary.

The Safe Harbors of a Virtuous Life

Like many people who vigorously pursue the American Dream, I believed I had it all figured out. I had meticulously followed the master plan for success, and it all began when my family landed on American soil in 1977. I was fifteen years old when we left Lebanon and moved to Boston. My siblings and I had been educated in an American school that was part of the regional Protestant mission that established the American University of Beirut, the oldest of its kind in the world. Other than being fluent in English, nothing could have prepared us for the culture shock we experienced when we moved to America.

To my surprise, upon our arrival in Boston I found that my childhood dreams had not made the trip. I had been delivered to a perfect new world where all my dreams had already been arranged, all my thoughts were already assorted, and all my virtues from then on were measured and weighed. What a strange thing to have experienced! Less than an hour after landing at Logan Airport, I heard these words that until this day still live in the recesses of my mind and that forever after have molded my life: "This is a finished world. Nothing is left to chance. This is a country of complete laws and pure order. Everything you do is covered by rules and guidelines of flawless accuracy. Follow these rules and work hard and you'll lead a happy life." This was the voice of our sponsor and my father's brother, Uncle Freddie. His words poured over me like a bucket of ice water would over a sleeping drunkard. It all transpired as we sat in the backseat of his gold 1972 Oldsmobile Cutlass headed to our new home. The ride on that rainy and sultry August evening turned into one of the longest journeys of my boyhood. From that day forth, I would no longer be allowed to draw on a blank white canvas. I could only stay within the confines of lines drawn by the greatest civilization and built on the hopes and dreams of immigrant families just like my own. On that August night, my childhood dreams were turned into a dull but virtuous reality. It shook me out of the deep slumber of youthful innocence and teenage rebellion and placed me into a world of structure and meaning.

Uncle Freddie was the family patriarch who had moved to Boston in the early 1950s and, to the dismay of his American wife, had sponsored many family members to come to the New World. His presence in our lives loomed large. There was no one my Dad admired more than Freddie, his oldest brother, whose birth name was Fareed. Just as millions of immigrants before him, upon his arrival to America Freddie had spent two weeks on Ellis Island. After his necessary quarantine, he was given papers with the name Fred and a shortened last name so that he could better assimilate into America's melting pot. A master tailor by trade, uncle Freddie always looked dapper in his own hand-tailored suits and camel-hair coats. He was the embodiment of an ordered life. For more than five decades, he punched the clock daily at the Filene's department store in downtown Boston. Every morning at 7:18 a.m., he walked out his front door on La Grange Street to catch the 34 East Forest Hills bus, which took him to the Orange Line train that dropped him off at Downtown Crossing, the heart of Boston shopping district. From there it was a hurried walk through a tunnel and up an elevator to the fifth floor of Filene's building. The elevator bell announced his arrival and that of many workers just a minute or so before the bells of nearby churches joined in a symphony announcing to the faithful of all faiths that the work day had begun.

My childhood innocence had been lost a few years before I became fifteen. Like all kids who grew up in Lebanon between 1974 and 1995, I had been deeply affected by the country's civil war. I had lost several close relatives and friends, and for several years our lives had been suspended between despair and hope, between death and life. The despair was the ever-present specter of death lurking ominously in the doorway of our ancestral home. The hope was for the fresh start that our sponsorship to America could provide. When we moved to the peaceful confines of United States, my parents hoped to restore some semblance of normalcy to our lives resembling the life they saw on American television programs such as "The Big Valley" and "Little House on the Prairie."

Boston was a divided city when we moved there. Violence, bigotry, and hatred expressed themselves in different forms than they did in Lebanon. The forced integration of public schools was ground zero for racial conflict at the time. We lived in the West Roxbury neighborhood, and our high school was in Roxbury. Although the names of the two communities sounded similar, the racial tensions between them told a different story. West Roxbury was primarily Irish, and kids my age projected their hatred on everyone else who wasn't. In my neighborhood I was beaten up and called the *N* word with the modifier *sand* in front of it. To my shock, one of my second cousins who was half Irish was consumed by the same hatred as he partook in verbal insults directed toward me and his own Arab heritage.

The racial composition of Roxbury, on the other hand, was diametrically opposite, but the hatred was just as deep. African-American kids in the neighborhood and in school used slightly less derogatory names toward my brother and me. Words such as *towel heads* and *camel jockeys* were hurled at us daily as we desperately tried to become invisible to avoid any forms of confrontation. Big fights at the school were brought to the principal's attention and were settled through physical prowess on the football field. The principal was a retired linebacker who had played for the New England Patriots and, as I learned in later years, had accepted this job only on the condition that he hire other ex-football players as teachers, administrators, and coaches in anticipation of racial violence at the school.

The contrast between this school and the small private school in Lebanon I had attended couldn't have been greater. In addition to the fear of daily harm, I was in shock at the size of the student body and the absence of meaningful academic standards. Fear, bewilderment, and confusion haunted me on every school day until one unexpected event took place: On a gloomy, snowy day, I was called to the principal's

office. Word had gotten to him that I had been correcting my geometry teacher, Mr. Antonellis, who had no business teaching geometry.
Mr. Antonellis could not tell the difference between a scalene triangle
and an isosceles triangle. Nevertheless, I was filled with fear as I waited
for the principal to speak. But when he did, he said, "Would you like
to earn some college credit while waiting to graduate?"

I couldn't believe my ears. To my surprise, that same question
had been asked of my older brother, Nassif, earlier in the day. We
were both elated. We didn't care that we had to walk through snow
and sleet across the football field and through one of Roxbury's
worse housing projects to get to classes on the other side of the
train tracks. Northeastern University saved us both from the slings
and arrows of an all-consuming racial divide. My brother and
I accumulated enough college credits in high school to go on to
graduate from college in three years.

Figure 1.1. The Dawlabani family at Nickolas's medical-
school graduation, 2004. Left to right: I myself; father, Elias;
brother, Nickolas; mother, Jamileh; brother, Nassif.

After college, Nassif went on to medical school and became a pediatrician; and, in later years, my younger brother, Nicholas, who had been born my last year in high school, also went to medical school and became a researcher in pediatric medicine. Unlike the two of them, right after college I started a career in real estate. For me, the ordered life began in earnest. This impressed Uncle Freddie but not my dad, who wanted all three of his boys to become doctors. I instead chose a career in the pursuit of wealth and the American Dream as I built a successful real-estate business in downtown Boston and at age twenty-six married my first wife, Rebecca. We were not in love, but we had two daughters, Chloe and Quinn, and the duty of being parents kept us together for nine years.

Figure 1.2. With my two daughters, Chloe (left) and Quinn, Easter, 1994.

In my chosen career, I had always balanced the routine and the mundane with the creative and the inventive. The dull monotony of brokerage and management responsibilities was offset by a healthy dose of creative work in the restoration of historic brownstones and the redesign of outdated spaces. The dullness was a necessity, and the creative was the escape that gave life meaning and balance.

But this fragile balance did not last. A decade into my chosen profession, the pursuit of financial success had become my sole preoccupation. The creative had given way to the dull, and I found myself increasingly uninterested in a meaningless office routine, regardless of how good the money was. In the twelfth year of my career, I sold my business and moved my young family to the Sonoran Desert, where sun, freedom, and creative opportunities abound. But alas, after a few years in Arizona pursuing my passion and creativity through meaningful work, happiness remained elusive—not because of the work itself, but because of all the other things I was ignoring while focusing on success.

The one issue I ignored the most was one that has been with me since childhood: I grew up with an alcoholic father, whom no one in the family dared to confront. He was what experts call a "functioning alcoholic." The verbal abuse he inflicted on us was hidden from the outside world. It festered just beneath the surface of what looked normal. Then, like the morning mist, it disappeared with the dawn of each day. After I married Rebecca, I discovered that she, too, had a problem with alcohol. Just as I grew up with the shame we felt in talking about my dad's drinking, I felt shame in talking about Rebecca's, which prevented me from seeking professional help. Instead, I chose to spend long hours in my office, hoping that the drinking would go away on its own. All that changed when too much drinking began to present a danger to our children. One day, some family members and I staged an intervention to get Rebecca into a rehab program. But she remained in deep denial of her problem, and after throwing our relatives out of the house that evening she had the police forcibly remove me from my home and family.

That night, the universe took everything I had built with my own hands and set it all on fire.

The First Journey into the Dark Night

The divorce was ugly, and our young children were traumatized by the ordeal. For two years, this unplanned journey into the dark night of the soul and the subconscious tore at everything I had known and loved. What I experienced during that time could only be described as an existential crisis, as the narrow window through which I had seen the universe gradually opened wider. Success in one area of life had unintentionally led me to vast areas that had previously remained outside my realm of conscious awareness. In the midst of that darkness, I began to question everything, and the more I questioned, the more unresolved issues appeared. Was I blindly pursuing success to prove my father wrong? If success was measured in financial terms, then my career in real estate had proven to be as lucrative as the field of medicine was. Yet, why had I failed to gain my father's approval? Did my choice of the woman I married have anything to do with how I saw my mother and what my perception of a caring parent was? If there had been any stability in my childhood, it was due to my mother's unyielding commitment to provide a nurturing and loving home. Like my mom, Rebecca was very content with rearing children. Did my eagerness to find the stability my mother provided make me overlook Rebecca's tendencies to drink? In a strange way, I began to uncover the weak self within me, the younger me who was shy and afraid and eager to please in order to gain acceptance and to avoid confrontation. I soon discovered that this was one of my default settings. It had to do with what Jungian therapists Hal and Sidra Stone call the "Primary Self," and my Primary Self in particular was what they call the "pleaser"[1] who defended human weaknesses—including alcoholism—as conditions that needed protection and love, when in reality what they needed was professional help and support.

Since very little in life made sense anymore, I began to question many of the assumptions I had about purpose and meaning. Nothing was left unexamined. What had made perfect sense in the past began to make far less sense during this period. My leisurely activities with friends and colleagues became increasingly mundane and uninteresting. I found more pleasure in reconnecting with poets and old dusty books than with bankers on a golf course. The drive for outer success had given way to a fuller world of inner enrichment and self-knowledge. Although nothing was said, my friends noticed the change, offered their opinions, and recommended a few books that could help ease my predicament. Of the books I read during that time, two became my companions through the early stages of my journey: Viktor Frankl's *Man's Search for Meaning* and Harold Kushner's *When Bad Things Happen to Good People*. The former helped put my experience in perspective, while the latter showed me the meaning of pain as a spiritual path for growth.

As I was going through these changes, my preferences for personal relationships began to change as well. Women whom I had found attractive a few years earlier I now had very little in common with. Power, pedigree, and outer beauty were a thing of the past. So was the satisfaction with the American Dream and all its superfluous extensions. Yet nothing in my new reality assured me of finding a higher purpose or a loving partner who appreciated the life changes I was going through. Like other facets of my life during this period, I decided to let go of my need for female companionship and trust the journey. This wasn't easy, as I had to overcome the fear of being alone. I had to quiet the voices of insecurity and feelings of inadequacy that were calling me back to the safety of my old life. These decisions added to all the unknowns and unrecognizable ambiguities to which I was surrendering. But, as scary as they were, with them came a new and exciting call to adventure. It was like a deluge that couldn't be stopped, as if I were standing in the rushing waters of a river and having to learn to let the torrents of life, past and present, go through me. Maybe it was the universe with its unknown mysteries pushing me forth. The past—with its limits meticulously planned, quantified, and measured to the point of blameless accuracy—became dull, mundane, and uninteresting. The future, although unknown and full of risks, spoke to me louder than any other voices ever had. Once I learned to trust the storm of my journey and let go of expectations and fear and embrace the unknown, the most wonderful thing that ever happened to me came knocking at my front door. Her name was Elza.

The Life of Possibility

Legend and myth often speak of the power of love and how it moves mountains and makes men do crazy things. It is a human emotion that transcends rational thought. It effects the unity of one's Self with another. It affords a glimpse of the possible that comes at a time when all around us seems impossible.

When I was thirty-six, a deeper love for life opened my eyes with its mysterious potion and touched my aching soul with its smoldering fingers. It was as if the goddess Ishtar herself had smiled upon me and awakened my spirit with her divine beauty. She had fashioned from herself an earthly splendor in the shape of a woman named Elza. She had empowered her with affection that contained the secrets of universal love that she sang with every movement of her lips. Only the luckiest of men have an "Elza" who appears in their lives as an unexpected answer to an unspoken prayer. She fills their loneliness with delight and makes their days pass by like dreams and their nights like an endless celebration. Few are those who are given the rare love that completes the union of the soul and the heart that makes the impossible possible. I was one of those lucky few.

Figure 1.3. Elza and I, 2000.

Before we met, I had been a rudderless soul languishing in obscurity, with no purpose other than to make money and accumulate material possessions. Elza, on the other hand, had been a force for change since the day she was born, and because of that she had always fought with the forces of the universe that opposed her. She had come with a mission, as if she had been predestined to fight for justice and the empowerment of women. She had stood up to patriarchal dominance her whole life. Like me, she had been born in the Middle East, where patriarchal authority permeates the wide expanse of the region. Repression of the feminine aspects of the universe is not unique to that part of the world. It has been one of humanity's greatest shortcomings since the dawn of Abrahamic religions. Even before then, stories from myth often vilified the feminine. This was a knowing of the women who would forever change the trajectory and purpose of my life. Many people around the world who know Elza believe that she has been a rare, modern-day warrior—a heroine fighting such historic forces—and are convinced that this has been her calling.

The Dark Night Returns

Our journey toward the life of possibility began to take an unexpected turn in 2014. It has been a slow, painful, and involuntary transition that has shaken my faith in every known truth I have encountered. It is a journey that makes grieving an unending process. How can a person process grief over any loss when the experience itself violates the loosest clinical definition of grief? How does one grieve the loss of essence of soul and of mind and spirit while the physical presence remains? People who are more grounded in their spirituality might say that the experience should be my teacher and that the lesson needs to be learned slowly over the span of many years. What has been upsetting is that Elza and I have been through parallel spiritual awakenings—our own baptisms by fire, so to speak—to get to where we were in life. This should have satisfied the heavens and given us safe passage to do our small share in contributing to humanity's welfare. What was happening was a clear violation of that universal covenant. The transformational lessons that placed us on this journey had already been learned, but the pain of what is happening today is too much to bear and too great to ignore.

I have repeatedly asked myself why I am in denial about what is going on. Has my ego and deep attachment to the work we were doing made inward reflection impossible? Have I forgotten who we are in relation to the great cosmos? Is it really the gods who became angry with Elza and decided to punish her and have me witness her painful decline as my own punishment for some unknown karmic debt I incurred in a past life? Or is this catastrophe supposed to be another lesson for my growth? Why has this new phase of our lives rendered me so weak? Why can't I explain to family and friends what it feels like when my beloved struggles to greet a friend or fails to answer a simple question?

For three years, such questions reflected the silent sorrow I carried, too embarrassed to share and too weak to overcome them. Then one night, at my darkest hour, I woke up from a strange dream, silently repeating the phrase "follow your bliss."[2] These were the words of American mythologist Joseph Campbell, whose teachings Elza and I had embraced as part of our transformational experiences and personal growth. Elza had discovered in earlier years that her bliss was in her ability to transform whomever she came in contact with into a better person. And I discovered that my bliss was in my ability to communicate through the tip of a pen or the strokes of a keyboard. It is in following my bliss that I was compelled to write this book while being a witness to my own pain and sorrow.

I write because it is who I am. I write because it is the most effective form of therapy I have known. I write because it is my inner growth made manifest. I write because I want my grieving words to tell those who are going through similar experiences that they are not alone. I write so those who are worthy of being remembered are not forgotten. I write because I want to feel deeply and love unconditionally. I write because it's an act that unites the heart and soul of the human race. I write so the life force in me knows that, when the powerful tale of the human journey is told, in my own little way I will have had a chance to contribute a line.

2
DAUGHTER OF THE PATRIARCHY

Me the woman he has filled with dismay...
Has filled me, the queen of heaven, with consternation...
I, the woman who circles the land—tell me where is my house,
Tell me where is the city in which I may live...
I, who am your daughter... the hierodule, who am your bridesmaid—
tell me where is my house...
The bird has its nesting place, but I—my young are dispersed,
The fish lies in calm waters, but I—my resting place exists not,
The dog kneels at the threshold, but I—I have no threshold...
—Epic of Gilgamesh

There are as many versions of Elza Maalouf as there are people who know her, and this version is about the Elza I know. She is the woman I have loved and treasured for two decades. The one who transformed my life in the most loving and mysterious ways. I have thought long and hard about the content of this chapter and whether or not I can do justice to who she is and the transcendent powers she represents. Indeed, I don't have that skill, nor can I begin to understand the divine nature of her presence in my life and in the lives of so many others. Hers is such a rare existence among us that the joys and the sorrows she brings are deeply felt and multiplied. Of course, we all express our biases when we speak of those we love, and I'm no exception. Throughout this book, I will speak from that place of love, but I will also allow Elza's own voice to speak, the voice that shows her greater transcendent purpose that she shared only with a few people. It was just recently that she had allowed me to read her personal journals and agreed to let me share some of their content. In addition, I will share some of her own perspective on life and the destiny that drove her from the unpublished manuscript of her book *Lifting the Veil*.

The Soul of a Warrior

The Elza I know is a heroine like no other. As her friend and colleague Dr. Don Beck describes her, "She came ready." Until recently, I had my own understanding of what that statement meant when he uttered it many years ago, but Elza's journal revealed an entirely different dimension. According to what she wrote there, his remark had been in response to her telling him she had been waiting her whole life for a genius like him to appear so that together they could make a significant difference in the problems of the Middle East. With Elza, nothing is ordinary.

From the West Bank and Israel to Kuwait and the United Arab Emirates, and from the Kurdish region of Iraq to the remote town of Bosra in southern Syria, people around the world know Elza Maalouf primarily for pioneering the use of Integral Theory and the Spiral Dynamics frameworks in the Middle East. Bosra in later years became ground zero for the Syrian civil war after the government failed to act on the recommendations of many of the human-development groups, including the one Elza was the head of—the Center for Human Emergence Middle East.

Figure 2.1 With the women of Bosra, 2007. Elza is second from the right.

Integral Theory and Spiral Dynamics are cutting-edge models that offer comprehensive approaches to solving the chronic issues that have historically plagued the region. Integral Theory is the brainchild of American philosopher Ken Wilber that offers a full and holistic approach to seeing and assessing problems. It's inclusive, balanced, and comprehensive. The model brilliantly weaves different disciplines and most known forms of human inquiry into one comprehensive map of human capacities. Spiral Dynamics creates a similar map based on levels of psychosocial development of individuals, groups, and cultures. The framework removes obstacles such as biases, ideologies, religion, and race and reframes challenges through the eight hierarchically ordered levels of development that form the Spiral. The theory is the creation of Dr. Don E. Beck and his associate and former graduate student, Christopher C. Cowan.

Beck and Cowan distilled the original academic work of Clare W. Graves, professor of developmental psychology at Union College in Schenectady, New York, into what became Spiral Dynamics. Graves was a colleague of Abraham Maslow, originator of the *hierarchy of needs* theory; according to Dr. Beck, the two shared many of their research subjects and were frequent guest lecturers in each other's classrooms. By the time Beck and Cowan had discovered Graves, he was in poor health and couldn't pursue his dreams of applying his theoretical work in the field. Under Graves's direction, Beck and Cowan began to apply his research into applications and chose to do so in South Africa. Elza chose to work with Beck because of his renown in using Graves's research and Spiral Dynamics to help South Africa transition from apartheid.

Tens of thousands of practitioners use both models in Western cultures, but nowhere has their application been more profound than in the Middle East.[1] Lucky are they who have the capacity to understand the full meaning of these frameworks, and luckier still are they who work with the frameworks' creators in applying them to solve real problems. Elza has been one of those lucky few.

Advocating for solutions based on these models was nothing new for someone whose life-long endeavors had rarely involved the acceptance of linear thinking that perpetuated the status quo. From childhood, Elza has always had that rare combination of rebellion and intelligence that sees a resilient simplicity beyond a foreboding complexity. This was especially true when politicians and people in power lulled the masses into accepting the status quo when, for many, injustice loomed just beneath the surface. For example, Elza has often referred to the actions of one of Lebanon's own political leaders who quietly oppressed the people of his own religious sect. When reporters asked the politician about his policies for not allowing any schools to be built in his region, his response was that there was no need for community-wide education; it was enough that his own son was being educated, and they should all rest assured that they would be taken care of. That absence of education was in the Shia community of southern Lebanon, and Elza believed it was one of the contributing factors that birthed Hezbollah.

Elza was born with a thirst for knowledge that is complex and cumulative. She didn't come to believe in the power of Integral Theory and Spiral Dynamics by accident but by methodical evaluation of their merits, which she combined with a rare spiritual awareness. These frameworks somehow contained all the knowledge she had acquired and elegantly organized it into a context that *explains everything*. It is the richness of her knowledge and her previous life experience that made these two frameworks so powerful for her.

There are over two thousand books that line the bookshelves of our home. I can honestly say that I'm familiar with the content of less than three hundred of them. Mine span the range of authors from Malcolm Gladwell and Thomas L. Freidman to my favorite poets and authors such as Kahlil Gibran and Ralph Waldo Emerson. In recent years, I've added books that address economics, complexity theory, and systems thinking. My latest additions are books on climate change. Others in my collection deal with other contemporary issues, but nothing of mine comes close to the diverse topics contained in the remaining books that represent the rich reservoir of Elza's knowledge and depth of her wisdom. There's a book for every subject one can think of—from contemporary leadership issues to deep esoteric topics on religion and the knowledge of the soul; from *Al Mathnawi,* the complete six-volume set of the collected works of Jalal Din Rumi written in Arabic to Raphael Patai's *The Jewish Mind;* from Michael Shermer's *The Believing Brain* to Sylvia Brinton Perera's *Descent to the Goddess;* from Flynt Leverett's *Inheriting Syria* to Bruce E. Wexler's *Brain and Culture*—and every subject in between.

Elza read constantly and studied at length. We had multiple shelves reserved for her favorite authors, from Joseph Campbell to Ken Wilber and Jean Houston and Deepak Chopra, some of whom she knew and worked with personally. There's an entire bookcase reserved for psychology and spirituality, where one can spend months exploring the works of C. G. Jung, Alan Watts, and the many saints and teachers of Eastern philosophy with an extensive collection on the subjects of mystic poetry, the science of the soul, and the law of karma.

Before embracing Integral Theory and Spiral Dynamics, Elza lived in the rich world of Eastern philosophy and mythology. Before Wilber and Beck, there were Rumi and Campbell. Even before them, there were the French existentialists and the Arab poets. Poetry runs in her blood. There are many poets from her Maalouf family who contributed to the Arab intellectual renaissance during the post-colonial period of the twentieth century. The annual gathering of Maalouf poets at Elza's ancestral home was the literary event of the season. Elza's earliest memory of her life is one of those events. Here's how she described it in her manuscript:

> I was two years old, and my oldest brother, Michel, was getting ready to recite his latest poem at the annual family gathering. He had already been anointed the family genius. At age nine, he had won several awards for poetry. Men filled every square inch of our living room, each taking his turn to recite his own poem.
>
> I wasn't having any of it. I went to the kitchen and dragged my mother's footstool, pushed my boy cousins out of the way, and placed myself in the middle of the room. Men and boys laughed

at me, but not my mom. She scolded everyone for their actions and then helped me to my own little dais, where I towered over my cousins. After quieting the room, she nodded her head and I began my recital. It was four words of rhyming gibberish that only a two-year-old could compose. The entire room broke into laughter, which made my mom angry. She ordered them all to stop, and those who didn't she asked to leave. That night, the woman who bore me became my first ally in my long fight against the patriarchy.

Kana Ma Kan

Fighting the patriarchy is a theme that has run throughout Elza's life. It is something that came to her as a calling and a knowing. She always sensed that her life had a bigger purpose and deeper meaning. What drove her in her earlier years, she thought, were factors that were a product of her environment; but, after suffering tragic personal losses, she found meaning that transcended the physical realms. That's when Eastern philosophy, the concept of karma, and the power of myth became a central part of who she is. That's when she discovered the archetypes that steered her passions, the awesome burden of karmic debt, and the gods and goddesses who helped her define her larger – than-life destiny. She believed that these were the same mystical forces that also admonished her for violating their heavenly rules of conduct. Here's how Elza describes her predestined journey to the physical world, the determining forces when her mother, May, gave birth to her, and what ultimately shaped her life:

KANA MA KAN—there was, there was not—long ago and far away in a place beyond space and time, on heavenly plains where gods and goddesses roam, the divine assembly was called to order. Gods and goddesses from every pantheon had gathered. The board ran endlessly with deities taking their seats in accordance with their heavenly rank. Those representing the matriarchy sat on the left, and the deities of the patriarchy sat on the right. Commotion and confusion filled the air, as storm clouds and lightening filled the heavens. Then, with one strike of his staff, Anu, the Supreme God, the source of all authority, brought silence to the heavens. With a roaring voice that shook all of creation, he said, "I demand to know. Who called this meeting?"

The goddess Athena rose from her seated position immediately to his left. "It was one of my own. She is none other than your daughter, Ishtar. I will let her speak."

Ishtar rose: "For months I've been hearing the prayers of a group of simple women in a small town in Lebanon for their friend, May, the mother of three boys. They plead: God, please give May a girl who can bring joy back to this poor woman's life. Their prayer was piercing and filled the firmament of my dominion, and I had to act."

"A feminine godly presence in the region of the world?" asked Anu as the patriarchy roared with laughter.

Athena rose again. "It is time," she declared as silence fell.

Debate ensued for eons, and deals were made and became memorialized in the heavenly record: May's daughter will have many obstacles to overcome. She cannot challenge too much of the power of the patriarchy. She will be given helpers, but she must understand her limits. If she doesn't take heed, the patriarchy will mete out punishment at its discretion.

With these conditions, the deities went to work. Anu separated a spirit from himself and gave it to Athena. The goddess took exceptional care of her precious gift, granting the soul of the baby girl virtue, strength, and courage and fashioning her into Beauty. She bestowed upon her wisdom from the heavens and placed in her heart an eye that sees the injustices of the physical world. She empowered her with goodness and affection toward all creation. Angels dressed the soul in clothes woven of hope and rainbows. As she descended from the heavenly plane, she wore the darker garments of mortality that prepared her for the physical world of life and death.

The Supreme God then took fire from the furnace of rage and punishing winds from the realms of ignorance. He reached into the cauldron of hypocrisy and selfishness, fashioned a flaming sphere of malevolence, and gave it to the patriarchy. The patriarchy bristled with contentment. Then God laughed and cried.

This passage was followed by a few pages of esoteric terms that Elza had mastered in her studies of Eastern philosophy and the role of karma. In these pages, she describes the journey of the soul through the different spiritual realms before it arrives at its final destination, the realm of physical existence in human form. Here's her description of the circumstances that surrounded her birth:

It was as if there were a tug of war between the patriarchal gods and the mythological goddesses disputing the outcome of May's pregnancy—the men wanting a fourth boy and the women hoping and praying for a girl. I believe my sense of purpose was created in those moments, as my soul was forming in my mother's womb.

My earthly journey began with my birth at the Tel Chiha Hospital in Zahle. It is said that on this treed knoll, sometime in the thirteenth century Prince Rizk of Bani Hilal burned his daughter Chiha at the stake believing that she had betrayed her family's honor. Till this day, the memory of her fate is preserved at Tel Chiha Hill, a reminder of the traditional tribal values of honor killings and ancestral loyalties—often upheld at the expense of girls and women—that continue to shape the Arab mind and heart till this day.

The morning of my birth, my father, who rarely left his lumber mill, had his driver take him up the hilly avenue to the large hospital overlooking Zahle. He sat outside the delivery room waiting for the news. "Mr. Maalouf, *Mabrouk!* Congratulations! You have a baby girl!" said the nurse. To that my father replied flatly, "I was hoping for a fourth boy, but whatever God provides we accept."

He hurried back to work weighed down by his growing family and the fact that his wife had just given birth to a girl. My father keenly felt the burden of a daughter. In his mind, just as in the collective mind of the culture in this part of the world, a girl brings only few returns. He would have to support me until I married, at which point I would follow my husband and become loyal to *his* family. On the other hand, sons—my father had three— would grow up to support his parents and help him with his business. Although we lived in modern times, the birth of another boy would also have meant the birth of a warrior always on the ready to fight nearby tribes should the ancient winds of hate and ignorance sweep in from the surrounding mountains. Since a girl couldn't fight, she was a burden. These were the values and the morals of a culture frozen in time, beholden to archaic traditions of questionable origins. Into that fray of injustice and patriarchal dominance was I thrown.

Elza would often speak about how she saw unfairness and injustice as imprints that directed her unconsciously from an early age. Her family's favorite story to share about her took place when she was five years old: taking her Christmas money, she walked to her uncle's clothing store, dragging behind her an entourage of poor kids and demanding that they be given nice clothes. She confidently placed the crumbled gob of Lebanese pounds at the cash register. It mattered not that her capital couldn't buy a single pair of socks. She stood blocking the entrance, face all puckered and hands on hips, until he relented.

Figure 2.2 Elza's family, 1972. From left: father, Said; brother, Habib; mother, May; Elza, age seven; and brother, Ghassan.

Her life before the age of eighteen is full of similar stories that in retrospect put her calling in greater perspective. One of profound impact occurred when Elza was sixteen and the publisher of the city's oldest newspaper recruited her to write a weekly column about the issues facing the youth in the town. She had caught his eye when he heard her recite a poem cleverly masking public corruption in rhyme at a public event, one of many she had written herself. It was one of her first stories published in that newspaper that forever altered the direction of her life and her relationship with her father and the patriarchy. Here's how she tells the story and about the transformational effect it had on her journey:

Everyone at home was running around frantically preparing for the arrival of the guest of honor. My brothers made sure everything inside and outside our front gate were in perfect condition. This was the man whom the entire Maalouf clan had supported in his run for office to represent our town in the Lebanese Parliament. My brothers announced his arrival, spotting his black limousine from the balcony on the second floor. At the gate, he motioned to his bodyguards to return to the car and wait.

Ahla Beyk—"Welcome, Your Honor"—was the phrase repeated several times as the member of Parliament parted the crowd in our large living room just as Moses had parted the seas. After a few minutes spent sipping Turkish coffee, he asked my dad for my whereabouts.

"So, you're Elza!" said the parliamentarian as he laughed. "You're so young. Where do you come up with this rubbish you write?" He turned to my dad: "You're not letting her young mind be corrupted by those evil communists, are you, Khaweja Said?"

To this intrusive inquiry, my mom immediately answered, "She is free to write about whatever she wants, Your Honor."

I wasn't sure what caused the man to become visibly upset at that moment. Was it what my mom said, or was it that my dad had failed to control the two females in his life in a world ruled by men?

24

The law maker turned to my dad in complete shock. "Are you going to let this stand?"

My dad answered calmly, "Your Honor, don't forget that the Maaloufs are one of the founding families of this town. We have protected it for three hundred years, and we're the ones who made it possible for families like yours to live in safety and prosperity here. Zaza can write about whatever she wants. Politicians who are not corrupt have nothing to worry about."

At that moment, I knew my dad had become my ally, one of the first and most important helpers along my early journey.

That night, I saw a different, more mature form of love from both parents. They had shown me the road forward and began to pave it with tenderness and unwavering support for their girl, defying the corrupt men who ran the country and the archaic patriarchy that informed them. It was on that night that I decided to become a human-rights lawyer and fight for justice for woman and against injustice everywhere. I could become a judge. I could run for Parliament. The possibilities were endless as I stood at the threshold of adventure.

A Heroine's Journey

Elza became obsessed with Joseph Campbell's work. After she became familiar with his writings, she started to frame everything in her life through the prism of what he called the hero's journey. The basic plot of the journey looks like this: A call to adventure propels a person on a quest whereon he or she passes a threshold into the unknown realm of the supernatural. There helpers and foes are encountered and trials and tribulations are faced; eventually, the hero overcomes all obstacles and returns home with a gift of knowledge or wisdom that benefits the entire community.[2] Elza fashioned several executive training programs based on the steps of the journey and even went to the extent of adapting the evolutionary models of Spiral Dynamics and Integral Theory to the steps and stages that we all face as heroes and heroines in our lives. Her ability to understand the role of myth in life was at the center of the transformational nature of her work and of who she is. The constant reminder of the higher purpose in one's life is what steered her passions. She often mused about the nature of the helpers the universe had sent her, especially the ones that appeared to help her with her specific calling.

Like most humans who choose to transcend ordinary existence, in addition to myth Elza subscribed to spirituality and the study of the unconscious. That's where those who choose to accept their calling align themselves with what Joseph Campbell calls the "rapture."[3] In this state, we leave the safety of the ordinary and sail the high seas of adventure. It is also the state in which we give in to our karmic destinies and place ourselves at the mercy of the gods. In framing her life through myth and karma, Elza believed that the support of her parents in beginning to facilitate her journey to become a change maker is what angered the patriarchy and presented her with the series of tragedies and setbacks that derailed her journey:

I graduated first in my class and scored second in my region on the national baccalaureate examinations required to graduate high school. No one was happier than sister Angelle, the head nun at my Catholic school. She boasted to other students about how I was the pride of Zahle. On her frequent visits to our home, she discussed my future with my parents. "If she's serious about the law, then the best place for her to go is the Sorbonne in Paris," she said repeatedly to my parents.

Lebanese law is based on the Napoleonic Code enacted when Lebanon became a French protectorate after the collapse of the Ottoman Empire. France gave the country its constitution, and there were two choices for my education: the Sorbonne in Paris or Saint Joseph University in Beirut. I decided to submit applications to both schools. The last thing that was needed was my dad's financial disclosures.

What happened as we sat at the bank waiting for the manager to produce the paperwork would come to change our lives forever. I could see the trepidation on her face as she brought in my dad's accounts. "I'm sorry," she said, "there isn't enough in all the accounts for the guarantee."

My mom and I were in shock and disbelief. We were rich. It had to be a mistake.

"I've been meaning to call you, May," the manager went on. "Khaweja Said has brought in many people over the last few months and lent them most of his money. I thought you knew."

Mom and I became numb as the banker kept pointing to the different account entries and the dates. We both turned to my dad for an answer, but he couldn't recall taking any of these actions. Ten days later, he was diagnosed with Alzheimer's disease.

My dad's illness plunged the whole family into darkness. The life we had all known had come to an end. My mom suffered a nervous breakdown and had to be hospitalized for a week. I remained in shocked disbelief for months. Sadness spread throughout the entire Maalouf clan and extended to those who knew us in Zahle, Beirut, and beyond. My older brother Michel had to drop out of his medical studies in France, and Habib and Ghassan had to abandon their lives and careers to attend to my dad's business. Everyone turned bitter and resentful for the fate that had found us. My brothers' sadness turned to anger when they discovered that, in addition to giving his fortune away, my dad had borrowed money and offered our home as collateral. Things couldn't have been any worse. This was the work of a vengeful god, and the damage was beyond belief. The man who had set the example for success and progress for us all had been struck by a disease that reversed all of our fortunes. The bravest helper that the universe had sent me lay wounded and disabled. The patriarchal gods had struck. They had drawn first blood, and the damage was immeasurable.

It took months for us to pick up the pieces and make sense of what remained. Lebanon's civil war was raging, and my brothers decided to join a local Christian militia to defend Zahle. Michel decided to stay in France, but there was no money to send him. Habib began to drink to ease his pain and to mourn the loss of his dream of becoming a commercial pilot. My mom was in denial of what was happening as she incessantly implored my dad to tell her where he hid his money. After a while, she fell into a protracted depression and rarely came out of her room. I was severely wounded and demoralized and had lost any sense of purpose. There was no "call to adventure." There were no goddesses to rescue me and no helpers who dared to reveal themselves. We all fell into an unconscious routine, waiting for the nightmare to end. My mom and I took turns taking care of my dad, hoping against all hope that his condition was temporary.

Months passed, and life had become a very dull routine. In addition to Alzheimer's, my dad was diagnosed with Parkinson's disease. My mom attended to his needs in the morning, and I took him for rides in the afternoon. We visited his lumber mill and spent time with the workers. We had Turkish coffee with the merchants who rented the storefronts he owned. We did all that not knowing if my brothers would be able to stop the banks from taking it all away. As uneasy as it all was, it became a safe routine in the midst of all the chaos. My dad's single favorite thing to do became mine. After coffee, we would drive to a small patch of land that overlooked the entire Bekaa' Valley, where we watched the sun set behind the western mountains before plunging the city into darkness. It was human misery playing against the beautiful backdrop of Mother Nature.

One morning, my darkness began to lift in the most unexpected way. After bathing my dad, my mom came into my room and pulled open the shades. "You can't do this to yourself," she proclaimed defiantly. We argued for hours about the desolation and the hopelessness we were in. Although our family now had no money, we were trying to maintain the appearance of wealth, which was futile. As hours passed, the argument between my mom and me became very heated.

"What would people say if they saw me attending public university? That's where poor families send their kids."

More time went by as our new reality took center stage. In the end, my mom had convinced me that my journey was not over, that what was inside me that made me who I am was not my dad's money. We laughed as she reminded me of the time I became the youngest poet in history at the age of two by pushing my boy cousins out of the way and towering over them. This was just another challenge to push out of the way so that I could tower over adversity again.

Two days later, I registered at the Bekaa' branch of the Lebanese University Law School.

Existentialism and Essence

In Lebanon, four years of studying law after graduating from high school allows a person to become a practicing attorney after passing the bar exam. From Elza's writings and from stories she told over the years, adjusting to tragedy emerged as a common theme. Her family slowly adjusted to their new reality. It was still depressing to be at home, so Elza spent as much time as she could on the university campus. She had shown remarkable intelligence from the day she arrived, researching and discussing the legal merits of cases that fourth-year students were debating. By her third year, she had become the school's center of attention and was allowed the privilege of taking courses at the school of sociology. That's where she met the man who would reignite her passion for rebellion and her sense of purpose.

During my last year at university, I became attracted to the work of one of the instructors at the sociology department, Professor Suhail. He had gotten his PhD from the Sorbonne in Paris, and I wanted to know more about the experience of attending the school that destiny had denied me. I had heard stories about him, about his progressive thinking and the well-regarded intellectuals he knew. He was a well-known philosopher who taught in France, Beirut, and Zahle and belonged to a group of Lebanese intellectuals who regularly traveled to Paris to meet with famous existentialist writers such as Simone De Beauvoir and Jean Paul Sartre. The professor was largely influenced by their work and by the ideals of postmodernism, existentialism, and Marxism.

Here was someone who was bringing to Lebanon the latest thinking from the West. This extraordinary intellectual seemed to span two worlds, embodying both the familial warmth of tribal culture and the sophistication of the post-modern West. He had transcended the patriarchal imprint and often spoke of the power of the feminine in healing the human condition. His world captivated mine. The first time I went to his office I found myself amidst ten-foot-high walls lined with shelves and filled with thousands of books. It was magical. I aspired to have that, to be like him. His office was a sacred space, an oasis for the thirsty mind. It celebrated knowledge, sanctified it, and honored the minds that gave the world such richness.

The chaos of the Lebanese civil war pushed many people in one of two directions—either into a rigid adherence to tribal and religious identity, or beyond the categories of religion and social affiliation. Professor Suhail let me into his world that belonged to the latter. I joined a group of socialist activists that became known as the first resistance to the Israeli occupation. Our backgrounds crossed the lines of different religious and nonreligious categories. There were Sunnis, Shiites, Christians, Druze, agnostics, and atheists, but none carried these descriptions as an identity. We were a secular gathering, and we all felt our higher calling. As I look back at that experience, I realize that it was being in their presence that prepared me to become a universal human being. It took me beyond the ethnocentric values I had inherited as a Christian Arab. To be a human being was becoming my identity, more so than the labels I had been born with.

While the country was being divided by bloody battles among Syria, Israel, the PLO, and the Christian militias, our group couldn't take sides and did not care who was right and who was wrong. We cared that people were suffering. We helped provide care to Palestinian and Shia families living in refugee camps at the edge of the Bekaa' Valley. We comforted Palestinian mothers who had lost their sons and daughters fighting against the Israeli soldiers who entered Lebanon in alliance with Christian militias. Despite the fact that I was Christian, and my two brothers had joined Christian militias, I had moved beyond taking sides. I was on the side of what was innately human.

In my last year of law school, my association with professor Suhail and the group of conscientious objectors had awakened me to a higher level of awareness and helped me rediscover my purpose through the lenses of maturity and a beauty that was unrestrained. The roadmap on how to fight the laws that were unjust became clearer. By the time graduation time came, I had a new resolve to continue this compassionate work and pursue my PhD in law, which would allow me to appeal directly to the United Nations on issues of woman equality and injustice.

I graduated law school first in my class and passed the bar exam with the second highest score in my region. The future looked bright as I began to consider my choices for graduate schools. One professor advised me to come back to teach as soon as I got my PhD, as the door was always open at the university. Another advised that if I wanted to run for Parliament, I should begin to befriend political families of my own faith, since the archaic Lebanese constitution still distributed parliamentary seats on confessional bases. The reformation work of the legal system was enormous, but I looked forward to the challenge.

I knew the Sorbonne was an impossible dream, but now that I could practice law, I could generate an income that put Saint Joseph University in Beirut within reach. Professor Suhail taught there on occasion, and one of my dad's cousins who had a successful legal practice in Beirut did also. Although my dad's memory was fading and the symptoms of his Parkinson's were becoming visible, we decided to pay my cousin, Professor Haj Shahine, a visit. His office had a commanding view of the Mediterranean, with books lining the walls of every room. He had requested my transcript and the results of the bar exam earlier.

"Elza is my cousin. She's the pride of Zahle. She will be working with me as a junior associate while in Beirut," he said as he introduced me to the dean of the law school. My cousin had submitted unofficial copies of my grades and the results of the bar exam to the dean. After giving us a tour of the campus, the dean instructed my cousin to have me finish my registration process while I was there. I could hardly believe what was happening. A future of new possibility was taking shape before my eyes. I projected my life into that future: I would work toward my PhD while gaining experience working as a lawyer. Then I would become a university law professor, run for Parliament, become a human-rights attorney working to fix injustices anywhere they surfaced. The sky was the limit as destiny began to erase the misfortunes of the last few years.

Ishtar and the Patriarchy

In her ambitious attempts to define her life through myth, Elza saw Joseph Campbell's hero's journey as essentially her own. Life mimicked legend in each and every experience and at every stage of her passage. As she further analyzed her situation in her manuscript, she left no doubt about what stage she was at on her journey: In breaking away from her old world and consciously committing to her calling, the so-called helpers appeared to her in law school. They bestowed upon her gifts that in later years came to define her life's calling, which took her back to the Middle East to help the Palestinians build their own state and create plans for the region to emerge from its archaic, patriarchal mores. At age twenty-one, she had crossed the first threshold, and the life that awaited her in Beirut assured her that there were no limits to what she could accomplish.

But just as she began to plan for the new stage of her adventure, she later believed that she angered the patriarchal gods again, for she was thrust into the Underworld where her life took a painful turn. It's what she has often called her baptism of fire, and it lasted for several years. It placed her in the metaphorical belly of the whale and forced upon her an inward journey of transformation that would test her resolve and prepare her to fulfill her destiny.

From this point on she began to identify with the archetype of Ishtar, the Semitic goddess associated with—among other powers— love, beauty, justice, and political power. Those familiar with ancient myths of the Middle East know this goddess by the name *Inanna*, but Ishtar, known also as *Ashtarout* in Phoenician myth, loomed large in Lebanese folklore for her love of the God Tammuz, or Adonis.

> The war and our financial predicament had made my brothers Ghassan and Habib into small angry men, shadows of who they used to be. In the months leading to my intended departure to Beirut, our home became another battleground, a minefield of bottled anger and range waiting to explode. In my brothers' case, the war had amplified their sexist cruelty toward me. They had each witnessed death; they each came close to dying. Theirs dominated my world and I wanted to escape. War does that. It often causes people to regress to the security of familiar, even primitive customs. In the process, rationality and humanity are abandoned. I wanted to escape it all as I prepared for my new life in Beirut.
>
> The day I was supposed to leave has been cinched into my memory forever. Shortly before I was to say goodbye to my parents, Ghassan and Habib came home, carrying their machine-guns after a night of guarding the city when they saw my packed bags waiting at the front door.
>
> "Say goodbye to your sister before she leaves," my mom said.
>
> Then came the first grenade: "She will go to St. Joseph's over our dead body!" They stood at the entrance to our home, blocking the door. "She will become a slut like all the other girls who live in Beirut. You can kiss the family's honor goodbye if she leaves this house."
>
> The second grenade came when my mom angrily tried to push them out of the way. Simultaneously they cocked their Kalashnikovs, training them at her feet ready to fire. My mom became hysterical as my dad stood there ambivalently. Habib shoved me back and I fell on the floor. I lay there lamenting and

screaming and then collapsed into stunned silence, watching through my tears my poor helpless parents.

My dreams came crashing down around me. At this critical juncture, my parents were unable to free me from the same tribal mores and traditions of which they themselves were victims. Just as I was about to embark on a new life, an ancient and stultifying belief system blocked my path. I became numb, reverting to the defense mechanism that was my default in times like these. I couldn't scream in rage and anger. God knows my brothers did enough of that. Again, I went into oblivion.

Even as I write this, the weight of the oppression from that day is still palpable. Despite years of therapy and psychospiritual work, I continue to struggle with the inner demons of anger and pain that resulted from the limitations imposed on me. I felt the weight of all the Arab women who have come before me—all the women whose impulses for self-actualization were forcefully squelched. I experienced their misery, their victimization, the cultural shackles placed on them by weak or manipulative mothers and men blinded by tribal tradition and power.

The White Knight and the Trojan Horse

At this stage of her life, Elza begins to show signs of resignation and surrender that she often described as feelings of utter numbness. "I was dead on the inside," she would say, "and dead people can't feel pain or judgment for the wrong decisions they make." Much like Ishtar at the threshold of every gate on her descent into the underworld, Elza willingly allowed herself to be stripped of power and will. Instead of being the heroine answering the call to adventure and charting a new course for justice and against the patriarchy, she succumbed to the old mores of mortals, living a life of ordinary existence. Below she describes the circumstances that led her to meet her first husband, a man who symbolized much of what she had sworn to change.

In my numb oblivion, I fell back into the old routine, taking turns with my mom in caring for my dad. I decided to clerk at the local court just to break the dark dullness of my life.

One day my mom called me at my office and asked if I would come home early. We had guests, she said, and she could not keep an eye on my father. From the hallway, I saw my mother speaking to two women, neither of whom I knew. She took me aside and whispered, "These women have been here for more than two hours, please ask them to leave."

When I entered the living room, the women immediately directed their attention toward me. They began to ask me questions about my education and work experience; they complimented me in all sorts of ways that were strangely gratuitous. I finally found the right moment to drop a hint for them to leave—we needed to attend to my father.

An hour later, there was a knock at the door. By that time, I had on my familiar uniform, an old, frayed shirt handed down from my brothers and worn-out pants that were too large for me. I had soap on my hair. This ignoble outfit was what I wore at home while I bathed and cared for my dad.

The knock came louder. Through the small window, I saw an unfamiliar but handsome man dressed in a stylish, three-piece suit. As I opened the door, he stood there with his gaze fixed on me. I wanted to hide. I looked miserable in my scruffy clothes, and my father was waiting for me to put him to bed. Under the circumstances, the last thing I desired was to entertain him.

"Are you May's daughter?" he asked.

"Yes. Please come in," I answered, bowing to the tribal injunction to be hospitable under all circumstances. There was no option for honesty. I could not ask him to come back another time.

"I am here to pick up my mother and aunt," he said.

"They left a little while ago," I responded.

He thanked me, looked intently at me again, and then departed. I learned that his name was Elie.

As I considered more carefully what had happened, I began to suspect that something was up. These people were focused far too keenly on me. In traditional culture, relatives—who for reasons of wealth, tribal connections, or physical attractiveness—are the ones who decide on who marries who. In most of the Middle East the ancient matchmaker is alive and well in the shadow of modernity. I began to connect the dots.

"As crazy as it sounds," I said to my mother, "I think they are sizing me up as a bride for their son and nephew. They don't know me from a hole in the wall, but I'm quite sure they are going to ask for my hand in marriage to Elie!" I added sarcastically.

My mother thought for a few moments, let out a laugh, and agreed.

The following evening, I had just put my father to bed when Elie's aunt telephoned my mother. She said that Elie wanted to see me. I stubbornly instructed her to say that I wasn't interested. I knew exactly what her motivation was. It all seemed so archaic to me. Here was the aunt of a grown man, trying to arrange a date for him.

Who exhibits this kind of behavior in our day and age? I thought to myself. My mom moved the phone away from her ear so I could hear the conversation.

"Why don't you let him meet her? What if he doesn't like her?"

That hit a raw nerve. Till this day, I don't know if this supposition was his aunt's ploy to lure me, or if she was sincere. Either way, it worked. Her suggestion that Elie might not find me attractive ignited every ounce of my feminine pride. He won't like me? I said to myself. I'll show him!

The following day, I met Elie at the place he chose, the most extravagant restaurant in town. He was tall, and I was physically attracted to him. At the same time, I saw no intellectual compatibility between us. Although he had spent many years in the United States, his beliefs were strikingly traditional.

"It is amazing to me," I remarked unabashedly, "that you, who have lived and studied in the West, are more traditional than I am. Why would you allow your aunt and mother to arrange your introduction to me?"

As the evening went on, many of my light-hearted jabs at his traditional mores went unanswered. He later commented that my manner of speaking was too intellectual for him; it unnerved him. And yet I had instinctively veered away from discussing politics or philosophy, knowing that he could not engage in informed dialog. I was amused by his questions: "What is your favorite flower? What is your favorite color? What is your favorite song? Who is your favorite actor?"

After coming home, I recounted the conversation to my mother and brother Ghassan, and they both laughed heartily. I wasn't sure why my brother laughed. This was the irony I was living with. It was only a few months earlier that he and Habib had acted from the same surface but stifling values as Elie had: the archaic patriarchy that killed all my hopes and dreams and left me only with the road to traditional marriage.

The House of Obedience

In her unpublished manuscript, Elza describes parts of the dark history of traditional Arab marriage in which the wife becomes the property of her husband and, by doing so, becomes an extension of his tribe. This was a part of a concept she describes called the "house of obedience." It is part of Sharia law that drew her attention in law school. She was so enraged by its cruelty toward helpless Muslim wives as they suffered unimaginable abuse at the hands of their husbands while the courts—full of religious men—did nothing to ease their pain. She writes that, as a Christian, she couldn't argue cases for a Muslim woman in Sharia court. Only a Muslim could do that. So, Elza did the next best thing: in her last year of law school, she began to coach younger Muslim female law students on building unique legal arguments that make abuses committed under the guise of the house-of-obedience law obsolete. She secretly became a cult hero for these young women, who stayed in touch with her for many years afterward. In her use of the term in this passage,

CHAPTER 2

Elza acknowledges that the abusive behavior of the patriarchy in the Middle East wasn't limited to Islam. The house of obedience ensnared men and tribes of every religion and in every part of the Middle East. Christian tribes in Lebanon were no exception.

The next day, Elie asked to visit me before he returned to his parents' home in Beirut. After some small talk and without hesitation, he asked for my hand in marriage. I became numb. It was an all-too-familiar feeling, the primal response to danger. I should have known. I should have heeded the warning signs. I knew I was about to create a very different future than the one I aspired to. He was attractive, popular, charismatic, and successful. Like untold women before me, I was about to act on the age-old programming that compels women to seek security, status, and the attention of a man. I was pulled by a powerful undertow that blinded me. I went unconscious.

Am I going along with this? What am I doing? I asked myself, as if trying to awaken from a dream. Why am I saying yes to this man? After all, I hardly knew him, and from what little I had seen, he unquestioningly ascribed to the traditional views I disdained. He had none of the intellectual or emotional depth I was looking for in a partner. I was inviting someone into my life who was just like my brothers. I knew I would suffer. Why was I walking into this mess?

I had no answers. Elie represented much of what I had vowed to change in my culture and myself. But that calling had become buried, hidden behind layers of pain and misery. I was numb. Very little of my ambition had remained in the face of an unyielding and punishing journey.

Before I woke from that nightmare, my mom threw me a lifeline. Not knowing my inner battles, in an effort to dissuade him she said, "To get my blessings, I want you to promise one thing. You have to allow Elza to finish her graduate education and fulfill her dream of becoming a professor or lawmaker. We could not help her continue, and I know that she will be miserable if she does not do this."

To this Elie responded, "I will support her in every way possible."

I couldn't believe my ears. I was wrong to prejudge this man, or so I convinced myself in order to escape my mundane existence. My brother quickly attended to my dad and brought him to the living room to formalize his approval and give us his blessing. While I remained emotionally ambivalent, the look of suspension and disappointment never left my mom's face.

Like many sons of wealthy families, Elie lived a double life. During the day he was the obedient son, the responsible manager of the family's businesses, and the caretaker of the extended family. At night, he was a different man. While we dated, I quickly became familiar with the life he led before we were engaged. He was a notorious drinker who had affairs with the wives of politicians and people in power. He dated famous pop singers and created enemies out of those who competed with him. Power gods come in all shapes and forms, and something in me was attracted to that dangerous behavior—perhaps because it looked a lot like the world of war that Ghassan and Habib lived in, which always affected me indirectly with oppression and forced limitations. Now I would get to be an equal in that dangerous world, even though it was going to hurt me. I had a front row seat in observing risky behavior, where with my brothers I was never allowed into their world; I just suffered the consequences.

This is how ambitious women took their revenge on a culture that oppressed them: they mimicked the behavior of self-absorbed men. They became the daughters of the oppressive patriarchy, the cocreators of misery and oppression. However irrational my thinking was, it took me out of the slow death spiral in Zahle and pointed me in an unknown direction full of rich spoils and material desires. The downshift from existentialism and the care for humanity all the way to the abyss of ugliness and darkness never happened so quickly.

In later years as I became a student of feminine myth, I realized that the circumstances that led me to marry Elie and my embrace of risky masculine behavior were patterns that women in patriarchal cultures embodied in order to survive. Even in Western culture, females are discouraged from claiming their full femininity. Instead, we are encouraged to be submissive and to relate to the patriarchal ways of things or run the risk of being shunned and ostracized. I came to learn through the wisdom of Margaret Mead and my friend Jean Houston that the wrongful way for modern feminism to reclaim its powers was by making women become second-rate men. Whether consciously or unconsciously, just as Ishtar had done in her descent to the Underworld, I had directed my entire being into what Arab culture calls the *House of Obedience*, where the patriarchy ruled with an iron fist and women were conspirators in maintaining the rule. My marriage to Elie represented my descent into Inanna's house of shadows. I had been swallowed into the belly of the whale on my life's journey, not knowing the challenges that awaited me as I parsed the darkness.

The Pride of the Tribe

Here in Elza's writings she began to describe this period of her life as the descent into the Underworld, manifesting in the most painful experiences that defined her marriage to her first husband. There are references throughout her unpublished manuscript to the seven gates through which Ishtar goes to gain wisdom for her return; but as life threw Elza painful obstacles, she also began to identify with the road of trials on the hero's journey. This is when her initiation, a new and more painful baptism of fire, began. It is said that the trials on the journey come in threes, and there were three events that again changed the trajectory of her life in the most painful transformative ways. In the part of the transcript that follows, Elza and Elie had moved to Virginia, where Elie's family had businesses and real estate holdings that he managed. After Elza became pregnant, Elie decided to stay in America until sometime after the child was born. The first child was a boy who, in the Arab tradition, would become the new pride of the tribe and carry on its bloodline.

I wasn't sure whether it was the gods and the patriarchy that wanted to punish me further, as if I hadn't been punished enough, or the goddesses who were angry because I had violated the heavenly covenants that birthed me. Maybe it was both. Maybe it was some unknown destiny that I had yet to uncover. Just as Ishtar needed to shed her worldly possessions at every gate in the Underworld, I came to shed the most precious possessions a marriage can give. Elie wanted to start a family shortly after we married, and I became pregnant with our first child.

Fawzi was born on November 5, 1988, in Virginia Beach hospital. From my bed I could hear the cries of joy Elie and his family experienced at the birth of a grandchild who would carry forward the family name. Fawzi was named after Elie's father. He was a gorgeous baby with big blue eyes that gazed at me with such calmness. The feeling was exhilarating. To hold a precious soul in my hands and to feel his warmth on my skin was to me like a poem rendered by angels. I had had very difficult relationships with most people in my life, but not with this amazing soul. After bathing him and putting him to the breast, I watched him sleep on my bosom with wonder and enchantment. I was always fascinated by the birth of ideas and philosophies. Holding my son in my arms turned the flames of knowledge into nothingness and him into a radiant sun.

I called my mother in Lebanon and said, "Mom, I don't know who this person is. When he looks at me, I feel that he is an adult who knows me. He speaks to my soul." Instinctually, I started thinking of ways to protect him as a mother.

When Fawzi was eight weeks old, we learned that there was a truce in the war in Lebanon and decided to visit Beirut. The day we arrived my mother called to say that my father's condition was deteriorating rapidly. I wanted to visit with my baby and to have my dad hold his first grandson, but Elie wouldn't let that happen. This was one of a million subjugations that a woman succumbs to when she enters the house of obedience. I left crying to my parent's house without my son. I think I lamented my weakness and my surrender to this abuse more than the abuse itself. I was observing my descent into a hole of despair with nothing to hold on to. I could not tell my parents how miserable I was, and I did not have the tools to dig myself out of that hole in spite of my newly found happiness with my son.

The Heavens Reclaim the Heroine's First Helper

Of the three trials that challenge a heroine on her journey, Elza was about to face her first. One of the very first helpers who had guided her way with love and tenderness was her father. From the stories she told about his wisdom and generosity, one can tell Elza had deep admiration and respect for the man who transformed his views on women and girls after seeing his own daughter excel in areas traditionally reserved for men. But the man who had been her caring guide had been ill for years.

As I arrived, my dad was lying on a hospital bed in our living room with an I.V. connected to his arm and an oxygen mask on his face. Life was slowly leaving him. The minute he heard my voice, he opened his eyes and a big smile came to his face. He mumbled a few words almost like a song. I hugged him and kissed him. His tears mixed with mine. It was a bittersweet moment.

"Dad, I have a son, he looks a lot like you ..."

He continued his unintelligible sounds and then collapsed into a deep sleep. My brother Michel had come back from Europe to be by my dad's side the last three months of his life. I stayed up with him reminiscing and talking about my son and went to sleep around 2 a.m. An hour had passed when Michel walked very calmly to my room. "Father's soul has left his body; let's pray."

I was amazed at how calm Michel was. He had spent the last three months meditating next to my dad and preparing his soul for its return to the heavens. He was practicing an Eastern tradition that wasn't familiar to me, but his presence was calming and serene.

I felt blessed to have spent those last precious moments with my father before he passed. The next day, I was bemoaning my condition, regarding both the passing of my father and my own journey. I was missing him and lamenting my new life, my disappointment with Elie, and the unknown future.

Michel, not knowing that I was suffering in my relationship, thought I was crying for my dad. He took me aside, and said, "Elza, you have to release Dad's soul. You were the one he loved most, and if you keep crying his soul might stay to comfort you. He needs to leave."

The splendor of that statement touched my heart. It helped me move from thinking about my victim state to caring about the soul that loved me.

During the next couple of days I spent in Zahle to help my family prepare for the wake, I asked Michel many questions and received the most insightful answers about life, about soul, and about karma. He gave me a book to take with me that contained much of this esoteric knowledge. It provided me with a new dimension that I could escape to every time I needed a reprieve from the shackles that held me. It opened my eyes to the deeper dimension the world of spirituality. Michel was a new helper who showed me how to make sense of the darkness I was in. Our conversations allowed me access to a whole new level of understanding, one that set mind and soul on fire. Little did I know that he was preparing me for what was to come next.

Karma and Destiny

As soon as Elza's first test on the road of trials came to an end, the universe in its own mysterious ways began to prepare her for the next cruel test. If this was the rage of the patriarchy, then it was targeting its own. First it was the father who had tried to help his daughter overcome patriarchal dominance; and now it was daughter's son who, if reared as Elza wanted to rear him, would have possessed a balance between the feminine and masculine attributes of humanity. But that, according to Elza manuscript below, was not how the patriarchal gods saw it.

The minute I returned to Beirut, Elie handed me our son, saying that he'd had a fever for the last three days and that no medicine was bringing his temperature down. We rushed him to the hospital. No one knew what was wrong with him. Doctors ran all the customary tests with no clear answers about the cause of his fever. After a few courses of antibiotics, they concluded that since his liver was enlarged he had hepatitis C and needed a blood transfusion. Catheters were hooked to his tiny body to supply it with blood to keep him alive. I became angry with the medical staff that couldn't assure me that my son was going to be okay. We all waited in the lobby while he rested. Hours became days and patience transformed back to anger.

"It's karma, Elza," said Michel every time I asked him why this loving god he spoke of would inflict so much pain on an innocent child. "It is said in Eastern philosophy that our soul comes into this world more than once, taking on a different mask every time, a different name, a different role. Souls return to learn lessons that will help them become one with God again." This wasn't helping my mournful state as he continued: "Some souls need a few months to burn their karma, and some need decades. Others have to come back in several lifetimes to erase their karmic debt. Who knows what Fawzi's destiny is?"

As days turned into weeks at the hospital, Michel's spiritual wisdom became the only remedy that calmed my nerves. Despite all the medical interventions, I became resigned to the power of karma and destiny.

Two months had passed, and my son had received several more blood transfusions. In spite of that, there was little improvement, and we began to lose faith.

"You should get some rest. I will stay with Fawzi and keep an eye on all the monitors," Michel said.

The moment I lay down, I saw my father in a dream holding Fawzi's hand and walking away, both wearing white. I woke up half an hour later to see my brother's worried face. The monitors where alarming and Fawzi could barely breathe. I held him in my arms as he breathed his last breath in my face.

I felt my heart ripping out of my chest. That beautiful angel had left, and with him left all the love that was lighting up my life. I think mothers experience death themselves when they lose a precious soul that was created in their womb. Again, remembering Michel's advice when my dad had died two months earlier, I tried not to cry. Even so, warm tears forced their way through, emptying with them any hope of continued happiness with Elie.

Life became very predictable after my son's death. There was a sense of resignation and an uncomfortable relief at the same time. Losing the ambition to become someone and to love someone made me feel ordinary for some reason, with nothing special to do or feel. *Emptiness* is a word that describes that feeling. At that time, I felt that my identity, my feelings and my emotions, my dreams and my hopes were carved out of me. My calling, like my son, was quickly dying, and I was becoming an empty vessel.

God's Light

In the middle of all the darkness Elza was going through, new glimmers of light began to present themselves through the spiritual teachings of her brother Michel. The intellectual and philosophical debates that had propelled her to pursue her calling had all but disappeared, but her soul's hunger to understand the mystery of life never faltered, especially after the death of the two males that meant the most to her at the time—her father and her son. Michel's teachings about Eastern philosophy and the knowledge of the soul became Elza's secret escape, her source of strength. She learned that the earliest manifestation of God was through light and music, and, as if reaching out to the gods, she wanted these attributes to be present in her daily life.

A year later, I became pregnant with a beautiful daughter. I decided to call her *Nour*, which means "God's light" in English. We lived in the Virginia at the time, and I would frequently talk to Michel, who had now moved to Canada. He would explain to me the principles of his spiritual path, who his teacher was, and the importance of having such teacher who can awaken one's soul and put the challenges of the physical realms of life and death in perspective. My brother had become one of his guru's important helpers. After being forced to drop out of medical school, he had studied languages, and after meeting the guru, he decided to become his official translator. He translated his books and lectures into three different languages, Arabic, French and Spanish.

The few times Michel sent me books and tapes about his meditative practices, Elie threw them away and threatened to cut off my relationship with my brother if he continued "to poison my head with such blasphemous ideas." Elie's control only made me want to explore more deeply the esoteric principles that became Michel's calling. People who had no capacity to understand deep spirituality were convinced he had joined a cult. He spoke of detachment from desires and of how desires are the cause of suffering.

"Think, Elza, that all the faculties we use turn into dust when we leave the body."

"What leaves the body?" I would ask him.

"The soul to rejoin with the universal Soul," Michel would answer calmly.

I was ready for Nour. I wanted to honor and love the soul coming into our life. The first few weeks with her were the happiest. A ray of hope reentered my life. She gave me a sense of purpose that I had lost. I could now prepare a girl to have a better life than the one I had.

Despite his parent's disappointment with me in having a girl, Elie became more caring and enjoyed his role as a father. He adored Nour, changing her diapers and watching her when I went to the gym. One day I came home to a worried look on Elie's face. He was holding her in his arms and asked me to press against her belly. I put my hand on her midsection and felt how swollen it was.

"Oh, God! This cannot happen again," I screamed.

We rushed her to the hospital, where the questions from a pediatric oncologist never stopped coming. The one question he asked at three different times was whether Elie and I were related. He then sat us down and said that he was almost positive Nour had what her brother had had, which was a rare genetic disease mostly observed in children whose parents were close blood relatives. The diagnosis was later confirmed as familial hemophagocytic lymphohistiocytosis, a rare disease of the blood, which had no cure. A treatment that followed the leukemia protocols would have to be administered if we had any hope of extending Nour's life by a few months. Without radiation and chemotherapy, we were told, she would die within weeks.

The first round of chemo brought her little body back to life as she screamed from the top of her lungs for three days in a row. The bad cells that had crept up to her brain and ravaged her tiny body were now being killed. Her doctor said that she might be experiencing a lot of pain but would be fine for a while.

Two months passed before we were allowed to bring her home. I wanted so desperately for this little soul to live and thrive. Her life became mine as I took her three times a week to the doctor and every time he injected her spine with drugs. She screamed every time, but the treatments worked. They had extended her life beyond anyone's expectations, and when she was eighteen months old the doctors declared her to be officially in remission.

God's Melody

In her unpublished transcript, Elza makes many references to an ancient philosophical concept called the "music of the spheres" that views the movements of celestial bodies—the sun, the moon, and the planets—as a form of music. It wasn't until I had a deeper comprehension of Michel's teachings that I understood the relationship between the microcosm and the macrocosm. According to the teachings, the music of the spheres exists within us as a manifestation of God's love. In Elza's mind, she had already made one aspect of God's manifestation present by naming her first daughter *Nour*. Now it was time to give God's melody a face.

I became pregnant again, and I didn't know whether I just didn't care anymore or I was acting on a subconscious wish to have another baby in case we needed a bone-marrow transplant for Nour at some point in the future. My systems were on overload. I had become the epitome of all that I criticized. I felt ignorant and weak with no say, just letting life happen to me. As I think back, I knew I could not handle the weight of my destiny anymore. Resistance was futile. I succumbed to a deep depression that was coated by the courage I showed in taking care of my ailing daughter. Nour and I were like buddies, but otherwise things looked very bleak. My only connections to my old life were books that I kept hidden in two boxes in a closet. When we moved to a bigger house, Elie told the movers to throw them all away. No books were allowed; neither were phone calls with Michel. Elie started drinking again. He had stopped for a while after our son died, but once Nour went into remission he found a new craving for drinking and smoking. There was only cigarette smoke and alcohol, and there was nothing I could do to convince him not to smoke around Nour, the unborn baby, and me.

Ghinwa was born on July 4, 1991, at 9:30 p.m. at Fairfax hospital in Falls Church, Virginia. Her Arabic name means "God's melody" in English. I chose the name because of Michel's Eastern philosophy that teaches that the universe and we are all made of light and music, the essence of the soul and the universal Soul. The bright light of Nour and the melodic sound of Ghinwa were now my universe. We could see the fireworks in DC from the delivery room. The free world was celebrating Ghinwa's birth and preparing her to become an independent American woman.

"Another girl!" said Elie's mother, sounding quite disappointed.

The arcane patriarchy was at it again. The tribe needed a healthy boy who would carry the family name forward, and all I could deliver was another girl who, in my mother-in-law's mind, was a burden. My mother, on the other hand, was the happiest grandmother on Earth. She bonded instantly with Ghinwa and felt a strong spiritual connection with her right after my delivery. All I wanted to know in that moment was whether she was healthy; I didn't feel much of anything else. My mind and heart were with Nour. She was the center of my universe. She needed to be saved.

With Nour in remission, we decided to spend Christmas that year in Lebanon. What was supposed to be a happy time with family and friends quickly turned into another crisis of faith. Nour suddenly relapsed and was rushed to the same dreaded hospital where her brother had died. I stayed by her side when one day she started throwing up blood and turned blue. A month had passed since her initial hospital stay, and the doctors were running out of options as to what to do for her.

One day, a cardiologist came into the room with a long syringe, telling us that this was their last recourse for resuscitating her failing heart. Against the doctor's advice, I decided to stay with my daughter. I knew her body was fighting its last round in a long and unfair fight, and I wanted to be there to comfort her soul. After they poked my baby's little heart with the needle, no visible improvement was showing, and they realized the battle was over. They asked if Elie and I wanted to be in the room with her for her last minutes of life. I held her in my arms, and Elie knelt down in prayer next to her bed as she breathed her last breath. Her soul left her body after being in this world for exactly two years. It was either my imagination or the imprint that Michel left on me, but as I closed my eyes in pain I saw the compassionate face of his teacher assuring me that her soul was going to a better place.

After Nour's death, we closed up our home in Virginia and moved back to Lebanon. Elie had been working on a deal with a major automotive company in Detroit. He had just become their exclusive representative in Lebanon and was working on extending that exclusively to the rest of region. In spite of that promising future, deep inside he knew that the move was going to place us at the mercy of his family's tribal impulses and create more tension in our marriage. Before leaving the States, I was corresponding secretly with Michel, who had taught me his meditation practice and arranged for me to be initiated into a path that widened my deeper knowledge of the soul and gave meaning to my existence. This and the fact that Ghinwa was healthy and didn't carry the gene that took my two other children would become my escape for several years.

Watching Ghinwa grow up was in my mind worth the sacrifices I had to make to adapt to an extremely confining, soul-crushing situation. The Elza in me that dreamt of a career as a professor and later as a legislator was barely alive. I was a wife, a mother, and a good citizen, but my real calling was hidden from sight.

Elie was happy as long as I catered to his needs and focused on his affairs and his business. The more demanding of my time he became, the more I began to realize that his world was no longer mine. He had become the man he had feared of becoming. My meditation became my escape from my outer destiny, but even that had it limits. The more I sacrificed, the more I grew resentful and contemptuous on the inside. Elie's long list of "do nots" drove me insane. Although Saint Joseph University was a few minutes away, I could not go back and pursue my dreams and my calling. No, I could not register for the graduate program, and no, I could not espouse a career in the legal or political arenas. No, I could not follow the guru that Michel followed. No, I could not meditate, because that was the deceitful practice of an Indian cult. No, I could not read spiritual books, and no, I could not go to psychotherapy, because people would say I was crazy. No, I could not teach Ghinwa how to meditate. No, I could not express any feminine powers or exhibit any signs of independence in defiance of the patriarchy that had returned with vengeance.

Figure 2.3. Elza and her daughter, Ghinwa, age
two, Falls Church, Virginia, 1993.

Dying to the World to be Reborn

The next section in Elza's unpublished manuscript shows a marked
shift in her perspective on destiny and the foreboding powers of the
patriarchy. In more than half those writings, her perspective about
herself is that of a deeply intelligent woman who had been victimized throughout her life by real and otherworldly powers that were
beyond her control. She ponders back and forth as to where her
destiny lies. Was the death of her second child the seventh and final
gate on Ishtar's journey to the Underworld? Or, after the death of
her father and her son, was Nour's death the third and final test
on her road of trials that finished her initiation and prepared her
for the return to her calling? She surmises that this is indeed her
return and that this type of return requires extraordinary sacrifice. It is at the seventh gate that Ishtar voluntarily sheds the final
remnants of the physical world before she's granted passage to the

other side. It is also at the end of the road of trials that the heroine begins to see glimpses of the world that awaits her.

While I dreamt of women's true emancipation, Elie's environment became all about women's submission. My breaking point came when he caved in to pressure from his parents about having more children. They wanted us to try for another boy. I was stunned. We were both so thankful for having a healthy and happy child such as Ghinwa, but his parents wanted a male heir to carry the family name. Forget the fact that I had buried two of my children and the emotional agony that comes from that. How could he put us through the same pain, knowing that another child had a high chance of suffering the same fate as Nour and Fawzi?

"How can you not enjoy raising Ghinwa with me? Why don't you spend more time with her and watch her grow up? What would a boy give you that she cannot?" I pleaded. Deep inside, I knew that another pregnancy, regardless of the health of the baby, would be an emotional death sentence for me. To Elie, it was about destiny and tribal honor and the continuity of the bloodline that only a boy can bring. To him, the traumas I had endured and the high emotional toll they took were secondary

Months passed, and Elie's drinking got worse, as did his verbal abuse. He had no shame about yelling at me in front of strangers. A friend who witnessed one of his tirades told one of Elie's aunts that I was so calm and masterful in deflecting his attacks.

"What a great and calm woman," he said to her. In Arab culture a great woman is one who takes abuse quietly and acts happy.

Elie started going to nightclubs with his friends again and coming home totally drunk. For months, I tried to talk to him about getting help, but he hopelessly defaulted to his old reckless, bachelor lifestyle. There was no way around his need to have a male heir, and his drinking was his way of showing his defiance. He went to the extent of proposing to convert to Islam, which, unlike the Catholic Church, allowed men to have several wives. He wanted to have a child with another woman and rear him as our own. That idea was creepy enough to make me scream in rage.

"Why don't we get a divorce, and Ghinwa and I can move out. You can marry the woman who can bear you a son," I said with genuine concern for the safety of both my daughter and me. To him the idea of divorce was a joke and a catastrophe that befalls Western families, not his.

"You will never get a divorce, and don't even think of taking Ghinwa anywhere," he warned me many times.

I knew that there was no way out of this—no counseling and no divorce. But he continued his destructive behavior at my emotional and spiritual expense.

"Elza, you have to take care of your soul. You can't save anyone, not even Ghinwa, if you don't save yourself," said Michel on one call. I had been seeking his spiritual advice on what to do about my situation and the emotions around leaving Elie and wanting to stay in Ghinwa's life. "It's all ego and attachment," he said. "Just meditate, and the right answers will come."

In my meditations, I realized that liberation takes on several forms. While my body was imprisoned, my mind was partially free, as was my soul. I learned to identify with my soul's purpose in the midst of all the emotional pain. The longer I meditated, the stronger my spiritual beliefs became. The patriarchy had imprisoned my body and my mind, but I wasn't going to allow it to imprison the essence of whom I am. I looked for strength in my meditations to overturn the tyranny that was forced on me. I prayed for salvation, I prayed for freedom. My guru's books, which I read in secret, reintroduced me to the mystical aspect of Christianity. I needed to derive strength from a place that was more powerful than money and coercion. Buddha's life story and the breaking of his bondage to attachment became my guide.

The longer I meditated, the stronger came the will to leave Lebanon. I gathered enough courage to rediscover my life's calling. I am the child of God who was born to sail the high seas and fulfill my life's purpose, my destiny, and my dream to make the world a better place. Ghinwa, who was four at the time, was my only connection to my old world, and I knew that leaving her would devastate us both emotionally. Even as I write this, tears well up in my eyes as I remember the last hours we spent together.

It was a cloudy day, and I asked my childhood friend Najla to take Ghinwa and me to our chalet located in a beach community just north of Beirut. I had been preparing for days. I couldn't be seen leaving with luggage, since the entrance to our home had security cameras. For the past week I had been sneaking luggage through the garage entrance in order not to be noticed.

Ghinwa wanted to watch her favorite movie, *Bambi*. The agony of the moment was tearing me apart as I sat by her side, waiting for the right time to say goodbye.

"Mommy, why did Bambi's mommy have to die?"

My heart was breaking, but I needed to stay strong. I needed to bring an end to this torture that no mother or daughter should ever go through. If I had any chance of saving her from the same fate that had found me, I needed to save myself first. If I had any chance to help the women of the Middle East break the shackles of oppression, then I had to free myself first.

"Ghinwa, Bambi's mommy is in a better place. Just like she had to leave, Mommy has to leave, too." She protested and cried and I held her for what seemed to be eternity. Then slowly I let her go.

This was the end to a chapter in Elza's manuscript that effectively signified the end to what she called the first half of her life. It closed the door on a torturous and tragic journey full of pain and dreams deferred. At age twenty-nine, she then moved to the United States and began doing volunteer work for her guru's spiritual organization. Gone were all the luxuries she had had: the chauffeurs, the shopping sprees in London and Paris, and all the trappings that had shackled her in chains of gold.

"Ah, freedom!" She sprinkles that statement generously throughout the remainder of her writings and whenever an oppressive memory resurfaced. It didn't matter that she was sleeping on someone's couch, didn't have a penny to her name, and had to take three buses to get to the spiritual center where she taught meditation, Eastern philosophy, and vegetarian cooking. Her only remaining sadness was about the absence of her daughter in her life. That very absence became a major motivation for her in later years to try to change the very culture that oppressed women and forced mothers to endure the pain of leaving their daughters.

With her newly found freedom, Elza's passion for the pursuit of knowledge returned. Glimpses of the possible life were reappearing in everything she read and with every new mentor she met. She lost her fear. She went to therapy. Optimism filled her life again and brought her clarity about her destiny and where she was in her journey. For most of the first half of her life, she had identified with being at the mercy of circumstances outside her control. It took an extraordinary act of courage to bring her out of her victim state. She had sacrificed an ordinary life with her own daughter to regain access to her extraordinary calling. Her courageous act cast the patriarchy in a mature light as she stood on the verge of her return.

Isn't it strange that most of the helpers the universe sent me were men? Fighting the injustice that comes with patriarchal rule can be bewildering. The helpers started with my dad, who opened the door to all my other teachers who held my hand and prepared me to answer the call to adventure. After him came Suhail, my law-school professor who taught me about existentialism and the true meaning of rebellion, followed by my spiritual teacher Thakar, who opened my soul to understanding karma and the transcendent meaning of life and death. Then came Richard, who opened my eyes to world philosophies and myth, which lead me to the wonders of Joseph Campbell. From the day I was born, I had heard the call to adventure, but were these teachers preparing me for something larger?

Indeed, they were. They were the guardians sent by the universe to rid me of all my fears and attachments and place me on the threshold of my true calling. The obstacles they threw on the path were gigantic, and the sacrifices were immeasurable. They had tested my ordinary existence, not for the purpose of stopping me, but to move me to the threshold of the Extraordinary. All these helpers—the gods and the goddesses, the mentors and the sages—had transitioned me from knowing myself as my ego to a place of humility, self-annihilation, and inward knowledge. I needed to die to my old self in order to be born again if I were to place myself at the threshold of the Extraordinary. Once I crossed the threshold, there was no going back.

It is on that other side that I saw the road ahead with clarity. That's where true warriors reside. That is the place where I would begin to care deeply about the plight of humanity and learn to become a part of the solution to human misery. That is the place where I met Ken Wilber, Don Beck, and Jean Houston. These were the gods and goddesses in human form, mentors whom I embraced with courage knowing they would be instrumental in deepening my own understanding of myself and prepare me to have a role in influencing the culture of the Middle East and help deliver women from the gripping hands of the patriarchy. Fate and destiny played their hand as well. They sent me that which completes the soul and makes the journey a pleasure, a soul mate endowed with boundless love. How appropriate that he shared the same name with my dad?

3

TIME, SPACE, AND ETERNAL FIRE

You are God's spirit everywhere;
You are stronger than the ages.
Do you have memory of the day we met when the halo
Of your spirit surrounded us, and the angels of love
Floated about singing the praise of the soul's deeds?
—Kahlil Gibran, *A Lover's Call*

It happened on a warm night in July in the year 1965. The young mother had just brought her newborn infant home and placed her on a child's bed as she rested in the adjacent room.

"Let's throw her off the balcony" said the six-year-old to his younger brother. "Yah, who needs girls?" mused the five-year-old enthusiastically.

The two boys hatched their plan as they helped each other on to the newborn's bed. She was bound in colorful swaddles as she slept peacefully. One tugged on her left side, while the other pushed from the opposite end till they brought her to the edge of the mattress. Part one of the plan was complete.

The heavily bundled infant dropped to the floor without making a single sound as the two boys proceeded with part two of their plan. They argued about who should push and who should pull. They took turns pushing and pulling, always being careful not to make a sound that might wake up other family members.

Then came the hard part. Who was going to open the door to the balcony? They whispered quietly. They knew the hinges on the old door were rusted and made those terrifying, shrilling noises the second it swung open. The five-year-old shied in fear, then slowly dropped to the floor and withdrew.

The older boy knew he had to do this alone. Rising bravely from the floor, he reached to the handle and turned it. The wind flung the door wide open, making the awful sounds that terrified both boys. After a minute of panic, they proceeded. The bundled infant had reached the wrought-iron rail, and the two boys struggled under her weight to prop her upright in order to complete the final act.

"Mom, wake up! They are throwing the baby from the balcony!" cried the boys' seven-year-old brother.

In horror, the mother kicked off the blankets on her bed, ran to the balcony, and threw herself at the girl. Terror and fury mixed with tears as she considered what her boys had done. A family meeting was hastily called.

"Where do you get these evil ideas?" the angry father implored his sons.

"From your evil brother," answered the mother.

Voices rose and arguments followed. In anger, the father's two older sisters chimed in, "You should have had another boy!" said one as the other completed her sister's sentence in unison. "She's going to be a burden to us all."

After quelling all the voices, the father took the baby girl in his arms, looked compassionately at her little face, and kissed her rosy cheeks. "Tonight, we are going to give this little girl a name."

Silence fell, then the father added, "we should call her Zkiyeh, after my mother."

Shouts rose simultaneously in protestation and adoration of the proposed name. "Why can't we call her Rose?" asked the mother.

Raucous protestations surged again and soon turned into a war of words between the old and the new, the archaic and the modern, the East and the West. Shouts of different names rose from every corner of the house; then everything fell silent as the seven-year-old boy came forth. He was the gifted one, the one who had been anointed the family genius who would carry forth a rare legacy. He held in his arms a French novel written by Louis Aragon. All eyes were trained on him. He pointed to the title and said, "We should call her Elza."

Life Calls Forth Adventure

On a warm July night in 1965, I awoke from a strange dream. I was three-and-half-years old and sat at the edge of my bed, rubbing my eyes as if parsing the darkness in search for something I had seen in my sleep. I had dreamt that I was being chased by a pack of ferocious wolves. They came at me from everywhere. The harder I ran, the more numerous they were.

Terror-stricken, I began to shout for help. The louder I screamed, the closer the beasts came. Exhausted, I stumbled and fell helplessly to the ground.

At that very moment, a strange light appeared. It was accompanied by equally strange music that drew me in a spellbinding fashion. In a trance, I began to follow the strange melody. The wolves ran in horror from what they had just seen and disappeared into the night. The music filled the sky as I began to search for its source. I walked and walked, but the closer my ears brought me to it, the further and more muffled the music became.

The road finally led me to a clearing where I saw a mountain on the horizon. At its peak a light was glimmering. The music intensified. It filled the valleys and echoed through the infinite canyons. I rested, as I knew I had found the source of both the light that had saved me and the music that had guided my passage.

I looked down and saw the turbulent waters of an angry river. I could not swim, but I was determined to reach the source and unveil the mysterious powers behind my journey. I rose, fully determined to wade into the river and cross it. But, as my toes touched the water, darkness fell and the music stopped. The silence was deafening.

I awoke, my heart pounding, my eyes searching for the light and my ears chasing for the melody. Failing to find either, I fell back into my bed, pulled the covers over my head, and fell into a deep sleep.

This dream haunted me for years. I could not explain it or make good rational sense of it. Throughout my childhood, vivid images of my attempt to cross the waters reappeared as nightmares that kept me up for hours. As an adult, I sought the counsel of dream experts and therapists who attributed it to the spiritual aspect of the psyche and the dream world. But why hadn't the nightmares disappeared? Was this more than a dream? Had the heavens who sent an angel to save Elza on that fateful night also sent me a spiritual enigma masquerading as a dream that could only be solved in due time?

In later years, as I gained a deeper understanding of Eastern philosophy and the common destiny of souls, I saw the connection of our two souls on that warm July night. While Elza was being saved from the murderous grip of the patriarchy immediately after her birth, and her soul was being prepared to fight injustice, I was being shown a glimpse of what an ordinary life would be as I was being chased by wolves who represented the physical world, the world of attachment and material possession. Then I was shown a glimpse of the Extraordinary. Light and music, the two manifestations of the soul and the oversoul, were the things that saved me. To complete the connection and begin to understand its full meaning took another thirty-three years.

Becoming a Madman

"Are you done being a cowboy?" asked my bother Nassif as we sat in his living room in New Jersey sipping on Heinekens and watching the football game while the Thanksgiving turkey slowly roasted. I chuckled, knowing what he was going to say next. To him, family and the sense of place were important. Although we had all left Boston, my two brothers had remained on the East Coast within a few hours drive to the city. That's where many extended family members had put down roots and reared children. Not me. I was the black sheep, and I had stormed out of my parents' home at age seventeen and never looked back. I had broken the shackles of duty dictated by the city's parochial heritage and its Puritan values that had shaped our adult lives. I had done something no one in the family dared to do: I moved west. I had given the person who bought my business a five-year lease, which was up for renewal at the end of that year. Everyone in the family had pushed me not to renew the lease and to take back the office space and move back to Boston where I could be closer to my old, virtuous life.

My dad sat anxiously awaiting my response in order to see if my adventure in Arizona was coming to a remorseful end. To him, selling my real-estate business was at the top of his list of reckless things I had done.

Half joking, I said, "When you're shoveling from under three feet of snow, I'll be in short sleeves sitting on the top of a mountain in the sun reading my favorite Gibran books."

Without batting an eye, my dad responded, "You're becoming like him, a madman."

I wasn't sure whether he was being disparaging or complimenting me on the progress I had made since my divorce. My dad and I didn't have much in common except for our love for Kahlil Gibran. We shared a favorite book by him entitled *The Madman*, originally published in 1918. It is Gibran's shortest collection of poems and parables, and, while my dad had infinite love for the poetry, from an early age I had been intrigued by its opening epigraph that had sent me on numerous inward adventures. I cannot do it literary justice by summarizing it, so I'm sharing it in the hopes that the reader gets a deeper spiritual sense of Gibran and his profound teachings:

You ask me how I became a madman. It happened thus: One day, long before many gods were born, I woke from a deep sleep and found all my masks were stolen—the seven masks I have fashioned and worn in seven lives,—I ran maskless through the crowded streets shouting, "Thieves, thieves, the cursed thieves."

Men and women laughed at me and some ran to their houses in fear of me.

And when I reached the market place, a youth standing on a house-top cried, "He is a madman." I looked up to behold him; the sun kissed my own naked face for the first time. For the first time the sun kissed my own naked face and my soul was inflamed with love for the sun, and I wanted my masks no more. And as if in a trance I cried, "Blessed, blessed are the thieves who stole my masks."

Thus I became a madman.[1]

On my first journey to self-discovery, I became Gibran's Madman. I often wondered if freeing myself from possessions and attachments represented the courageous act of removing the masks that I had so carefully fashioned. I have worn several masks in my life—some out of necessity, others out of the need to belong—but none had allowed me the room for true exploration of the Self. Before my first journey into the dark night, I had known myself only by the identity thrust upon me by my parents, my church, my schooling, my work, and society. But this wasn't who I am; it's what others needed me to be. It is what most of us ascribe to unconsciously as a survival mechanism in order to belong.

Throughout my life, I've had glimpses of what lay beyond that identity. It was an awareness that comes to a person when chaos and uncertainty threatens his or her ordinary existence. It is the authentic Self, the soul that waits on the other side of identity. Those were the times that my true calling in life tugged at the masks I had so tightly worn, the masks that had prevented my full inward discovery.

On my own hero's journey, until the age of thirty-six, I had refused my soul's call. I had known very little beyond the masks I wore. But, on that Thanksgiving Day, I had already been wading in the river of darkness and change for two years. Darkness was giving way to new light. Life had removed several of my masks, and I was no longer resisting the call to my own adventure. I had waded fully into the torrents of madness, where I began to see glimpses of my authentic Self.

Other than my favorite books, helpers along my way had been few. It was more the absence of the old that was placing me into a state of bliss I had not known before. What I had identified with in the past was also how others identified me, and, to them, change was a violation of that knowing. Thus, to my friends, my family, and to all I had known, I had indeed become a madman. Beyond the trappings of identity, the universe was revealing to me the vast world of the Self, and my search for soul and meaning had begun.

On that Thanksgiving Day with my family, the questions that I had often asked myself whenever I read those opening lines to Gibran's book took center stage: Were all the seven masks aspects of one's identity that needed to be transcended in order for the authentic Self to rise? Was there something higher that lay in the great beyond? Is there such a thing as a past life? *Can* there be seven past lives? Could there have been existence beyond time and space before any gods had been born?

The Goddess in Disguise

The tryptophan from the turkey had done its job and, after the obligatory nap, I decided to check my emails. I had been testing the waters of being a single man again. The Internet was a new phenomenon that was disrupting everything I had known, and part of what was being disrupted was the old way in which people met. Earlier that year, I had placed a personal ad on a dating site on America On Line. I had quickly become disheartened after meeting the first few women face to face. Something about that medium and experience was amiss. Maybe it was the absence of spontaneity, the attraction at first sight. The Internet had removed that which comes with being innately human, the *je ne se qua* of the unspoken subtleties of love and attraction. Although I had not responded to many inquiries, I had also not removed my personal profile.

The email I received that day was from a user named Ishtar65. There was nothing in it that was boastful—no mention of pedigree, educational background, or professional accomplishments. The degree of humility and honesty were greatly disarming. I didn't know how to react, so I decided not to respond. The user stated her name as Elza; she said she was of Lebanese origin and had been on a soulful journey of self-discovery while doing volunteer work for a spiritual organization. In her unpublished book, Elza tells a more accurate version of our initial interaction through the Internet.

"Biker Chick Where Art Thou?" read the AOL personal ad. Not knowing the difference between American *chick* and French *chic*, I read on. I had led a life of solitude for over five years; and, except for the occasional date and a platonic relationship with a coworker, my personal life had naturally taken a back seat as I put together the pieces of the broken life I had left behind. After dedicating so much time to healing, inner growth, and service to others, a shift to becoming a woman again was happening. I had the desire again to look pretty and feminine and to seek a fulfilling relationship.

I had benefited tremendously from two psychotherapists who frequented our meditation center and who lovingly offered to help me make sense of the emotional traumas I have been through. I came to believe that deepening my consciousness and my spiritual practice had to be accompanied by a psychological understanding of myself in order for me to become whole. This process gave me the confidence that I can love again and not project my subconscious thoughts about men onto a new relationship. Two of my closest friends, a Lebanese-American social worker and a rabbi, insisted that I could find my man on the Internet. They had searched dating sites themselves and were a living proof that this could work. Both of them ended up marrying their Internet sweethearts. As much as I admired them, a part of me thought that I was a Lebanese Princess and that the man should come knocking at my door. I was willing to forego the white horse.

One night, after working on a project until 2 a.m., I wanted to give this Internet thing a try. I looked at the profiles of vegetarian-spiritual men first, then Arab men second. Eerily, the two groups had something in common: they were both militant about their views on life. Arabs flaunted their material possessions and their lifestyle of instant gratification, while vegetarians took pride in how small the size of their carbon footprint was. Now I knew for sure that this was not for me. But before logging off at 4 a.m., I ventured on one last search that omitted the age criteria.

"Thirty-six-year-old male looking for a conscious and athletic female. Please respond only if you have good family values."

He mentioned that he was Lebanese-American. From the list of authors he admired—Gibran, Thoreau, and Emerson—I knew he was different. Still, thirty-six years old. Only three years older than me! What could he possibly have of life experience that would come close to mine?

I decided to write him an email, making sure I mentioned my work with my guru first. I would have perfectly understood if I never had a response. But there was a certain attraction about this man. I had developed my own theory that night that the Internet could be the place where two souls can meet before meeting face to face. My belief in the law of karma and reincarnation explains how people might have had a past destiny together and might meet again to complete a journey toward wholeness. This rang true in my dreams that night.

A week passed, and not a word from my virtual contact. This confirmed my cynical beliefs about the openness of Lebanese men. After all, I was married to one who had lived in the United States and claimed to have family values, yet he could not stomach the idea of meditation or of anything else outside his tribal norms. I kept quiet about my cyberspace missteps to all my friends, but I never let go of the belief that the right man for me was out there.

Two weeks had passed when I received an email in which this man apologized for not responding promptly as he had been away on business and visiting family on the East Coast for the Thanksgiving holiday. He also stated that he had been born in Zahle and came to the States at a young age and wanted to know more about the spiritual work I was involved in. He ended his email saying, "I really look forward to hearing from you, Said."

I had to read these two parts over again several times. Of all the men in the world, this man is from my hometown and has my dad's first name. Could this be a coincidence, or was it part of a divine plan? I quickly answered him, and, after acknowledging our commonalities, I described the transformational nature of my work.

In contrast to the confined mindset of the Arab culture I come from, in the five years since I had left Lebanon my work had exposed me to a post-modern American lifestyle that allowed for a comfortable level of psychological intimacy with people in general. Relationships between members of the opposite sex in my culture were always viewed with suspicion and the ever-present moral judgment of sayings such as, "If a man and a woman gather, the devil is the third person present." In the West, friendship between a man and a woman is the norm.

It was this new mindset that made me comfortable in taking the conversation with Said to a deeper level. From our first contact, I expressed the psychospiritual nature of my work rather than playing the dating game at which I had never been good anyway.

I'm not sure what a divine plan looks or feels like, but from our second correspondence through the magic of the Internet, our vastly different worlds came together to reunite us in a tribal remembrance of place and time. In addition to being born in the same city and my having her dad's first name, we were born in the same hospital. Furthermore, it was my grandfather who built the maternity ward of that hospital. Two of Elza's brothers had attended the same school that my brothers and I had, and one of them, Ghassan, was Nassif's classmate. To add to the serendipity of it all, before moving to the United States my dad had built an addition to her dad's lumber mill and constructed several commercial storefronts for him.

But if our meeting were part of a divine plan, I was in denial of it at first. After leaving Lebanon, I had disowned everything about the place, its people, its heritage, and the horrible memories of war and death. Nothing in my conscious awareness allowed for the possibility of being with a Lebanese woman. Maybe there was a stereotype in my head about the archaic practices of arranged marriages that left incompatible couples with miserable lives in order to uphold tradition and their parents' tribal will. Since my divorce from Rebecca, my dad had spoken to several families in Zahle, including a second cousin, about giving their daughter in marriage to me. Maybe it was my rejection of what he had done without my knowledge that caused him to call me a madman; nonetheless, I knew traditional marriage was not going to be part of my future.

The existential changes I was going through at the time had placed me on the threshold of new adventure; but, other than reading about such transformation, I had no guide or community to show me the way forward. On my own hero's journey, I had thought that I was in the belly of the whale, where I had transcended the impermanence of a world based on attachments and material possessions. I was seeking an elusive, earthly paradise where saints and philosophers dwelt, but I had no map or guide to take me there. The fact that Elza had been on that road for some time gave me a glimpse of the remainder of my journey and what was possible. It quelled all my perceived notions and manias that arose from the different identities I had lived and from the repressed, shadow aspects of my character as we both began to reveal parts of our authentic selves to each other.

The Brilliant City Within

"Do you like to dance?" she asked in an email. "Yes!"

"Do you know Rumi?"

"No, should I?" I answered.

Her response, accompanied by a poem by the thirteenth-century Sufi poet, gave me the first glimpse of Elza's transcendent depth and spirituality.

"Here's what I teach," she said.

Dance, when you're broken open.
Dance, if you've torn the bandage off.

Dance in the middle of fighting.
Dance in your blood.
Dance, when you're perfectly free.

Struck,
The dancers hear the tambourine inside them,
As a wave turns the foam on its very top, begin.

Maybe you don't hear that tambourine,
All the tree leaves clapping time.

Close the ears on your head
That listen mostly to lies
And cynical jokes.

There are other things to hear and see:
Dance, music and a brilliant city inside the soul.[2]

Could this be? I asked myself. Could the search for the soul peel away the layers of identity and bring me closer to knowing my authentic Self? I had been at a standstill seeking the unknown, and suddenly a poem from the thirteenth century pointed to the vastness of what lies beyond identity. It engulfed me. It sent me on a quest in search for answers: Where is the soul? Where is the brilliant city?

Until then, my search had yielded only a myriad of worldly expressions that didn't satisfy. I wanted to move beyond the confines of the physical world, and the search had to shift from an outwardly focused life to an inwardly directed quest for the knowledge of the soul, the face in the brilliant sun beyond the earthly masks. I was indeed in the belly of the whale, and, if I wanted to be born again, I had to pass into my own inner temple.

That night I had a dream. It was the same dream I had had when I was three-and-a-half-years old. I was standing on the banks of the same angry river with my eyes fixed on the same glimmering light shining from the same mountaintop. The angry torrents of the water were deafening. As I had in the first dream, again I tried to cross, but the second I put my toes in the current, alligators appeared from the dark waters savagely snapping at my feet. They looked at me with the same evil eyes as had the wolves that chased me in the first dream. I quickly withdrew. At that moment, the light shining from the mountain intensified. It transformed into a beautiful maiden dressed in flowing, white robes. She extended her hand across the vast river and placed it before me. As I reached my hand to take hers, my surroundings became engulfed in flames that quickly turned into a towering inferno. I awoke.

The next morning, between sleep and awakening, I contemplated the dream I had just had. Did the appearance of the maiden represent the world that awaited me farther along on my journey? Did the consuming fire symbolize the painful transition between the physical world and the world of spirituality? Was Elza the maiden in disguise, the goddess the heavens were sending to rescue me? It was too much to process and too much to accept all at once.

Finding God in Miami

I wanted to play it safe and not delve further into the unconscious in search of the deeper meaning of my dream. A part of me wanted to shut the door on what was happening, as the self that identified with safety arose with the sun and morning coffee. I wanted to know more about spirituality from Elza, but I also wanted her to see it from my own perspective. In her unpublished manuscript, she tells a far better story about what we revealed to each other:

"Elza, I'm at a crossroad in my life. Everything I believed in is being shaken at its core. I have spent my life pursuing the American Dream, and I had a hollow feeling when I got there…"

Disbelief mixed with delight as I read every word in this email that revealed the soul of this man. Could he really be from Zahle? Could another conscious soul have been sent to that same place where tradition and the patriarchy had killed all souls?

This man was on a spiritual quest to find God. He ended his email by saying that he planned on taking time off to travel to Turkey to find God. A spiritual quest of sorts to connect with the soul of his great uncle, a bishop who was considered a saint by many for saving thousands of Christians from the Ottoman massacres during the last days of their reign.

"You don't have to go to Turkey to find God—you can find him here in Miami," I answered back with smug cleverness. After all, I believed that the true journey to finding God was an internal one.

I had picked the right books and packed the right gear in anticipation of a journey of a lifetime. I could disappear for months after I handed the management of my properties in Boston and Arizona to trustworthy professionals. I was waiting for my house to sell so that I could be free from the last few things that tied me to a physical place. I had thought that Mardin, Turkey, held many of the answers for my spiritual quest. The trip would expose me to my family's roots and the noble work that my ancestor Bishop Yohana Dawlabani had undertaken in saving thousands of lives in the final days of World War I. The Bishop was an orthodox biblical scholar who had translated over sixty works of Christianity from Latin and Greek to Arabic and Aramaic.[3] At the height of the war, he had arranged for the safe passage of thousands of Christians, including members of his own family, from Turkey to Syria and Lebanon. He had stayed in Turkey in order to save those Christians who wouldn't leave by allowing them to convert to Islam; then, after the war, he rebaptized them in mass ceremonies. In 1919, he led a group of Eastern Christian clergy to testify at the 1919–20 Paris Peace Conference on the brutality of the Ottomans and their systemic and indiscriminate starvation and slaughter of Near Eastern Christians.

Oxford University's Syriac Studies scholar Sebastian Brock knew and admired Bishop Dawlabani. He included him in many of his writings and, as I learned from a biographical sketch of Brock written in 2004, he even established a fund for students at Oxford in the bishop's name. Here is an excerpt from that piece (*Dolabani* is one of various spellings for *Dawlabani*):

It was on a momentous trip to Tur Abdin that the young scholar Sebastian met Mor (Mar) Philoxenos Yuhannon

Dolabani, Syrian Orthodox Bishop of Mardin. Bishop Dolabani being a scholar himself with a vast knowledge of his own heritage took interest in the young English scholar. The bishop apparently had made a memorable impression on Brock as, years later, he would comment on this experience indicating that he saw in Dolabani a good-natured humble scholar, a humanist who led a simple life of scholarship and devotion. Perhaps it was then that Brock subconsciously recognized a kindred spirit in Dolabani and seized Dolabani as a role model. In fact it was not long ago that Brock was instrumental in establishing the Oxford-based Dolabani Fund to help students of the Syriac tradition to study at Oxford. Within each academic year, a few students from all denominations of the heritage from India, the Middle East, and the diaspora benefit from this fund.[4]

Figure 3.1. Bishop Yohana Dawlabani with others in the older generation of our family, 1959. In this photograph, taken in front of our home in Zahle, Bishop Dawlabani is seated second from the left. On his right is my grandfather, Said Ephraim Dawlabani, and on the Bishop's left is my grandfather's brother, Abdo. In the back row, my father, Elias, is third from the left; his brothers Philip and Jamil are fifth and sixth from the left. My mother, Jamileh, is second from the right. My dad's sister Laurice is third from right, and my paternal grandmother, Victoria, is fourth from the right.

Bishop Dawlabani was my great grandfather's first cousin, and the monastery in which he had served held all his scholarly works. It sat on a historic site dedicated to Shamash, the Assyrian sun god and, as I found out later, the brother of the goddess Ishtar. This would be a perfect place for the deep reflection and quietude I was anticipating. But, just in case I didn't find God there, I had planned a pilgrimage to Mount Ararat, just a day's drive from the monastery. Surely the place where Noah's ark came to rest would hold many of the answers to my questions.

Something profound happened to me the minute I read Elza's email that morning. Suddenly, the outer pilgrimage looked mundane and repetitive. Like many of my other pilgrimages to mountaintops, it would surely satisfy my senses and expand my understanding of the human condition, but would it really enrich my soul? And, while others would laugh at the idea of God being in Miami, Elza's statement appeared as a simple answer from an entirely different realm—the universe within. It hit me as a knowing. God was everywhere. It began to reveal to me that to know my soul is to know the god within me and that my journey forward is a journey inward. It will involve no outer travels and no mountaintops. Rumi's tambourines and his twirling dance began to play in my head. I wanted to know what it felt like to tear off the many faces I had worn, the bandages that had shielded me from true knowing, and what it really felt like to dance in my own blood. I wanted to find the music and a brilliant city inside myself.

Until that time, Elza and I had only exchanged emails. But that day I asked her if we could speak on the phone. A conversation would reveal much more of who a person is than a carefully prepared email ever could. She had seen a picture of me, but I had not seen any of her.

I dialed the number and she answered. Her voice was angelic and Beirut-cosmopolitan all at once. Gregorian chants played in the background at my home, and the first words out of her mouth were, "My god, you *are* looking for answers."

A profoundly meaningful conversation ensued. Laughter and happiness flung my heart and my soul wide open. She spoke half in English and half in Arabic. I spoke in English, which added to her delight in that I wasn't the stereotypical Arab male. To me, Arab culture and language were just other things I had disowned in order to forget. To her, I had the desirable American mindset that she sought.

If there is such a thing as love at first sight, then this was love at first conversation. If love moved mountains, then the most important mountain in all the Abrahamic scriptures was reduced to dust. If love made men do crazy things, then what I did next was one of the craziest things I had ever done. Within two hours of our conversation I booked a flight to Miami. A part of me was filled with anticipation, while another part began to raise doubts about who she could be. The critic in me chastised me for the hasty way in which I decided to meet her.

She had already told me that she now lived free of material possessions after having left a life of glamor and wealth. I don't know if that is the dying-to-your-old-self part of every spiritual journey, but where she was is where I wanted to be. All I was hoping for was that she didn't show up at the airport wearing an Indian saree with a dot on her forehead and driving a broken-down Yugo.

I waited at the curb. She was late. Twenty minutes passed before a fast-moving, late-model sports car pulled to the side. This surely couldn't be her.

The woman exited the car. She had light, long, curly hair and wore high heels and a miniskirt that revealed the body the gods had given her. She couldn't have been more than eighteen, I thought. She beckoned in my direction. I wasn't sure whether she had motioned to me or not, as a much younger man standing next to me started to walk in her direction. Then she motioned again, calling my name. It felt unreal and ecstatic. A thousand emotions lifted me, and I felt Cupid, the god of love, carry me to the car. The only words that played in my head as I approached her were, "Yes! God is indeed in Miami."

My soul had fallen in love with Elza's soul from her first email to me. It took my mind and my heart three weeks to know what that felt like. If I weren't looking for deeper answers to life's mysteries, I would have not picked up on the subtleties of our parallel journeys. She had seduced my soul and my intellect from three thousand miles away, and now I had fallen head over heels for her physical beauty. The package of wholeness was complete. As we left the airport, I heard Ishtar, the queen of the heavens, laughing.

In her unpublished book, here's how Elza describes our first meeting:

The day Said was supposed to arrive in Miami for our first face-to-face meeting, I was fraught with nerves. I couldn't sleep the night before or focus on my work. I had my childhood friend Najla with me on the phone all day:

"He must be the one," Najla said, "I have never seen you so unsettled before. You were always the levelheaded friend who had all the answers, especially when we talked about boys and teenage crushes. Who's the teenager with the crush now?"

The moment we exited the airport, I told him I wanted to pull over to the side to see his face. He smiled at me but did not understand what I really meant. My heart and soul were busy telling me that this was not our first meeting, as if wanting to see how he looked like in this lifetime. An eerie feeling of familiarity overcame me, along with a confirmation of a yet-we-meet-again promise made many life times ago. I had decided not to proselytize my spiritual practice and philosophy before we both had a chance to know each other better during his stay.

The next day he visited my apartment, which was bare of any signs of consumerism. A second-hand twin mattress lay on the floor, and a borrowed desk and dinosaur computer made up the other noticeable material things. Cushions were spread on the floor for seats. Like many volunteers who serve in spiritual organizations, I have gotten used to a simplified lifestyle that allowed me to dig deep and find beauty beyond the material world. At times it was very difficult though; I still craved all the luxuries and every gadget known.

I had one big bookcase that was bursting at the seams with esoteric books, and Said immediately gravitated to them. He managed to find a videotape that I had hidden behind one of the books. The title on the case read "The Journey Within" and had a picture of my compassionate guru on the cover.

"Who is this man?" he asked. "What is this journey? Can we watch this?"

There went my plan of not mixing work and pleasure. He brought it onto himself. His eyes were tearing up as the words in that video spoke truth to him. We did not have to talk much on his first visit. There was a deep knowing between us, as he spent the rest of his stay fully immersed in the books of Kirpal Singh, Rumi, and other Sufi teachers.

One book that grabbed his attention was entitled *Many Lives, Many Masters* by Brian L. Weiss, a psychiatrist who specialized in past-life regression. The book tells the story of Dr. Weiss's own spiritual transformation as he treated a patient who recalled past-life childhood traumas that seemed to explain her anxiety attacks and repeated nightmares. Said sat on the balcony of my apartment on the seventeenth floor for two days engulfed in the pages of the book.

"He's a hunk!" uttered my friend Steven, who is a meditator and a successful businessman. My friends Eva and Lynn, who helped me prepare our lectures and meditation sessions, gave Said an exuberant nod of approval. "Tall, handsome, and intelligent!" both whispered to me.

Did they expect me to let go of my standards for a partner the way I did for my material lifestyle? Maybe that level of saintliness might come to me in a few more lifetimes.

I extended my stay for another day, but I needed to return to a world that no longer interested me. I was in the final stages of negotiating a lease on some office space in a building I had finished constructing a few months earlier. My soul was in love. It was the heavens that had brought us together and the goodbye was difficult for both of us.

Elza had known about my love for Gibran. She played a song by the famous Lebanese singer Fairuz that was adapted from Gibran's book *The Prophet*. It played in the background every day I was there. I held her tight as we danced to the profound words and melodies in it. As we embraced for our first goodbye, her eyes welled up with tears. I looked deeply into them and, without forethought, I uttered words that were in Gibran's book but not in the song: "Love knows not its own depth until the hour of separation." With those words, she melted into my arms as we held each other in a long embrace.

A few minutes after I got home, the phone rang. "I figured it out," she said enthusiastically.

"Figured what out?" I asked.

"Who we were in past lives! I am the soul of May and you are the soul of Gibran."

The *May* to whom she was referring was May Ziade, who was Gibran's contemporary and the Susan B. Anthony of the Arab world. She was a prolific Lebanese Palestinian writer, poet, and essayist who lived in Cairo and wrote extensively on the issues of women emancipation in Arab culture. Although the two never met, they maintained an extensive correspondence that, according to some literary critics, became a long-distance romance. They remained literary pen pals until Gibran's passing in 1931.

Slowly a pattern began to emerge. On my first visit, Elza explained to me the circumstances under which she was given her name. At the time she was born, the Middle Eastern literary world had been in uproar over the Arabic translation of Louis Aragon's book *Le Fou d'Elsa*, and our town was ground zero. The translator was poet and essayist Said Akl, who was from Zahle and who, in later years, became one of the most famous Arab poets and philosophers of the twentieth century. In the book, Aragon describes the clash of civilizations between East and West, Muslim and Christian, set during the Spanish Inquisition. It was in poetry and in prose. In one of the most known poems in the book, the writer announces the arrival of Elsa, whose character represents the transformative powers of the feminine. She had also told me that Akl had intentionally translated *Elsa* to *Elza* in defiance of the French colonial influence that resulted in so many Christians in Lebanon giving that name to their daughters. He replaced the letter *s* with the letter *z* for the first letter in the name of our town, *Zahle*, in order to leave its literary legacy with the reader.

Apotheosis

That week, I began to feel the heavy burden of my calling. As must be apparent by now, I had fallen deeply in love with Elza. The gods and goddesses had answered my call and sent me my long-lost soul mate, but did she have to be such a clear-headed warrior?

I began to ask myself those questions that only fools ask when they don't understand the gift they've been given. In my longing for true companionship, had I summoned the same divine Assembly that had rebirthed her soul in the brutal way reflected by her early life? Were the gods sending me unequipped to join in some battle against inequality about which I knew very little? What did the soulful connection I felt with her have to do with fighting the patriarchy and injustice over women's rights? Was her oldest brother, Michel, the guardian angel whom the heavens had sent to guide her way?

My questions were many, but, just as with so many other unknowns that were calling me, I decided to trust the divine forces that had brought us together and wade into the torturous waters of change.

During one of our many philosophical discussions, I wanted to know how Elza's esoteric teachings interpreted the seven masks in Gibran's *Madman*.

"The masks are not selves or parts of the physical identity," she said. "They are the different spiritual realms to which the soul ascends on its way to Nirvana, or *Naam* in the Sant Mat tradition."

She then proceeded to name the different realms on the spiritual path known as *Sant Mat,* or the "Path of the Saints." The realms had different names in Sanskrit, but Elza named them in English in descending order:

"Nirvana is the realm of the Unknowable," she said, "followed by Oneness, which is the realm of Infinite Being and Cosmic Consciousness." With confidence in her voice, she continued, "Then comes the Supra-Causal realm, identified as the Whirling Cave, and then the two causal realms, the first identified as the Great Void and the second as Emptiness. Then comes the Astral realm, which is halfway between the intelligent soul and the mental body. And finally, there is the physical realm—"

"And that's where we clueless humans roam!" I interrupted.

She laughed and added, "Not only that; the physical realm is where time, space, and matter are made manifest. It is the lowest and densest form of existence."

My soul was hungry to learn more. I decided to learn the meditation techniques that she taught and was initiated into the traditions of the Path of the Saints. Poets such as Rumi and Kabir were some of the earliest teachers of this tradition. It is deep and esoteric, and I came to learn the similarities between the microcosm and the macrocosm, the universe within and the universe without. Everything in the cosmos is all one, and what ties it together is karma. Karma is the omnipotent power that came into existence when the universe was created. Its earliest form manifested in light and in sound. The teachings say that when we enter the physical realm, we become disconnected from our source. The only way to reconnect to it is through meditations, whereby one can identify with the universal Soul, Nirvana itself.

To me, these revelations were profound and scary all at once. Could the dream I had had when I was three-and-a-half and that reappeared thirty-four years later be from one of the spiritual realms where souls exist as one and where everything transcends time and space? Did the beasts in those dreams represent the seductive powers of the ordinary life that kills a soul's purpose?

In my meditations, I heard the same music that in the dream drew me away from the claws of death. It was played by bagpipes that sang the rare melody that was seducing every fiber of my being. Was my soul's purpose being revealed to me at this stage of my life? If the microcosm is the same as the macrocosm, could the universal Soul exist within me? Was I entering the world of the collective unconscious, where heroes and archetypes of the psyche reside? The questions were many, and my love for them and for Elza grew feverishly.

The months that followed were full of bliss—the type of delight that occurs when the body, mind, and soul of two lovers become one. Our friend Bruce Lipton, the evolutionary biologist, best describes this feeling in his book *The Honeymoon Effect.* We spent months in what he calls the state of bliss that comes from enormous love. Our lives were so joyful that we both couldn't wait to get up and start a new day, thanking the universe that we were alive.

One day, that blissful state led my heart and soul to speak: "I want to spend eternity with you."

Elza answered, "That's wonderful. How much money do you have?" She explained the reasons for that answer in her unpublished book:

> When I saw the look on his face after I asked the question, I realized that what I had just asked was a faux pas in mainstream culture. Oops! I had to explain, saying that his statement triggered my thought of every plan I had in mind to transform the world into a better place; and, therefore, he had to have enough money to support a volunteer with such an expensive habit of serving. Transforming the world would be an awesome challenge, but what was coming to me was more my continued personal transformation. I had been to the depth of esoteric understanding, and now with the help of a partner I was ready to venture forth into the real world to apply it.

After six months of our traveling between Miami and Phoenix, Elza made the painful decision to close the meditation center she had started in Miami and move in with me. This was an agonizing sacrifice for her, since the center was the first city prototype for the spiritual organization that had ashrams in rural areas all over the world. While the organization wanted to expand its reach to inner cities, Elza's own spiritual awakening was leading her in a different direction. She wanted to apply the enlightenment that came with the deeper knowledge of the soul to solving real problems. And without knowing it at the outset, I was going to be her partner on the journey. First, I needed to be in the same spiritual space she was in. Her sacrifices on her journey had been many, and mine paled in comparison. But while my dying to my old self had been partial until we moved in together, that is when my true surrender began.

One of the first things Elza embarked on when she moved with me was to transform the rest of what hadn't already been transformed in my life. Our meditations and spiritual practices made me aware of how a soul incurs karmic debt, and I knew which practices to adopt to minimize my karmic footprint. It is said that we incur karma just by being born. It is by living a life of selfless service—the life of soul—that karma is mitigated. Practicing nonviolence in thought and in action, truthfulness, and love for all of humanity were virtues that I began to nurture from the time we met.

I had also understood from a karmic perspective the importance of maintaining a vegetarian diet and the high karmic cost in continuing to eat meat. In spite of this new awareness, I had not given much thought to adopting a wider perspective on health. I had been a runner for years and hadn't thought much of good health being anything beyond physical exercise. With Elza, the issue of health, like anything else, was a whole-systems approach. Her introspective spirituality had provided her with a fully integrated philosophy that she brought to our lives. She was the embodiment of the saying "Physician, heal thyself." She believed that food was energy and that what we put in our bodies affected us physically, mentally, and spiritually. This was the new path of awareness toward which I continued in my own transformation. Being vegetarians was just the beginning, which grew into the proactive practices of eating only organically grown fruits and vegetables. I discovered the wonderful healing powers of herbs and supplements and developed the awareness of the energy of food that nurtured our bodies, minds, and souls. We planted an organic garden, completing the circle of whole health that began to define our lives together.

Since my divorce from Rebecca, I had remained in the small suburban town of Fountain Hills in Arizona. I wanted to stay close to my two young daughters and watch them grow. A colleague of mine from my Boston days had moved to San Diego and had been luring me to move there from the time he heard that I was selling my business. Over the course of many visits, I had fallen in love with the coastal California city. After the divorce, I wanted to move to San Diego with my children, and now, with Elza. Rebecca and I had joint custody and the children couldn't leave the state permanently without a court-approved agreement. In spite of my ex-wife's known abuse of alcohol, I still faced an uphill battle to get the court to grant me full custody. My attorney advised me that courts only granted such requests to fathers in extreme cases. Rebecca's drinking had gotten worse, and my lawyer and I had figured that a charge against her of driving under the influence would constitute an extreme case. For three years, I waited for the law to confirm what most of my friends and neighbors in Fountain Hills already knew about Rebecca's alcoholism, but, alas, that day never came.

Fountain Hills was becoming increasing small for me, even before I met Elza. Everyone's life in this suburban desert oasis was an open book, and mine was no exception. Rumors were going around that I was dating a woman much younger than I was, and, after Elza moved in, the intrusions into our lives went into high gear.

"I hope she's not a gold digger," said my friend Bob as we putted on the greens at the local golf course.

Women intruded differently. Kathy was newly divorced from her husband, who was a pilot for Southwest Airlines. She showed up at my front door wearing a colorful Christmas sweater and bearing a tray of Christmas cookies. She lingered until Elza came to the kitchen and joined us. An hour passed before she left with enough gossip to keep the town buzzing beyond the year-end holidays. This was purgatory, and we were both suffocating. The need for change had become palpable.

There were exactly three things that kept us in Fountain Hills: the first two gave us a glimpse of what our future life together would be like, and the third was preventing us from moving forward into that future.

The first peek at that future was a weekly radio program in Phoenix that Elza had agreed to host. She called it "Soul Talk," and in it she interviewed people from diverse backgrounds to speak about transcendence and the knowledge of the soul. We prepared and edited the show's content together. Over the course of the show, she had interviewed prominent figures who had deep knowledge about the subject matter. They included scientists and doctors such as Andrew Newberg and Bruce Lipton, who both had done research and written extensively on brain science and the biology of belief, as well as Coleman Barks and Daniel Ladinski, prominent scholars in the field of Sufism who had translated the works of Jalal Din Rumi and Hafez, respectively.

The other activity we pursued that became a gateway to our future was a course on comparative philosophies taught by Richard Dance, who became a lifelong friend. Richard opened us both to the work of Joseph Campbell and the perennial philosophers of the East and the West. The Buddha, Lao Tzu, and Socrates were never so alive as they were in Richard's classes and at the philosophical salons he held at his home in Scottsdale. But, as exciting as the radio show and the philosophical salons were, they were both a transitory undertaking while we waited for an upcoming court hearing that would decide the custody issue and allow us to move to San Diego with my two daughters.

The Departure

From the first time Elza met Chloe and Quinn, she fell in love with them and their sense of independence. She was careful not to act as if she were replacing their mother and encouraged them to express their feelings and individuality while carefully navigating the minefield of becoming a stepmom. Their living situation alternated weekly between our home and Rebecca's. The week they lived with us, we went to therapy in order to process all the changes we were going through and the lingering trauma from the divorce. But sadly, the weekly progress that was made in therapy became unraveled as they spent time with Rebecca. She had grown increasingly paranoid about my new lifestyle, the therapy, and the new woman to whom the kids were taking a liking. This tug of war with the children had been going on for months before the therapist became frustrated and acknowledged that, without Rebecca being a part of the therapy, no further progress could be made.

In October of 2000, Rebecca's illness and level of neglect toward our children had reached its limits, as one of her closest friends observed. Initially, Sherry hadn't believed that Rebecca abused alcohol and, because of Sherry's love for Chloe and Quinn, she had not supported my legal efforts to gain their full custody. Her kids were best friends with mine, and she knew that if I moved them to San Diego the loss would be immeasurable. But after three years of observing Rebecca's illness first hand, she had come to believe in my cause. She had filed a report of neglect with the child welfare authorities after repeatedly witnessing an environment at Rebecca's home that wasn't conducive for rearing children. All I needed was a finding of facts that proved negligence for the legal system to grand me full custody. My attorney and I were ready to take the appropriate court action as the date for the decision drew near.

Sherry was in tears when she called after receiving the report with findings that didn't meet the authorities' narrow definition of neglect. I became despondent as sadness and disbelief reached new depths. My lawyer had run out of legal tricks, and life had become a waiting game, the kind of game that risked the lives of our children as the authorities became enablers of all forms of child abuse. To this day, I still don't know whether it was Sherry's anger toward her friend or her guilt from the years of not believing me, but what she said next alleviated my own feelings of guilt over my biggest burden at the time. She encouraged me to move with Elza and assured me that she would keep a watchful eye on Rebecca and the kids. We both hoped for one of two outcomes: the first was for Rebecca to voluntarily enter a rehab program; and the other, with the help of Sherry, was for the courts to accumulate new evidence that Rebecca was an unfit parent, granting me what I had sought for the past three years—a normal life for my children.

There I was—in the same torturous place that Elza had been in when she made the decision to leave her daughter. Just as her ex-husband inflicted abuse on both her and Ghinwa, Rebecca's alcoholism and an incompetent legal system inflicted abuse on Chloe, Quinn, and me. In projecting her problems onto others, Rebecca had told everyone, including the teachers at our kids' school, that Elza and I had joined a cult. Fountain Hills became a lot smaller, a suburban hell from which there was no ordinary escape.

What had moved me to Arizona was now choking me and negating whatever progress I had made on my own inner journey. I caught myself falling into the safety of the ordinary again, the numbness of not being conscious. What was scarier is that I was luring Elza's soul into the same place of the ordinary and the complacent. I knew that in order for us both to pursue a journey toward the highest human possibility, a journey of selfless service, I needed to be extraordinary in my actions. I needed to die to my old self in order to be born again. I needed to place us both at the threshold of the Extraordinary, and that required an incredible act of courage. As painful as it was to leave my two young daughters, I needed to cross a new threshold to where destiny had called me. Once I crossed, there would be no going back. There was no greater grief or deeper sorrow than what I experienced on that day—the day Elza and I drove west to California.

Figure 3.2. Our favorite hiking spot—Squaw Peak, in Phoenix, Arizona, where, after our move to California, we kept a second home.

4

THE LIFE OF POSSIBILITY

In this universe of ours, from the tiniest particles to the Galaxies of galaxies, everything is rhythm, pulse, beat, music. It emerged out of an infinite deep domain of Being's vast intelligence, creativity, and energy. Allow yourself to marvel at the immensity of this picture for a moment and then ask yourself: Where does my life fit into the consciousness of a universal reality? What can I do to play my part?
—Jean Houston, *Jump Time*

"Are you up? You have to listen to this."

After Elza nudged me several times, I woke up, eyes heavy with sleep, searching for the clock.

"It's 3:30 a.m. What could be so important that it couldn't wait until morning?"

Assured that she had an audience, she began: "OK, this guy Ken Wilber says that in order for us to save humanity we have to resurrect the goddess Gaia, which the patriarchy has brutally repressed for millennia. Do you understand what this means? This is the reawakening of the Feminine! I'm marking all the important stuff for you to read."

"That's great," I said dismissively as I rolled over to the other side of the bed, trying to recapture what was left of a lucid dream.

"OK, you have to listen to this!" she said a few minutes later as she flicked the ceiling lights on, making it impossible for anyone to remain in a sleep state.

87

As I looked over at her, Elza was busy doing what she was born to do— highlighting critical passages in a book with yellow marker and making notes in the margins. These are the activities that added to her incredible reservoir of knowledge that made her so extraordinary. It was time for me to make coffee and prepare for a discussion of some unknown nature dictated by some unknown author.

"OK, listen," she continued as she quoted from the book. "Development is not linear. It's full of spirals, streams, and waves…"

The more she spoke, the more my brain fell asleep. Maybe a second cup would help, I thought.

"…he talks about a model called Spiral Dynamics that says the psychology of a mature human being is an unfolding, emergent, oscillating spiraling process…."

No amount of coffee was going to be useful. We'd had our share of philosophical and intellectual debates, but this was something far more complex than I'd ever encountered, and I couldn't comprehend much of what she was saying—maybe because it was 4:00 a.m., or maybe because the wiring in my brain at that time didn't allow for complexity of this magnitude.

Destiny in the Bargain Bin

The book Elza was reading was Ken Wilber's *A Theory of Everything*, which she had picked from the bargain bin at an independent bookstore that was closing its doors. It was August 2002, and we had been in San Diego for almost two years. From the day we settled into our first home in the coastal community of La Jolla, Elza began to come out of her self-imposed spiritual exile. She worked on diversifying her knowledge and began to explore subjects such as depth psychology, myth, and human development. She wanted to find answers that her own journey thus far had failed to provide. But it was her more explicitly spiritual teachings—such as detachment from the ego and the material world—that had attracted me to her, and I began to feel a sense of betrayal. I was a newcomer to spirituality, and she had been my guide, my loving helper who was going to lead me to the promised land and to the heaven on earth that lay beyond the life I had known. But with Elza's new interests, I felt a sense of abandonment and began to question my new reality. Was the new field into which I had crossed after leaving my world of known limits actually one of *false* adventure? Was my soul mate the trickster who had brought me to the threshold of self-understanding only to abandon me in the realms of the unknown? Was this the beginning of my own road of torturous trials? I had wanted so desperately to be in Elza's universe, but as I committed to uproot myself to join her on a spiritual journey, it seemed to me that she had decided to circumnavigate that quest and come back to the ordinary world again.

What Enlightenment?

This was yet another new obstacle for me to overcome, another layer to peel on my path to wholeness. Was I playing the victim because I didn't want to take responsibility for my continued conscious transformation?

Every time I questioned our journey together, Elza would tell me that I still needed to empty myself from my ego in order to find my own answers. All I had done since we moved was spent time emptying myself from myself. In addition to meditating, reading spiritual books and mystic poetry, Elza suggested that I explore Buddhism and read the works of renowned authors in the field such as Alan Watts and Jack Kornfield to know how to let go of attachment. Being the good pupil, I did just that. I delved into the Middle Way and read many books. Over several months, I began to see glimpses of nondual consciousness, the emptiness that lies beyond the ego. Every time I shared my insights with Elza, she would respond with the phrase "chop wood, carry water," which was a shortened version of a saying from the Buddha: "Before enlightenment; chop wood, carry water. After enlightenment; chop wood, carry water." This was the essence of the Middle Way that brought me humility and the understanding of the very nature of being.

CHAPTER 4

After reading Jack Kornfield's *After the Ecstasy, the Laundry,* the stages of my own journey became a bit clearer. I had glimpses of what humility felt like if I could only remain in the state of transcendence—of being at one with everything—and return to daily life. After freeing my soul from the bondage of identity and self-imposed limitations and experiencing oneness with the universal Soul, I was still faced with the daily tasks of being human. I had believed that my transcendental experiences had made me so enlightened that I was no longer directed by the powers of my ego and the different masks I had worn. But dirty laundry and spiritual awakening are both part of the human condition that is not to be judged. They are two sides of the same coin, and on both sides the enlightened one chops wood and carries water just the same. It is that simple.

This truth required a new state of acceptance that had yet challenged my journey toward wholeness. To place all my past masks of identity in the same, nonjudgmental space as my Higher Self became my new challenge. In that space of stillness, I learned to watch the grass grow and contemplate the distant blue ocean that lay beyond the beautiful sandstone canyon flanking our backyard. This had to have been heaven on earth, especially at sunset when the orange rays hit the sandstone, making the outcroppings look otherworldly. When it rained, there was only the rain, and when the winds blew, there was only the wind. I learned to live in the now and to open myself to above and below, trusting that everything would fall into place.

In the months that followed, it became clear to me that conscious awakening had many helpers, but the path from that point forward was a solemn and unique journey of the individual. The arduous search to find the universal Soul was only the halfway mark on the quest. My soul mate had brought me to the threshold of that understanding, and then must come the homecoming, the part of the journey when the hero returns to the ordinary world, bearing transcendent powers and teachings to bestow upon others.

While my first two years in San Diego were defined by my struggles to deepen my own self-knowledge and the nature of being, for

Elza they were the years when she began to put her spiritual awareness to work to improve the human condition. The comfortable lifestyle we had gave her the security and safety to revisit much of the philosophical acuities she had set aside after law school and helped open her up to acquiring new knowledge. However, her financial dependence on me weighed heavily on her, and she wanted to become financially independent as quickly as possible. She had thought that her return to the ordinary world would be a return to the Middle East and began to explore ways for that return. A childhood friend of hers, Rabih, had become a renowned interior designer in Kuwait. He had worked for a famous Italian designer and, as a result, had accumulated several rich and powerful clients in the Middle East. Rabih was very familiar with Elza's journey and her spiritual awakening. He related to her the stories of many of his wealthy clients about the spiritual void they felt that no money or power could satisfy. He implored her to become a personal coach to those who were hungry for the kind of knowledge she possessed. She promised him to fulfill his request when the time was right.

Elza hit the ground running when we moved to San Diego. She pursued change the only way she knew how; she read books on the subject matter and pursued the practical applications in all that she read. One of the first books that placed her on the road to a new path was *Frames of Mind: The Theory of Multiple Intelligences* by Harvard-trained, developmental psychologist Howard Gardner. After finishing the book, she understood the need to nurture other innate intelligences in addition to the spiritual intelligence she already possessed. Within weeks she enrolled in an emotional-intelligence certification program and became a certified coach within a few months thereafter. Subsequently she became fascinated with the work of Hal and Sidra Stone, two Jungian psychologists who pioneered a theoretical framework called the Psychology of the Selves. The practical aspect of their work is the model known as Voice Dialogue. Within months of attending a seminar with the Stones and reading their books, she became a certified practitioner in Voice Dialogue. These were enough tools for her to create the first consultancy that launched her into her return and into a new career. She called her business Selfwork. By the end of that year, with the help of her friend in Kuwait she became financially independent and a sought-after life coach for wealthy Arab families.

A New Existential Crisis

While my soul mate continued to explore different methods to augment her return, I was beginning to falter on my own journey. Without her being a part of it, I felt my quest was coming to an end. I began to languish. I had emptied myself from my ego to find the Middle Way, but instead of being in that place of bliss, I had awakened some of my past selves and parts of my ego instead. The only difference now was that I was on my own in sorting it all out. Elza had needed my emotional and financial support to begin anew, but in less than a year she had liberated herself from those dependencies.

Alone, I slowly observed my state of enlightenment giving way to matters of security and the safety of the old and the familiar. I found myself making contingency plans: just as I had done when I moved to Arizona, I now pursued the goal of becoming a licensed real-estate broker in California. This was the secure and safe pattern I had adopted many years earlier. It was honorable, and it left nothing to chance. First came the real-estate license, then the builder's license. Those were the sure ways of building a solid career and a virtuous life. I took all the necessary courses to become a broker, and by August 2001 had passed the licensing exams. All I needed was the license itself, a piece of paper to hang on the wall of my new downtown office that overlooked San Diego Bay. It would announce to the community—but more importantly to me—that I had returned to the world in the pursuit of material possessions, augmented now by a marginal understanding of spirituality and self-knowledge.

One of the last requirements before my license could be issued was for me to pass a background check conducted by the FBI. This was a routine task and I had nothing to fear, since the same checks were conducted routinely for a number of other professional licenses I had kept active from the two other states in which I had lived. But while waiting for my California license to arrive, the world as we knew it changed. The attacks of 9/11 took place, and all background checks on Arab-Americans became much more extensive. The backlog took over a year to process, and by the time my license arrived, I had subleased my office space and lost all interest in returning to the real-estate profession.

When the events of 9/11 took place, something shook us to the core. First it was the shock from the event itself, then it was the aftermath of living-while-Arab in the United States. It mattered not that both Elza and I were US citizens; to us racism and bigotry were quite palpable. The winds of war began to blow, and we felt it everywhere, from the awkward looks we got when a barista at Starbuck's called my name to when our table was ready at a restaurant. Then came the insensitive jokes our friends told about Arabs when they innocently thought we identified only as Americans.

The biggest sower of discord, however, was the media, which divided everything into us-versus-them scenarios. In traditional societies, the clergy, the nobility, and the commoners had been considered the three estates of the realm. Now the power of the media—sometimes called the fourth estate—was evident and in full force. The degree of ignorance about Arab culture being disseminated by newspapers and television news made us both cringe. It was clear that most American leaders and citizens alike had little understanding of the Arab world. The numerous cultural compositions and the varying values of tribal life in the Middle East were mostly absent from American conscious. To accuse an entire race of being at war with the West was as absurd as believing the earth is still flat. It was so odd to experience firsthand a culture that thrived on free speech being manipulated by those who held authority, power, and influence. The US media had joined hands with the political establishment to wage unnecessary wars based on deception, manipulation of facts, and the stereotyping of a religion with more than a billion followers. These were the powers that controlled the narrative, and those who had power controlled the degree to which speech was free.

I had never experienced something so contentious and on such a large scale. Discrimination began to rear its ugly head everywhere I looked, from the added disclosure requirements when I tried to open a new business banking account, to the endless list of questions about having any affiliation with terrorist groups every time I drove across the Arizona border to visit my kids. Suddenly I became "them." I had always thought of myself as an American and a patriot, but I rarely wore my heart on my sleeve. To me, the hundreds of jobs I had provided throughout my career was my way of showing my patriotism, but in a post-9/11 world, that wasn't going to be enough. The random checks of our luggage at airports became laughable. It was as random as the sun rising every day. The books we carried with us to read on long trips, books by Rumi and Gibran, became a national security threat. It all seemed like a nightmare, as I felt the great divide between East and West come to America's shores. As an American, I felt both the pain and the ignorance of my nation. I wanted to do *something*, but I was at a loss as to what that something could be.

Elza, on the other hand, felt that the events of 9/11 represented a long-awaited, personal call for action. No one around us had cared to know about Arab culture and the factors that led to the events, but Elza understood them fully. She understood them from the political, social, religious, and cultural perspectives. She has had a front-row seat to this clash of civilizations for decades. It started for her in law school, when on the university campus she had witnessed the birth of Hezbollah, the extremist Shia Muslim militant group that became based in Lebanon. She had known then that a meme was emerging that would take the Middle East by storm and present a growing threat to the West. She gives a detailed analysis of that phenomenon in her book *Emerge*:

> During my second year of law school, something strange appeared on our campus. Over the summer, our Shia classmates completely transformed their appearances. These

were young men who had been full of enterprising ambition the year before. They had been indistinguishable from other students. They wore Levi jeans and Nike sneakers and freely conversed with women. They participated in heated debates about the nature of governing and how Lebanon's so-called democracy left out the fair and equal participation of the Shia sect. All that was gone. Dialogue had disappeared. Eye contact and hand shaking with women became a thing of the past, and so were many common goals these young men had shared with their classmates just a few short months before.

What had happened? These young men could no longer identify with a secular society that denied them equal rights. Now they had a new identity that gave them a holy sense of purpose. Prominent were their bearded faces, their black suits, their buttoned-up, white collars. This was the unmistakable attire of Iranian revolutionaries. The Islamic Revolution that had swept through Iran a few years earlier became a new *meme* (ideology) for the oppressed Shia in the region. All the ideology had needed was a new Arab voice to spread its values and justify its legitimacy as the first modern-day Islamic Revolution. That Arab face was the Shia of Southern Lebanon and the Bekaa Valley.

Most national boundaries in the Arab world today were drawn by colonial powers. The design of these nations did not emerge naturally through the creation of common goals and values that bound the people under a common flag. Colonial clerks who, first and foremost, sought the interest of their own empire imposed arbitrary geographic boundaries that forced feuding tribes to compete and claim the new land and its natural resources for their own tribes. Instead of helping these new nations move forward, Western interference only constrained their progress.

The values of the Islamic Revolution spoke much louder to these young men and women than did a model for governance designed by French colonialists. The revolution inspired them. It gave them common purpose and a personal sense of identity. Suddenly the secular form of resistance to Israel disappeared. It was replaced by an ideology with the Shia brand of Islam at its core. This was the birth of an organization that became known the world over as the Party of God, or Hezbollah.[1]

Although Elza's analysis in her book was about the birth of Hezbollah, a Shia militant group, the meme for a new Islamic revolution spread across both Shia and Sunni branches of the religion. This was a rebellion against the Western influence on Islam, and Elza understood it at a profound level. She had known intuitively that there would come a time when her love for Middle Eastern politics would call her back and she would have a chance to contribute to making the Middle East a better place. She understood the teachings of Wahhabism—the ultraconservative Sunni religious movement—and the threat its followers presented to the world. In law school, she studied everything pertinent to Islam from Sharia Law and the Quran to the Hadith and Nahjul Balagha. After the events of 9/11, I found her reading Islamic scripture and literature again, and I wasn't sure what to make of it.

The events of that day had shaken us from the safety of our new life together. It sent us both on a search for deeper answers steered by questions of identity and purpose. We each felt the heavy burden of what needed to be done for both the Middle East and the West to understand each other better, and we looked for how to affect change in any way we could. Maybe this had been our calling all along, a common cause for us both in which we could affect change having deepened our understanding of ourselves, and of the oneness of humanity. In terms of the hero's journey, this work would amount to a return on a quest that had been driven by inner forces for change. For me, it was my opportunity to reclaim a big part of myself—my Arab identity—that I had abandoned and repressed from age fifteen. For the two of us, the work would constitute our joint return to the ordinary world bearing the wisdom we had gleaned from all our spiritual search over the past several years. The road ahead looked daunting, but our determination to travel it was undeterred.

Winning the Blessings of the Gods

While Elza continued her coaching work in the Middle East, through her connections she began to reach out to influential people and offer her services to affect social change. The more she searched, the more she recognized that the starting point to the transformation of the region was the Israeli-Palestinian conflict.

"Arabs have the knack to blame everything on the far enemy," she said. "They project all their problems onto the Zionists and the imperial Americans, and that has to change."

She believed that reason to be mainly what stopped any meaningful conversation about political or religious reform from taking place. It enabled the culture and its leaders to continue in their complacency and their projections on the "other" instead of doing the hard work of introspection. For Elza, it was high time to pull the rug out from under that excuse in order for the region to begin to emerge into higher values. This realization steered her passions beyond any consulting or coaching activities. Working on this conflict would bring her full circle to where she had started with the group of Lebanese existentialists in her third year of law school. She had since seen all the treaties and peace accords between the Israelis and the Palestinians falter, and she knew there needed to be a more wholesome approach to a lasting peace. The summer of 2002 was the time the gods and goddesses had marked for us both to meet our helpers on this new common quest, a journey of possibility that was like no other.

Elza's exuberance in reading Ken Wilber's *A Theory of Everything* marked a profound shift in her thinking. Wilber details the nature of his Integral Theory and offers a comparative analysis of different human-development models. Throughout the book, he keeps coming back to the Spiral-Dynamics model and the work of Don Beck, the model's coauthor and the successor to the legacy of Clare W. Graves, the academic who had been behind the original research.

Figure 4.1. Dr. Don Beck (left) and Clare Graves, 1978.

What interested Elza was Beck's application of the model in South Africa that helped the nation's transition from Apartheid. This was developmental psychology applied at the level of nations, and she knew that the same methodologies would offer a more comprehensive approach for solving the Israeli-Palestinian problem and address the greater issue of the region's arrested development. She became consumed with both Wilber and Beck. She purchased all the books they had published. We spent the rest of that year enriching ourselves with new knowledge about the nature of psychosocial development and states and stages of conscious. There were colors that Beck used as designations for levels of development that removed all stereotypes and compelled us both to learn about human and social development through different lenses.

Turquoise to My Yellow

In later years, I asked Dr. Beck about his motivation to use colors to designate the levels of human psychosocial development instead of the numbers in the hierarchy that Graves developed. Dr. Beck said that in the past Graves had told him about the academic and the institutional resistance that Graves's colleague Abraham Maslow had experienced in using terms such as *hierarchy* and *evolution*. The 1960s and 1970s were times when egalitarian values were on the rise. That was especially true in the ivory towers of academia, and anything academic that used these two terms was frowned upon. Hence, Graves became hesitant in formally introducing another model that espoused a developmental hierarchy. This, Dr. Beck believes, was one of the primary reasons why Graves didn't submit his work for peer review during his lifetime. Beck and Cowan, however, saw beyond the egalitarian values that dominated academia at the time and chose to use colors instead of levels in order to lessen the appearance of hierarchy.

As a result, they came up with the following color scheme that represents the eight different levels of development in their Spiral Dynamics model: The color beige represents the first level of psychosocial development that deals with survivalistic existence, while the purple color represents the second level that deals with tribalistic existence. The color red represents the third level of heroic and egocentric values of existence, while blue represents the values of the absolutistic fourth level. The color orange represents the multiplistic and scientific values of the fifth level, while the color green represents the relativistic, humanitarian, and the egalitarian values of the sixth level. According to both Graves and the Spiral Dynamics theory, the first six levels of existence—beige through green, or the first through the sixth levels—are the values of a subsistent humanity that form the first tier of values. The last two levels, seven and eight, which Graves called "the being values" or "the values of magnificence," form the still-emerging second tier of values and are commonly known throughout the Spiral Dynamics community as "the emerging values of humanity." The seventh level is designated by the color yellow, and it represents the integrative values that see the big picture of life on the planet, while the eighth and final level, designated by the color turquoise, represents holistic values that integrate mind and spirit where everything connects to everything else in ecological alignment.[2]

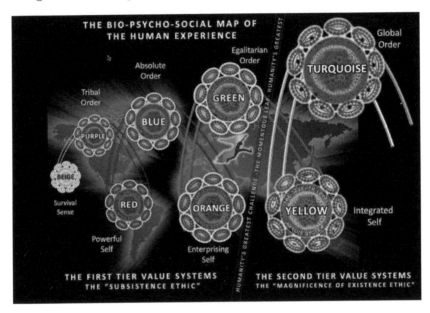

Figure 4.2. The Graves Spiral Dynamics Model by Said E. Dawlabani and the MEMEnomics Group. Used by permission.

To Elza, Beck and Wilber became the guides on the next phase of her new journey. Their theories had provided the answers to the new existential questions she was asking. She had sent both of them several emails requesting their input or a meeting at which she could discuss the application of their respective knowledge to the Middle East, but had received no response. One day, an Internet search led her to a white paper that Beck had authored about the Israeli-Palestinian conflict. It was as if she had found the Holy Grail. Finally, she thought, the theorist she had admired was presenting her with the tools for the deeper understanding of the structures that prevented Arab culture from moving forward and providing her with a comprehensive explanation of the psychosocial dynamics that cause conflict and war. To her, the paper provided the answers to the failure of leadership in governance that had eluded most world leaders. Intuitively, she knew that she would be working with Beck; it was just a matter of how and when. She had also discovered that Beck and Wilber had collaborated to create a hybrid model that combined their two frameworks into one. They called it the Four Quadrants Eight Levels Model, 4Q8L for short. In later years the model evolved further and became the "All Quadrants, All Levels" model, or AQAL. After that collaboration, Beck joined hands with other leaders in the human-evolutionary movement to help Wilber form the Integral Institute in Boulder, Colorado.

The institute's first official leadership training is what brought Elza closer to beginning her journey toward new possibilities. It was dubbed the flagship program for students of evolutionary consciousness looking to change the world. Elza thought she would meet both Beck and Wilber there and have a chance to discuss the Middle East. That chance never came: Wilber was at the training session, but Beck wasn't. However, in addition to learning about Integral Theory directly from its author, Elza got to learn indirectly about Spiral Dynamics and Beck's work in South Africa. She was surprised that Beck wasn't teaching at the Integral Institute at the time. He was instead traveling the world spreading the gospel of large-scale integral design and psychosocial change to governments and world leaders. At the training, a video recording of Beck showed him introducing his latest conception, called Stratified Democracy, to a group of executives at the World Bank. To Elza, this was the answer to most of the questions she had sought. She immediately signed up for the Spiral Dynamics training Beck offered.

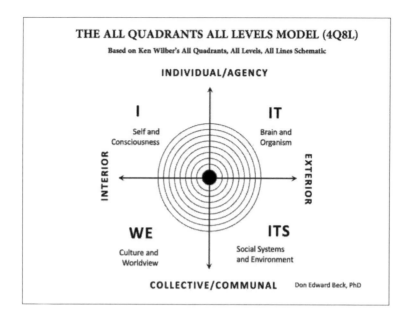

Figure 4.3. The Spiral Dynamics Integral Model. Copyright by the Spiral Dynamics Group and Don E. Beck, PhD. Used by permission from Don E. Beck.

It was at that Spiral Dynamics training in Boulder that an extraordinary partnership was forged. Elza had dissected every aspect of Beck's white paper and gave her analysis that provided what she saw as the missing pieces of the puzzle—the cultural and religious nuances that only a native of the region would possess. At the end of the training program, she told Beck that she had been looking for someone like him her whole life. Beck responded, "I've been looking for you since 9/11."

"You have to take the Spiral Dynamics training as soon as possible. We're going to be working with Don Beck in the Middle East!" Those were the first words out of Elza's mouth when I picked her up from the airport that week. It was the spring of 2003, and I had never seen Elza as animated and as happy as she was during the months of April and May of that year.

During the training, Dr. Beck had asked her whether she would set aside her consulting work if he could find the funding to start an initiative in the Middle East similar to the work he had done in South Africa. Elza agreed, and in the following months I got to meet the man who forever changed the trajectory of our lives.

Dr. Beck was the consummate academic; and, as soon as I was trained, he began to mold our thinking in order for us to see the world differently. He became the guide for our return to the ordinary world, where we carried the fruits of knowledge that integrated all we had acquired on our transformational quest. His guidance contained all the wisdom we had sought and delivered it in the most disarming form.

He spoke in simple language peppered with a Texas drawl using color in a disarming way: "South Africa is not about black and white; it's about value systems. It's about red and blue-orange. The Middle East is not about Jews and Arabs; it's about value systems. It's red and early blue on one side and orange and green on the other."

Those were the common refrains that recolored the lenses through which we saw the world. It was evolutionary and revolutionary all at once. We were consumed by colors that added richness, humor, and the instant delivery of a psychological profile. "Is there anything I should know about this person before I meet him?" I would ask Elza. And if her response was, "He's mostly green with high rejection of orange," I would then know with a high degree of certainty how the meeting was going to go.

At home we spoke in colors. When I was being stubborn about an issue, Elza would tell me to examine my red, or to stop being a "red ass." On her birthday or on our wedding anniversary, I would always add the words, "You are the turquoise to my yellow," to a cake or a card. While people often struggle to describe how they feel about their significant other, their soulmate, the yin to their yang, people in the Integral and Spiral community knew the depth and breadth of what it meant to be the yellow to your partner's turquoise.

SPIRAL DYNAMICS: THE EIGHT VALUE SYSTEMS

COLOR, LEVEL, SUMMARY OF VALUES AND PERCENT GLOBAL POPULATION

TURQUOISE 8	**GLOBAL ORDER:** Holistic and intuitive. Meshing of mind and spirit. Global brain. Aligned with ecological systems. Interconnected and interdependent.	<1%
YELLOW 7	**INTEGRATED SELF:** Integrative. Big-picture perspectives. Complex systems. Chaos. Multiple realities. Functional and evolutionary flows. Flexibility and spontaneity.	5%
GREEN 6	**EGALITARIAN ORDER:** Relativistic. Seeks peace and consensus. Humanitarian. Free of greed and dogma. Equal sharing of resources. Communitarian. Harmonious.	10%
ORANGE 5	**ENTERPRISING SELF:** Multiplistic. Strategic. Objective. Competitive. Driven. Scientific. Optimistic. Self-reliant. Seeks best solutions. Manipulative. Risk-taking.	16%
BLUE 4	**ABSOLUTE ORDER:** The one true way. Law and order. Rigid ideology. Everyone has their proper place. Transcendent causes. Discipline. Truth. Righteous living.	22%
RED 3	**POWERFUL SELF:** Heroic. Impulsive. Exploitive. Egocentric. Guilt-free. Break free. Conquer. Dominate. Call the shots. Demand respect. Expect attention.	32%
PURPLE 2	**TRIBAL ORDER:** Seeks kinship. Mystical and superstitious. Rites of passage. Family bonds, warmth and safety . Loyalty to chief, elders and clan.	15%
BEIGE 1	**SURVIVAL SENSE:** Automatic-instinctive. Lives off the land. Seeks food, water and safety as priority.	<1%

Figure 4.4. Summary of the Spiral Dynamics Model. Copyrighted by Dr. Don E. Beck and Said E. Dawlabani. Used by permission from Dr. Don E. Beck.

The gospel of Spiral Dynamics began to transform who we were and uplifted our vision of who we could become. If we had captured the so-called elixir of life, or any enlightenment on the first half of our respective journeys, then the return to the ordinary world was manifesting through our new map of reality—the knowledge of Spiral Dynamics being taught to us by the master himself.

On the Threshold of the Return

While Dr. Beck was searching for someone like Elza to help him bring Spiral Dynamics to the Middle East, after the events of 9/11 many in the consciousness and human development communities turned to him for answers. They wanted him to duplicate what he had done in South Africa in this troubled part of the world. The Middle East steered the passions of several conscientious leaders, including Ken Wilber and many in the Integral and Spiral Dynamics communities. After the events of 9/11 and the ensuing wars in Iraq and Afghanistan, the search for more conscious and sustainable solutions went into high gear. And, while Dr. Beck was known the world over for his involvement in South Africa's transition from apartheid, the details of his ten-year involvement had remained obscure to those outside his circle of influence. In 1991, with South African journalist Graham Linscott he wrote what amounted to an academic book about the experience. The book was titled *The Crucible, Forging South Africa's Future,* which he dedicated to his friend and mentor, Clare W. Graves. Its content and the experience were the predecessors to the book *Spiral Dynamics,* which brought forth the value systems framework to the world. By the early 2000s, Dr. Beck was witnessing the global success of the Spiral Dynamics framework and, based on its teachings, he was becoming a renowned geopolitical advisor. But, as he told Elza during their first meeting, he was itching to apply it in the field where it made a difference in people's lives as it had in South Africa. She recalled his paraphrasing a statement by Graves that had led him to give up his tenured career as a professor at the University of North Texas. It was something about his being extraordinary and having the rare ability to know what change the world needs. She couldn't recall the exact Graves quote, but she remembers Dr. Beck rephrasing it to her in this disarming way: "Consultants are a dime a dozen, but there's only one Elza who knows how to bring real change."

On our respective journeys, the two years that followed could only be described as the culmination of all of our experiences, transformative and otherwise, in preparation for the extraordinary return to the world of the ordinary. It was a labor of love that translated whatever wisdom we had acquired into practical tools needed to renew our professions, our communities, and the larger world. We forged a partnership that utilized the best of our collective talents. We collaborated on position papers on the Middle East that included Elza's in-depth knowledge of the culture, my knowledge of economic systems, and Dr. Beck genius in shaping it all into new models for leadership in economics and in governance. The Middle East became the next frontier for Dr. Beck and, for him, everything else faded away. Elza became the resident expert on seeing the region through his model. We became his most sought-after guest lecturers in his trainings and conferences that sought a deeper understanding of the conditions that created conflict and the underlying dynamics that fostered terrorism and a culture of death.

Figure 4.5. The first Spiral Dynamics *integral* certification in the Middle East, 2005. Elza and Don are seated in the front row.

These were indeed the times the universe had circled for us on the calendar, as the most conscious helpers began to appear with hands extended. The Beck–Wilber partnership reached new heights between 2000 and 2004 as Dr Beck's training programs were transformed to include the word *integral* in their title. "Spiral Dynamics" became "Spiral Dynamics *integral*" and, in the process, became the new transformative tool that brought integral theory to many areas of human and cultural development. More importantly, it applied the theory to an area where it hadn't been applied before—that is, to culture. And *culture* at this particular time meant the Middle East, as Elza began to pioneer the use of both frameworks in the region.

Figure 4.6. Don Beck and Ken Wilber, 2001.

While waiting for funding to start their work in the Middle East, Elza continued her consulting activities with families and businesses in the region. After mastering the organizational applications of both Integral Theory and Spiral Dynamics, she formed her consulting firm, The Integral Insights Consulting Group, which quickly became the name to know in Middle Eastern corporate circles. Her connections in the Middle East had led her to conduct executive training at several medium and large-size companies. The programs became the standard by which much of the region's executive development was judged. At joint training programs with Dr. Beck and me in the United States and Europe, Elza spoke of her efforts to transform the Middle-Eastern corporate world as a precursor to the transformation of the region. She would repeat that the structure was holonic, comprised of the *micro*, the *meso*, and the *macro*—the *micro* being the transformation of the individual, the *meso* being the transformation of the work environment, and the *macro* being the transformation of whole countries and eventually the region. In a short period of time, her work garnered the attention of many who believed in the pioneering nature of her approach.

Ken Wilber himself agreed to be on the board of advisers of her company, which lent depth and breadth to her work.[3] Then another prominent person took notice of our joint work who in later years became a proponent of my work in economics as well: During a training session in Boulder Colorado, we met Belgian economist Bernard Lietaer, at the time a visiting scholar at nearby Naropa University. He had been a prominent figure in the central banking world before he embarked on designing the university's center for business and economics. The author of many books on currencies and global financial systems, Bernard had attained global prominence for being one of the main architects behind the design of the European single currency, the euro.[4] During the training, Elza, Dr. Beck and I got to spent time with Bernard, who by then was more concerned with the conscious evolution of humanity than he was with the design of currency. We both joked about the dismal nature of the field of economics and thought of ways to make it more conscious through the prisms of Spiral Dynamics and Integral Theory. That weekend, I asked Bernard whether he would have done things differently if he had known Spiral Dynamics while he was working on designing the euro. Together we revisited the wisdom that placed the financial integration of an entire continent before its political and economic integration. Bernard was a brilliant person open for learning, and, once I explained the logic behind my thinking through Spiral Dynamics, he immediately understood my rationale. A unifying currency should be the last step in a sequence of steps that took decades to achieve. It was the higher-value system that was the reward confirming the much harder work that the lower systems had to do first.

I explained that when we apply Spiral Dynamics to nations, the fourth-level value system—blue—is the most crucial stage of development. That's the stage at which nations build the right institutions to create political and economic platforms with long-term, institutional outlooks. It's known as the hardest transition, during which power moves from the hands of the egocentric leader to being vested in the institutions of a culture. I recall Bernard listening intently as I continued: Ideological transitions are as challenging as the developmental movement up to a new stage on the spiral. Countries in Europe that were formerly communistic must have their blue systems ripped out by their roots and replaced with a new blue system in order for democracy and free-market forces to thrive. That stage of development, we both agreed, had not been given enough attention and time.

We both laughed as I repeated a common refrain that filled some of the missing gaps in the integral framework: "before integration comes differentiation." The differentiation in this case was the political and economic reformations within each member country before they were all integrated into one monetary system. Bernard and I ended our conversation that weekend with the deep knowledge that our paths would cross again. Before we parted, Elza asked him if he would do her the honor of joining her company's board of advisers. He responded: "The honor will be all mine!"

The training work with Dr. Beck, along with Elza's consulting activities in the Middle East, filled our time while waiting to start the long-anticipated work on the reformation of the Middle East through the cultural applications of the two frameworks. During those years, Elza did not waver from her calling to empower woman and to fight the injustice caused by patriarchal dominance. Her work in personal coaching took on a new form. She had been a close personal coach to one particular family and had brought change to their lives that no therapy or money had done in the past. Her work led one of the daughters to start a successful business and another to obtain a graduate degree in a field of studies that reignited her passion for life. The matriarch in the family had drawn close to Elza during the personal-development work Elza had done with her, and now she needed Elza's guidance into the next phase of her psychospiritual quest. She was an enterprising woman who created one of the very first chain restaurants in the Middle East, but in a culture dominated by patriarchal values, she found herself ceding control of her venture to her brothers, who squandered away the potential of the business. The matriarch's father was behind the creation of several multimillion-dollar companies, and she wanted to reclaim her rightful place in the family enterprise.

I remember the day Elza met with this client for this specific purpose. She had set aside a busy schedule to come to La Jolla and spend a week working with Elza. An hour after leaving home to meet with her client, Elza returned abruptly and announced that she would no longer work with the woman. Only recently, after Elza gave me permission to read her diary, did I discover the reason why. When it came to the issue of the family business, the client had projected all her problems onto others—her father, her brothers, and the numerous male executives who marginalized her and made her feel unworthy. To Elza, this attitude was at the heart of what was wrong with the Middle East. It was the woman's acceptance of being victimized because she was feminine; and, after working with this client for years, Elza wasn't willing to lead her down a new path of oppression and undo all the progress they had achieved. As she described the meeting in her journal, the woman had been full of resignation, victimization, and blaming the other. Elza wanted nothing to do with a person who refused to take responsibility for her own journey.

The shock from Elza's actions must have awakened her client from whatever state of denial she was in. On the third day of her visit, Elza spent the entire day with her and, after coming home, announced her intention to work exclusively with this client and to discontinue all her other work with coaching other corporate clients.

Elza has a strong sense of intuition and a rare stubbornness that makes her stand tall among her peers. As unconventional as decisions like the ones she made about helping that woman were, I learned to trust them. This is the way she had behaved her whole life. It is the essence of what made her extraordinary, and all I could do was be supportive. The decision she made to work with her client that day was the beginning of a partnership that cast both women into a future of boundless possibility.

The Appearance of the Goddess

Few are those in the world who know the meaning of evolutionary consciousness, and fewer yet are those who embody it fully in life.

Jean Houston is one of those rare and remarkable people. She has been described as a mystic, a philosopher, a historian, and a scholar, but, above all, she is the embodiment of the Feminine, the one who redefined Campbell's hero's journey through feminine myth and consciousness. She had collaborated with Dr. Beck in offering seminars at the graduate-level training in Spiral Dynamics. Those gatherings are where ideas become mythic possibilities that empower the extraordinary in all of us. Elza had used some of Jean's ideas in seminars intended to bring back the spirit of the Feminine in the Middle East. After Dr. Beck mentioned the work Elza was doing in the region, Jean wanted to meet her. Here is how Elza described the circumstances surrounding their first meeting in her journal:

> Today, Athena herself asked to meet me. I couldn't believe my luck. I called and we talked for over an hour. I felt her hold my hand on my own mythic journey as Ishtar continued her return from the Underworld. This was destiny that had transcended all the feminine powers I had known and placed me at the source of all that is Feminine. It empowered me in ways that assured me that I wasn't alone on my quest. I told her about my calling and sense of purpose and my lifelong struggle to take the Middle East out of the grip of the patriarchy. She told me of her long-held view about women in the region having the power to transform the world. The Goddess of all goddesses had spoken, two old souls reuniting to bring change to the world. She invited me to attend one of her weekend empowerment retreats that is taking place next month. I'm overjoyed!

I drove Elza to that retreat and had a chance to meet Jean Houston myself. Just as Elza had associated my face with the karmic powers and the greatness of past lives, at first sight Jean described me as having "the ancient face of a Phoenician god."

In that instant, I felt the transcended power of myth, both the masculine and the feminine, in union. It took me out of the many masks of identity and placed me at the center of a godly partnership where Elza and I would continue our journey and living through the mythic dimensions of our lives. During that brief encounter, I remembered Ken Wilber's words as Elza had first paraphrased them to me in the middle of the night: "In order for us to save humanity, we have to resurrect the goddess Gaia, which the patriarchy has brutally repressed for millennia."

That thought is what had cast us both on this remarkable new quest. To me, Jean Houston was the embodiment of the goddess Gaia, the ancestral mother of all life and of Mother Earth. Her words empowered me to become the cocreator and supporter of Elza's quest in fighting injustice and patriarchal dominance wherever they might exist.

Figure 4.7. Elza with Jean Houston at Jean's home, 2009. The eight-foot statue of the Greek warrior goddess of wisdom, Athena, was carved from a single tree. Used with Jean Houston's permission.

The Return

"We have funding to begin our work in the Middle East. You need to clear your calendar so we can get started." Those words of Dr. Beck's were the words Elza had waited for over two years to hear. It was in late 2005, and the beginning of Elza's extraordinary return on her heroine's journey had begun. By then the region had become resigned to a predictable future of failed peace treaties and continued violence. In preparation for this new adventure, Dr. Beck, Elza, and I formed the Center for Human Emergence Middle East (CHE-ME). I agreed to handle all the center's needs and administrative tasks in the United States, while Elza and Dr. Beck did the work on the ground.

This was one of several CHEs Dr. Beck formed in collaboration with a handful of global change agents who had trained with him for years. The centers dotted the globe from Canada and Mexico to the Netherlands, the United Kingdom, and South Africa. We all felt the awesome responsibility that Dr. Beck had bestowed upon the centers. We formed a network of cofacilitators for no less than the conscious emergence of the human species. We were the newest think tanks using the latest breakthroughs in human knowledge and capabilities and utilizing meta-integration methods that expanded the capacities of the whole mind and of human consciousness. Moreover, these centers weren't just think tanks; they were think-and-do-tanks, which made conscious change visible in our respective communities and regions of the world. The first was established in South Africa, where Dr. Beck and his colleagues designed parts of the transit from the apartheid system. Dr. Beck worked closely with F.W. de Klerk and Nelson Mandela, while Mandela was still in prison, on preparing the country for the transition of power. Beck's advice on how to build national cohesion was summarized in the movie *Invictus*, in which he counselled the coach of the South African rugby team, the Springboks, on developing the winning strategy that brought the country together.[5] Further, his work with Peter Merry, the head of the CHE in The Netherlands, introduced a new organizing principle to help Dutch society become more accepting of new immigrants. They called it Societal Mesh Works, and it created a new tapestry that overarched the entire society and the mutual sharing of accountability and responsibility.[6]

By the time our work in the Middle East began, Dr. Beck's had garnered the attention of many global leaders, including George Bush and Tony Blair. He had worked with President Bush from the time he was the governor of Texas and had advised Tony Blair's policy unit. In the Middle East, however, he was mostly known for his work in helping dismantle the Apartheid system in South Africa. Several intellectuals on both the Israeli and the Palestinian sides had known about Dr. Beck's work with Nelson Mandela and F. W. de Klerk and were looking forward to being part of an initiative that sought to break the stalemate of failed negotiations and bloody violence. Hopes were high that the same thinking that helped dismantle Apartheid would be spread in the Middle East to help resolve a conflict of historic proportions.

From their first visit, Dr. Beck and Elza hit the ground running. They met with stakeholders on both sides. They made presentations to the intellectual elites at Israeli and Palestinian universities. They recruited leaders from both sides who knew the two local cultures well but were hungry for a fresh approach to solve the conflict. They trained them on how to become experts in the value-systems methodologies and its applications to nations. There were brilliant engineers and successful entrepreneurs on the Israeli side who cared about both the Israelis and the Palestinians equally. There were Palestinians intellectuals who spent time in Israeli jails and were transformed by the experience and after leaving prison decided to dedicate the rest of their lives in pursuit of peace.

In her book *Emerge*, Elza chronicles the applications and the developments on the ground between the years 2005 and 2008. By the start of the second year of work, we had gathered enough data from both cultures to determine the causes of failure of past peace treaties. Our research had uncovered that there were vast developmental gaps between Israel and Palestine that were at the core of the failure of all the past peace treaties. It was an asymmetry in institutional capacities that unfairly prevented the Palestinians from meeting the conditions for peace. These findings compelled the CHE-ME and our Palestinian and Israeli partners to begin helping the Palestinians build the needed capacities that would eventually lead them to have an independent and resilient state. Our mission became known as the Build Palestine Initiative.

Figure 4.8. Elza and Dr. Beck (in the back row, left) with members of the Fatah movement, 2006.

Like a wild fire being fanned by the media, the goal of our mission spread quickly. It represented both the hunger for something new and the excitement of peaceful coexistence. There were meetings with governors and Knesset members and university professors working on the science and the anatomy of peace. No stakeholders on either side were left out. Our work first began with members of the Third Generation Fatah movement. The movement was founded as a socialist democratic party by the Palestinian diaspora who were primarily well-educated professionals. Over the years it became the main moderate political party to which many young Palestinians belonged. To the dismay of our Fatah partners, we engaged with the radical Hamas movement as well in order for them to begin to see the conflict through different eyes and for us to gain a full perspective on the dynamics that fueled their radicalization. There were powerful Israeli and Palestinian business leaders who saw the wisdom of peace through commerce and committed to hiring Palestinians in their factories. By the third year, every town and hamlet in the Palestinian territories had heard of the work that was being done. They called our Palestinian partners and us *the people of the spiral*. Officials in the Israeli government took notice as well. There were more meetings with Knesset members and at the Israeli Ministry of Defense. The office of the president of Israel had taken notice and had given us the nod of approval.

Figure 4.9. Elza and I with Don, United Nations, June, 2007.

Elza and Dr. Beck also did the work that needed to be done on the ground in the United States. In the summer of 2007, they presented their work as a study to the United Nations through its Values Caucus. By the beginning of 2008, the movement had reached critical mass, and no one was happier than Elza. In February of that year, along with our Palestinian partners, we organized a Nation Building Conference where over seven hundred community leaders came from every part of the West Bank to engage in a first-of-a-kind exercise to design a future state informed by the new and powerful paradigm of value systems. Most of the attendees identified as members of the Third Generation Fatah party made up of young, college-educated professionals who held the greatest promise for a resilient and peaceful future. As Elza describes this critical event in her book, before taking to the stage at that conference she had asked herself if the grassroots, collaborative work that was being done might become a template that could transform the region.

This possibility would be the fulfillment of a dream born out of an unwavering commitment to stay true to her calling.

Figure 4.10. Don and Elza at the opening ceremony of the Nation Building Conference as part of the Build Palestine Initiative, Bethlehem, February, 2008.

The Lift and the Freedom to Be

At some level, the extraordinary work we were engaged in had shown us both the fruits of the transformational journeys we had taken. The deepening of our understanding of humanity had made it possible for us both to participate in such an adventure without fear and without the impositions and limitations of our egos. The absence of fear was quite noticeable in Elza when she began to fight the forces she had fully expected to fight on her return to the Middle East. She had refused to accept the victimizations and the projections each side made onto the other. She had confronted the patriarchy and the injustices it generated head on with both the Israelis and the Arabs. She knew first hand that such action was the key to the region's long journey toward healthy emergence. The more prominent and misogynistic the man was, the more she partook in deconstructing his ego. Nafiz Al Rifai, our Palestinian friend and colleague at the CHE, summed up her fearlessness as a rare ability to take apart the Arab male and put him back together in the most mysterious ways that made him more evolved and well adjusted. Similarly, our Israeli friend and partner Neri Bar On described Elza's fearlessness as disarming when she confronted right-wing

Knesset members such as Avigdor Lieberman, who unreasonably projected Israel's problems on the Palestinians.

We had seen the miracles that were already occurring as well as those that still awaited us once we let go of our personal limitations and saw ourselves as parts of the oneness of humanity. We had crossed the threshold into unimaginable possibilities and moved freely between our two worlds, the ordinary and the extraordinary, the individual and the collective conscious. Our personal ambitions had dissolved and became part of a universal quest toward that oneness. Ego had given way to a higher calling in the service of humanity. There were constant reminders that kept the two worlds in balance.

What had begun as a teacher-student relationship with Dr. Beck a few years earlier had evolved into a dynamic partnership that none of us had imagined possible. It became a life-long relationship that defied all expectations. We became friends and often exchanged visits with the Becks. It was during one of the Beck's visits to La Jolla that Dr. Beck's wife, Pat, told me that his engagement with us in the Middle East had brought new purpose to his life.

Referring to Clare Graves, Dr. Beck's mentor and the academic behind the Spiral Dynamics original research, Pat said, "Just like he willed Clare to give him another ten years, Elza willed him to live at least another ten years to work on the Middle East."

This was something Dr. Beck had said many times about Graves, who by then had retired from academia and was in poor health after suffering several heart attacks. I told Elza what Pat had said, but, instead of being boastful, Elza reminded me that it wasn't her personally but the work we were doing that had led Pat to say what she had. It was another of the constant reminders of humility and centeredness that made Elza who she is. Every time I boasted about our accomplishments, Elza would remind me to chop wood and carry water and to remember the laundry after the ecstasy. We learned to continue living in the moment. The Middle Way replaced the highs and the lows that came from the work that became us.

It was at this stage of our lives that the US economy began to show signs of weakness, and the funding we had counted on to continue the work in Israel and Palestine began to dwindle. This presented us with new dimensions of what was possible. Dr. Beck and Elza shifted their focus to influence powerbrokers in Washington. The Build Palestine Initiative became a case study they presented to all who would listen. At the State Department they met with the office of the assistant secretary of state for the region, which subsequently sent personnel to train in Spiral Dynamics. At the Washington Institute, they met with President Clinton's past envoy to the Middle East, Dennis Ross, who had heard about our work and wanted to know more about the merits of our approach. Elza offered edits to Mr. Ross's book, *Statecraft*, about Sharia Law and cultural misconceptions about Arabs in general and Palestinians in particular. They submitted a proposal to the American Psychological Association (APA) to create a new branch of psychology that Dr. Beck named Psychology at the Large Scale. The three of us worked together on the proposal that sought to bring together the work of three prominent psychologists: Muzafer Sherif, the father of social psychology and Dr. Beck's PhD advisor; Clare Graves, Dr. Beck's associate and the brilliant developmental psychologist behind the academic work on value systems; and Dr. Beck himself, focusing on his own work in developing the Spiral Dynamics framework and the Sherif-Graves hybrid models he created and applied in South Africa and through the Middle East. The proposal was accepted, and all it needed was enough signatures from APA members to become official. But as we began that work, the global economy was plunged into the worst economic crisis since the Great Depression, forcing us to put the plan on hold.

The financial crisis of 2008 presented both Elza and me with new and unimaginable possibilities that were different from what we had worked on at the CHE up until that time. I wasn't sure whether it was my newly acquired knowledge of concepts that explained everything to me or the deepening of my psychospiritual capabilities that made me fearless in taking on new adventures. Spiral Dynamics had given me a deeper understanding of the psychosocial forces that drove the housing market, and during the time that

I developed the last parcel of land I had in Arizona, I witnessed the price of the homes I was building double as they were being built. This was an unprecedented and unsustainable phenomenon being steered by economic forces beyond the normal boundaries of healthy supply and demand. Wall Street was coming to Main Street to destroy it. The predatory hands of investment bankers were behind the endless supply of money that had corrupted one of the last bastions of the American Dream. Investors bought the majority of my new homes without ever seeing them. This was happening all over the country, and I knew it would end only in disaster.

That fall, I shared my views with Dr. Beck on what was happening in housing and in our economy through the prism of value systems. In preparation for a Spiral Dynamics training at the Adizes Graduate School in Santa Barbara, he asked me to speak to the graduate students and trainees about these views and what had led to the financial crisis. What was supposed to be a twenty-minute analysis of the housing market and the state of our financial system quickly evolved into a lively and heated debate about the capitalist system itself that consumed the entire afternoon session.

As we had dinner that evening, Dr. Beck said something that forever changed the trajectory of my life: "Forget the Middle East. This is your passion. Drop everything you're doing and start writing a book about this." He reminded me of how animated I had been in discussing global finance and macroeconomic issues with economist Bernard Lietaer in Boulder a few years earlier.

I didn't get much sleep that night as his words set my heart and my mind on fire. Yes, the Middle East had consumed my heart, but economics and finance were subjects with which I was very familiar. I had made the conscious decision not to return to building homes, but my knowledge of business and economics still steered my passions. No one had applied the value-systems framework to economics, and no one who practiced Spiral Dynamics had the same academic and business background in finance and economics that I did. The first time I ever spoke about economics and global finance through the prism of my new knowledge, it had moved the passions of the designer of the euro and contributed to his evolved understanding of monetary systems and their necessary connection to political and economic reforms.

Expanding my interpretation of macroeconomics through Spiral Dynamics very quickly became my new vocation. To write about it became a further refinement of my bliss, and I took up the cause in earnest. From that day forward at all our joint appearances, Elza and Dr. Beck spoke about the Middle East and I spoke about economics in the context of evolutionary values. For a few years I kept refining my research and adding to the concepts that eventually became the book *MEMEnomics: The Next Generation Economic System*, released in September, 2013.

Figure 4.11. Don Beck, who wrote the foreword, and his wife, Pat, were the first recipients of my book, *MEMEnomics*.

With the book came the expansion of what was possible. The world that I knew had taken notice, and the framework I had put forth became our community's battle cry for change and progress. It quickly expanded beyond our community of practitioners and reached those who were searching for deeper answers to what ailed a capitalist culture. It wasn't about economics as much as it was about the evolutionary values of humanity as those values were being expressed through economic policies. It was about the long-term effect of economics on culture and the need to strike a balance between success and meritocracy on one side and the care for humanity and the need for inclusion on the other. Without my ever intending for my work to be moralistic, to many it became the scientific argument for higher consciousness and greater inclusion. The framework of evolutionary values was challenging the dismal science of modern economics and its proprietary nature, and for those who sought higher consciousness, my writings became an affirmation of the greater good in humanity.

With all the positive book reviews and interviews with the media, it was difficult to keep my ego in check. There were appearances on National Public Radio, the Voice of America, and an endless number of podcasts. *Newsweek Magazine*, the *Christian Science Monitor*, the *International Business Times*, and other print media interviewed me and wrote about my work. The widely respected *Library Journal Book Review* called my approach to solving problems bold and creative, triggering the interest of hundreds of libraries around the world to add the book to their stacks. Seeking Alpha, an online financial services website with seventeen million subscribers, compared my writings to those of Warren Buffet and Peter Lynch. The book was translated to Korean, and my name was proposed as a keynote speaker for the 2015 Asian Leadership Conference, which was hosting several past and present world leaders as keynote speakers for that year. The Taiwan Ministry of Culture chose the book as one of a handful of English – language books to add to their libraries in that same year. In the short years that followed, I became the embodiment of the work that I loved. I delivered keynote addresses in many parts of the world, from the largest gathering of financial planners to the gathering of the most powerful global bankers and influential politicians looking to design the next financial system.

In what seemed to be a blink of an eye, I had experienced success beyond my dreams. The years of inward growth were being rewarded by outer success that made a difference in the world. The pearl was mine for the taking, and following my bliss had brought me unimaginable joy.

The 2008 financial crisis brought a new dimension of possibility for Elza as well. Her Middle Eastern client's family businesses were being affected negatively by the crisis, and her client sought her advice on what to do. In her personal journal, Elza describes their first conversation about this issue as her client's golden opportunity to separate the business entities she was passionate about from her family's remaining enterprises and assert her own powers. Everything was being run by men who were driven by their egos and made decisions impulsively. Although Elza dedicates an entire chapter in her book *Emerge!: The Rise of Functional Democracy and the Future of the Middle East* to her long-term involvement in her client's enterprise, she describes her greater drive to empower the feminine in the Middle East through business in more detail in her journal. Her coaching of her client for this extraordinary feat was intense, and the patriarchal resistance to breaking its grip on the enterprise was powerful. It was a microcosm of the challenges facing the entire region. As Elza began to identify the organizational changes that needed to happen, she simultaneously sought to embolden the feminine powers of her client. As she describes in her journal, she called on the Goddess of all goddesses to help her:

> Today, Athena herself—Jean Houston—came to my office to meet the extraordinary female I have been working with. The heavens must have circled that week for us on the calendar. After a three-hour private meeting with Jean, my client decided to extend her stay for a few days to reconnect with that which has been dormant in her and in every woman in the Middle East.

A week later, there was this entry:

> I was overjoyed today to hear from my client that she has decided to separate the food-services operations from other family businesses and run it herself. I will be returning to Kuwait for three weeks next month to help her begin this process.

Elza became obsessed with transforming her client's organization. Bringing change to the region by influencing the thinking of four thousand, five hundred employees became her focus. She called her first years of engagement "righting the ship," and, as she details in her book, there was much to right. She initiated processes and procedures where there had been none; and, as time went by, those who made decisions outside the parameters of the new policies found it difficult to stay. Impulsivity and the individual ego were gradually replaced by temperance and the way of the organization. Employee rank and pay had been based on country of origin— a custom that Elza began to change immediately. She promoted women who held MBAs but were doing secretarial work because of their nationality. Meritocracy replaced tradition. Old thinking was purged and replaced with the newest cutting-edge practices that sought long-term sustainability and resilience.

This work was Elza's way of introducing whole-systems practices culturewide and of affecting regional change through business. With the support of her visionary client, the two of them sought to show leaders in the region how to approach change positively and what needed to be done for the region to move toward greater resilience and sustainability beyond the age of oil.

This enormous effort called on every capacity and source of knowledge and skill that Elza had. She created training programs in both Spiral Dynamics and Integral Theory at the company's headquarters in Kuwait City that were specifically tailored for the cultural and developmental sensitivities of the region. She adopted Joseph Campbell's paradigm of the hero's journey to Spiral Dynamics and trained executives to face their shadows and follow their bliss on each of their unique journeys. She trained managers in emotional intelligence. She always thought that children held the key to the future of the region, so she created training programs called Integral Parenting that were popular among workers and executives alike. That led her to expand the personal development of employees and create an Integral Relationships training program, which made her the resident expert on issues affecting the whole employee. Like her mentor, Dr. Beck, she always took the latest innovations in management practices and brilliantly wove them into the Spiral Dynamics model to augment it and keep it current. After years of hard work, she was being acknowledged through many parts of the Middle East for the work she was doing.

Her client's family wanted her to transform their other companies as well. Old friends working for large businesses in Lebanon heard consultants speak about her work as the next thing that would transform the region's corporate practices. Other companies in the Gulf solicited her services, promising to double her pay.

But higher pay or the quick empowerment of businessmen was secondary to Elza's goal. With her coaching and the systems she had put into place, she had transformed her and her client's vision into a reality. Jointly they had transformed a workplace into an oasis that fostered an ecosystem for the highest human potential that was like no other in the Arab world. The business expanded to Europe and other parts of the Middle East. By 2014, revenues had more than doubled, and the company had upward of seven thousand, five hundred employees. All this reached its height in the following two years when *Forbes Magazine* took notice of Elza's client's leadership qualities and named her one of the most powerful businesswomen in the Middle East for 2014 and 2015, respectively.

This, Too, Shall Pass

Elza's extraordinary accomplishments over the years had garnered her much deserved attention. Magazines that were on the cutting edge of consciousness practices in Europe and the Middle East were featuring her work. She was also featured in the book, *Lawyers as Changemakers: A Global Integrative Law Movement*, by J. Kim Wright, a self-described legal rebel who is one of the best-selling authors of books published by the American Bar Association. Wright included Elza as one of only one hundred attorneys around the world featured for the cutting edge work she was doing in bringing change to the Middle East. She had dodged bullets in the West Bank to help Western aid agencies understand the needs of Palestinian women and girls. She did what no one in the Integral community dared to do: she challenged Ken Wilber publicly on his wisdom in conducting a series of interviews with spiritual guru Andrew Cohen on the powers of the feminine without even inviting a female to be part of the discussion!

Her reservoir of courage was endless, and it got her noticed in the community that mattered to her the most. She was unanimously elected to become a member of the Source of Energy Foundation's Evolutionary Leaders in Service to Conscious Evolution, a global initiative founded by Deepak Chopra and Diane Williams. This group included the Who's Who of people who had steered Elza's passions for decades, from Deepak Chopra, Ervin Laszlo, and Barbara Max Hubbard to evolutionary biologists Bruce Lipton and Elisabet Sahtouris. The two extraordinary people who have guided her journey, Don Beck and Jean Houston, were the members of the group who nominated her for inclusion.

At the height of her consulting career and after her inclusion into the Evolutionary Leaders organization, Elza set her sights on a much higher goal. She wanted to formalize her experiences in ways that serve as a platform for the next phase of her calling: the transformation of the Middle East. Her next logical step was to document her experiences in a book. Just as I had brought a fresh perspective on evolutionary economics through my book *MEMEnomics*, she began to put together all the elements of her experience for the world to read. Dr. Beck, being the consummate cheerleader, assured her that anything she wrote would mark another groundbreaking milestone that would bring evolutionary values to politics and organizations alike. In earnest she began the venture to document the application of Spiral Dynamics to peace in the Middle East and the transformation of organizational practices in the Arab world. With Dr. Beck's blessings, she added all the

concepts they submitted jointly in earlier years to the APA to create the new branch of psychology that Dr. Beck called Psychology
at the Large Scale, which made for one of the largest chapters in
the book. The largest chapter, however, was reserved for her work
on the Palestinian–Israeli initiative. As a part of her vision of the
future, she added a chapter on the design, training, and certification criteria of value systems for those who wanted to become
experts in the field. This was part of a greater vision that the three
of us—Elza, Dr. Beck, and I—had formulated for an entity that
will carry forth the legacy of Dr. Graves, Dr. Beck, and the work of
all the CHEs around the world. The entity will train world leaders
and aspiring change agents alike in the methodologies of large-
scale transformation, and Elza's book was the first place where such
plans were made public.

Her work documenting organizational transformation comprised another chapter. It also became the basis for a chapter that
set forth Elza's future goals for the methodical transformation of
the entire Middle East. She called it the Arab Memome Project, and
it sought the mapping of the value systems of the entire region as
a way to begin the long-awaited transformation of that part of the
world. Her life had come full circle as we stood on the cusp of a new
phase that promised a new journey into another world of possibility.

These were the extraordinary lives we were living by choosing to follow our greater destiny—our bliss—and it all felt right.
We were bringing positive change to the world, and every time I
boasted about our work Elza would remind me of the Middle Way.
"Enjoy this, but keep your ego in check," she would say lovingly. It
was humbling and amazing all at once. It was remarkable to see
the things that can happen once the ego gives way to the greater
Self. Empathy, compassion, and selfless service were the things that
steered the passions of those who had the courage to remove all
the masks worn of necessity. We became one with the madmen and
madwomen who saw beyond ordinary existence. We became the
observers of our lives and our work, witnessing the hand of destiny
working through us. We moved freely between the ordinary and the

extraordinary and learned to live in the moment, neither anticipating the future nor regretting the past.

Elza's book *Emerge!* was to be released in October, 2014. At the time, I was in Berlin delivering a keynote speech at a global gathering on sustainability practices, and Elza and Dr. Beck were in Moscow delivering a Spiral Dynamics training and laying the groundwork for a Russia-based CHE, the newest in the constellation. The three of us spoke on the phone before heading to Washington DC for the book launch. It was at that launch that I felt the patriarchy begin to rumble and the universe begin to chuckle.

Figure 4.12. Delivering a keynote speech at the 3.0
Reporting Conference, Berlin, 2014.

Figure 4.13. Spiral Dynamics training, Moscow, 2014. In the second row from
the bottom, Dr. Beck is in the center, and Elza is second from the right.

5

TRICKSTER GODS AND
FALSE PROPHETS

I would not for a moment have you suppose that I am one of those idiots who scorns Science, merely because it is always twisting and turning, and sometimes shedding its skin, like the serpent that is its symbol. It is a powerful god indeed but it is what the students of ancient gods called a shape-shifter, and sometimes a trickster.
—Robertson Davies

The final stage on Joseph Campbell's hero's journey is the state of bliss that comes from being the master of both worlds; the material and the spiritual, the inner and the outer. This is the happily-ever-after end of the road that completes the journey and makes the ordinary in us extraordinary. It is a place of being where all transformational lessons have been learned and integrated into one's higher being. It is the atonement with that Higher Self that brings the adventurer face to face with his or her calling and purpose. At this stage, there are no more dragons to slay and no more thresholds to cross. The metaphorical rebirth after having been in the belly of the whale and the subsequent road of trials have all been conquered, and the hero enjoys the earthly paradise he or she has worked so hard to reach. End of story. Full stop. Except that real life rarely follows Campbell's monomyth, or at least it doesn't factor in the full power of other forces that can derail the journey—even after the adventurer has reached the final destination.

Outside the strict confines of the hero's journey, the world is full of archetypes and gods that can easily derail one's quest. The trickster archetype is one such power that appears in the myth of many cultures. Trickster gods are defined as boundary crossers who often break both physical and societal rules and violate the principles of social and natural order, playfully disrupting normal life and then reestablishing it on a new basis.[1] The trickster is also a clever shape shifter who holds a great degree of intellect and knowledge. The fox and the serpent are just a few examples in myth. The trickster is the peddler of false prophecy. He lures us into a place of hope just to see us suffer.

Such trickster power began to visit our lives in 2014. It hid behind the different faces of the all-knowing medical professionals in order to conceal its sinister plans. It was as if the patriarchy had sent the god Shiva, the supreme destroyer, for no other purpose than to disrupt the very cherished lives we had so carefully built.

The Impermanence of Being

The trickster gods slowly began to derail our journey when Elza began having symptoms of cognitive decline in early 2014. To the outside world, everything appeared normal. While the signs were inconspicuous and rarely noticeable to others, to me they foretold something ominous. This was a new experience, and the symptoms were different from those of her small depressions in the past.

Elza dealt with depressions most effectively through her spiritual practices. Every time she came back from a trip to the Middle East, she felt depressed. Her rationale was that she had taken on some karma from the negative forces that opposed her work in the region and that rest and meditation would mitigate her suffering.

But this time was different, and she wasn't bouncing back as quickly as she had in the past. I had witnessed some odd and subtle changes in her behavior for months, but I couldn't make sense of them. They began to manifest as a mild loss in interest in the activities that defined who she is. First came the disinterest in reading, her favorite scholarly activity. If this had happened to an average person who read an occasional book, the change wouldn't have been noticeable, but Elza read constantly. Even before we met, she had had a ferocious appetite for knowledge and felt an obligation to teach that knowledge to whomever had the curiosity to ask—from the local grocery-store clerk to F. W. de Clerk at a peace conference in Oslo.

From the day we met, Elza reignited my passion for intellectual curiosity, which had become dormant in me after my college years. She was the living embodiment of Prophet Mohammad's saying from the Hadith to *seek knowledge from cradle to grave*. Her books were her favorite teachers, who continuously brought her a new understanding of the human condition. In years past a new book would drop at our front door once a week. To Elza, the day a book arrived was like Christmas morning to a child. She would tear open the packaging and sit on the front steps, completely absorbed in the subject matter. Whether it was a prerelease copy of the latest work of her friend Deepak Chopra, or a pocket-size classic by C. G. Jung about the undiscovered self that she bought from some obscure, used bookstore, her quest for knowledge never wavered.

But in early 2014, while the books kept coming, an increasing number of them went unread. By April, not a single book was being delivered to our front door. These were significant changes and in direct contrast to everything I'd known Elza to be. Even the books that our friend Dr. Beck sent to her sat in their original packaging at the corner of her desk, collecting dust. I tried to convince myself that this behavior was temporary and that she was overwhelmed by writing her own book, or maybe the responsibilities from the increased workload in her consulting work had overwhelmed her.

As the months went by, she gradually began to favor the safety of the knowledge she already had and her familiar routine over the adventure of new discoveries. This was a form of intellectual laziness I had not seen in her before. In years past, she would burst into my office, newest book in hand, marked in a million places with color-coordinated tabs and notes in margins to justify her own expanded reinterpretation of the author's work. I would protest the disturbance since I needed complete silence to focus on my own work. She would ignore my objections and try to break my focus by twisting my swivel chair. If that failed, she would close my laptop and—like a teacher scolding a child—order me to pay attention because "this was important." Those sweet interruptions were my gateway to my Higher Self, both spiritually and intellectually. After getting over the upset from the interruption, we would sit like children on the couch in my office in awe of new discoveries. From the latest findings in complexity theory to the hyper-intellectual and spiritual depth and breadth of Ken Wilber, nothing could quench Elza's thirst for deep exploration of mind and soul. Nothing in her being would have stopped her from sharing that knowledge and spiritual wisdom with those she loved and cared about. But now, all the books sat silently on their shelves like inanimate remains at eternal rest.

The outside world knew very little about the changes in Elza. Her closest friends and colleagues were aware of her occasional bouts with depression and always afforded her the time and space to deal with it. She had worked her way through tens of depressive episodes like this, but this time it was different.

The Healthcare Industrial Complex

At my urging in March 2014, Elza agreed to see her primary-care physician about her symptoms. This was a milestone, since in general she believed that alternative treatments and natural supplements were the only anecdote we needed for all that ailed us. I had known that she would turn to Western medicine only if all alternative treatments failed.

Until that time, and as she had been doing for many years before we met, Elza had relied on naturopathy and Ayurvedic medicine to provide needed cures. For her, good health was whole health. Under her influence, I had become a vegetarian, and food consciousness had become as important to us as the conscious nurturing of our minds and souls. We grew our own wheatgrass and planted our own organic garden. We exercised our bodies daily and took supplements and herbal remedies to complete the wholeness of mind, body, and spirit. But in 2014, no diet or supplements or alternative treatment—no herbal remedy or targeted acupuncture—was proving effective in slowing Elza's cognitive decline.

I waited outside the examination room during her first appointment with her primary-care physician. She emerged a half-hour later and swiftly clutched my hand and ushered us both out of the cold and sterile confines of the concrete and glass that defined her doctor's office. With prescription in hand, as we drove away she told me the doctor had diagnosed her with a mild depression. The doctor had only prescribed the minimum dose after Elza explained her views on Western medicine and her reluctance to take prescription medications. For the following few months, her mood improved slightly, but other subtle symptoms remained.

March of 2014 marked the beginning of our slide into the clutches of the American healthcare system. In the summer of that year, one of Elza's friends had noticed that her antidepressant had stopped working. She had experienced similar symptoms herself and suggested it could be an issue with her thyroid gland, recommending a specialist she knew. This new doctor carried the newest badge of merit called "functional medicine." He soon determined that Elza's problems were indeed tied to her thyroid and prescribed a cocktail of medications that were available only through a compounding pharmacy. As Elza's symptoms got worse, the doses got higher, and since this was functional medicine, the doctor only focused on the function of the thyroid gland, leaving out all other symptoms and organs of the body that determine whole health.

A few months into that treatment, Elza began to look like an addict coming off a high. Her condition played on a loop of perpetual helplessness. She had lost weight and become very jittery, but she refused to acknowledge that yet another diagnosis had failed to restore her to health. I believe that, at some level, she knew what the problem really was. But, as evolved and as conscious as she was, she just couldn't begin to contemplate a worse diagnosis than the one she had been given.

Elza's slow decline continued, but she stubbornly resisted the idea of seeing a new doctor or changing her course of treatment. It was now the middle of 2015, and I could tell she was losing her valiant battle against whatever was causing her decline. I was torn between praising her fighting spirit and persuading her to consider a new course. Elza, the strongest women I have ever known, was by now becoming weak and vulnerable, both physically and emotionally. As painful as this was for me to witness, I decided not to rock the boat and to provide her with love and comfort instead.

At Christmas that year we saw my brother Nassif, the pediatrician, who immediately expressed concern about Elza's fidgety state and the amount of weight she had lost. When I moved to dismiss him halfway through his sentence, he interjected, "You know, she tried several times to have me call in those compounded prescriptions to my pharmacy."

At that point, I knew that her desperation had gone too far. She wanted so much for the hypothyroidism diagnosis to be the right one and was trying everything within her reach to make it so.

In the early days of 2016 over several conversations, I convinced her to find a new endocrinologist. On our first visit, after feeling her thyroid gland and reviewing her list of medications for a second time, the new doctor had a bewildered look on his face. He dismissed the diagnosis given by the functional medicine doctor altogether. To confirm his topical diagnosis and to ascertain the cause of Elza's jitteriness, he ordered several blood tests. These tests confirmed that the medications she had been prescribed—Armour, T3, and T4—were all at dangerously high levels. Elza had also been following a nutritionist's advice for brain health by taking vitamin B12, which was shown in the blood tests to be at extreme high levels as well.

After I explained Elza's recent battles with cognitive decline, the endocrinologist suggested that the issue could be neurological and that we consult with her primary-care physician about next steps. To me, this was the first meaningful push toward ending this mystery, but to Elza it was the beginning of the end of her denial about what her ailment could be. After two years of ambiguity, misdiagnosis, and not knowing, I wanted certainty regardless of the consequences.

We visited her primary-care physician. Afterward, the tension in the car was heavy and unmistakable. Elza's silence and facial expressions spoke louder than any words could. When we got home I asked her if everything was okay. At that question she unleashed the worst tirade of profanity and insults toward me—words that came from a space within her that I had never known before. Soon after, she started breaking whatever was in her way, among them several framed pictures taken with prominent people. There was the one with members of the Israeli Knesset, and another with Palestinian leaders. There was the one in the large antique frame taken at a retreat with her colleagues from the Evolutionary Leaders Circle. There was another with the undersecretary of state, as well as her favorite, the one with Dr. Michael DeBakey. The framed images that highlighted her career, her rise to fulfill her hopes and dreams for a better world, her greater calling—all smashed and scattered into a million pieces on the floor.

In her fit of rage, she moved to the kitchen as I slowly followed her. Anything I said only fueled her anger. To her I was the curator of the worse possible scenario about her health. I was the executioner of whatever hope she had held for reversing her decline. The more I tried to comfort her, the angrier she got. She reached for an orange in the fruit bowl and hurled it at me. Then she fell to the floor weeping and wailing until she became fully exhausted and spent.

There's a saying that doctors make the worst patients. This is true across many professions, especially those requiring deep knowledge of psychology and spirituality. Elza had extensive knowledge and expertise in both these areas. She had counseled many political and community leaders and heads of corporations. Jungian shadow work was her favorite approach in helping people overcome obstacles and reach their potential. But, in her own battle to overcome health difficulties, she failed to apply any of these skills to herself. Daily meditations that expanded her bandwidth for tolerance and rejuvenated her spirit and recharged her soul were all but gone. Her own adventures in bringing conscious awareness to issues in the unconscious had all but disappeared. I couldn't allow myself to feel the effects of these horrible changes. The woman who had made me a better man needed my full support; and, as much as I needed to engage my own spirituality and consciousness to deal with these changes, I couldn't relinquish the dreadful duty of being a caregiver.

In the spring of 2016, Elza's decline began to be reflected in her professional life. The transformational work she had done in the Arabian Gulf had become a beacon for corporate wisdom and resilience. This, and her pro bono work with Dr. Beck for the Israelis and the Palestinians, had become her passion and her calling. Among the tens of thousands of practitioners in Spiral Dynamics and the much larger Integral Theory, Elza had been the first to pioneer both applications in the Middle East and in corporate practices and for large-scale cultural change. This was the legacy that she had so desperately sought to continue.

In years past, her consultancy work had caused her to spend two to three months a year traveling to different parts of the Gulf and Europe to train company executives in the latest in management practices and whole-systems strategies. The empowerment of the feminine in that region of the world had taken root through Mideast corporate practices, and Elza's work had become a beacon for change. With the help of her newly published book at the beginning of 2014, her passion had moved her to empower other female leaders in the region and in other areas of leadership. She had hoped to get every powerful woman in the region on *Forbes's* list, just as she had done for her client. She had surmised that the empowerment of the feminine had to follow this route in order for the patriarchy to loosen its choking grip on the region. The female CEO she had coached had become her primary ally in this ambitious endeavor.

Unfortunately, though, those plans would never materialize. Elza's first visit in 2016 to the corporation she had helped transform lasted for less than two weeks. Earlier that year, she had asked for my help in designing some of her training material. This was yet another sign that something was amiss, since I knew very little about the corporate culture she had so carefully crafted for that company over the years.

Modern Gods and the Twisting Serpent

In April of 2016, we saw a neurologist for the first time. He ran some initial tests and quizzed Elza in areas of memory and problem solving. What came next was the beginning of our descent into a deeper layer of mystery and incompetence perpetrated by the American healthcare system. Immediately after concluding his examination, the neurologist assured us that her symptoms were not indicative of memory loss and that, therefore, the nature of the problem was unlikely to be neurological in nature. The three-word summary of his initial neurological evaluation was "results were unremarkable." However, since Elza scored below average on some of the math and the problem-solving exercises, he ordered several MRIs of her brain. The assurance he gave us that her symptoms were not a sign of early Alzheimer's disease gave us a new lease on life. We could breathe easier as we prepared for a large conference where we both were keynote speakers.

Held in early May 2016, the conference took place at a hotel on the shores of Lake Balaton in Hungary, and it was the largest gathering of Integral Theory practitioners in the world. The conference was organized by clinical psychologist Bence Ganti, a Hungarian native who also held US citizenship. Bence is a friend and a conscious therapist who uses integral practices in his work and spends half of his time in the United States and half in Hungary. He had cofounded the organization that administered such events, and in 2014 he launched the first Integral European Conference. Bence also founded the Integral Academy in Budapest in 2006 as a post – graduate institute to teach integral theory and the AQAL model in practice. The conference was called the Integral European Conference (IEC), which in later years grew to become the sole global event where people on the cutting edge of consciousness practices gather every two years to learn about the latest advancements in Integral and Spiral Dynamics applications. Dr. Beck, Elza, and I were scheduled to speak, and at Bence's request we arrived in Budapest a week early to offer a Spiral Dynamics certification course to students at the academy.

Figure 5.1. Bence Ganti and I at the Integral
Academy training in Budapest, May 2016.

I had worked for months helping Elza prepare for both the training and the conference. In the past, at events of this magnitude she would recite from memory all the pioneering work she had done in politics and in organizations in the Middle East, but by then those abilities were slowly diminishing. Her book *Emerge* had been out for two years, and many students at the academy were anxious to learn directly from her about the work she had done in applying both Spiral Dynamics and Integral Theory at the Kuwaiti corporation that she had worked to transform. I had helped her highlight those accomplishments and printed them on paper for her to remember, but throughout the training, she was hesitant in engaging with participants and I found myself needing to speak on her behalf. She had shown signs of stress throughout the week, but I gave that no heed, knowing that we would soon be spending time away from stressful circumstances.

The following week the conference took place on the shores of the lake, which was a few hours drive from Budapest. After the training, we had a few days to relax before we were both scheduled to speak, and I could see Elza becoming relieved from the stress of the week before as we took long walks along the edges of the water. Europe was dealing with the an unprecedent deluge of refugees coming to its shores and across its borders from all parts of the Middle East, and Elza had decided months earlier that her presentation at the conference would be about employing the methodologies of everything she knew to address the crisis. For months I had helped her memorize the entire fifty-minute presentation. She received three standing ovations for her insights. One came only ten minutes into her presentation after she had reframed the entire history of Islam through the lens of Spiral Dynamics, pointing to epochal turning points that marked the evolutionary periods and the eras of stagnation that have defined the religion for more than fourteen centuries.

Figure 5.2. Elza delivering keynote speech at the Integral
European Conference, Lake Balaton, Hungary, May, 2016.

CHAPTER 5

My own presentation was about the applications of my work to the economics of the European Union, and it, too, impressed many attendees. More than four years have passed since the conference and of the hundreds of speakers who appeared at the IEC, the three presentations by Dr. Beck, Elza, and me remain some of the most popular presentations ever made.

But my focus at the time was not on our success or furthering our careers. It was on something more elemental. After the conference, we went on a well-deserved vacation, indulging in our relief over the latest medical findings regarding Elza's health. We reimagined a return to the life we had enjoyed a few years earlier and the recommencement of our journey toward the possible. I was elated at the idea that hard science had finally spoken and that her cognitive decline was not neurological in nature and remained treatable through psychotherapy. We started planning for a period of recovery. Along with the anticipated time in therapy, we began to plan for vacations full of recreational activities and balanced with soulful meditation retreats.

But alas, instead of being joyous about our new start, Elza fell into a deeper depression. Her appointment for the MRIs was drawing near, and I surmised that once the images from her brain scans confirmed the diagnosis of depression, she would let go of any remaining doubt about her neurological health. I told myself that with the help of the right therapist she could easily emerge from this depression.

A week passed during the hot and sultry days of July until we were summoned for the results of the MRIs. As we sat nervously in the waiting room, I held Elza's hand, assuring her that everything was going to be okay.

"Although the loss of brain tissue is higher than average for your age, you're very likely suffering from depression."

These words of the neurologist afforded us, in a somewhat definitive way, a reinvigorated perspective on life. He dismissed our concern about Elza's loss of brain tissue and hastily ushered us into the reception area. This was a respected neurologist at a local research clinic, and his assurances dissuaded us of the need for a second opinion. He instructed his assistant to help us make an appointment for a neuro-psych evaluation.

That night was reserved for celebration. This was the best news we had received in over two years! After making several exhilarating calls to weary family members, we dined lavishly at one of our favorite restaurants on the edge of the Pacific. For a few weeks, our joyous days gave way to blissful nights that lured us back to the life we had once known.

We set an appointment for the neuro-psych evaluation in September, and I drove Elza to the appointment. This was an impressive battery of tests named after the institutions or the doctors who had created them. They were given to Elza to determine the type of depression she was suffering from. The five-hour session had assessments ranging from simple problems in arithmetic and shape configurations to word association and story memory. Elza was exhausted by the time I picked her up. We went out to dinner and wanted to bring closure to the day as quickly as possible.

We received the results in the mail the following week. In a seven-page memorandum, the doctor described the details of the test and the corresponding results. In the last paragraph, he concluded that her previous diagnosis of mild depression had been wrong and that Elza was suffering from "a prolonged exacerbation of a major depressive disorder." Her condition, he claimed, was not being adequately addressed with her current psychiatric treatment. He recommended a full reevaluation of her symptoms and the antidepressant medication she was taking.

The last three diagnoses that found no neurological basis for Elza's decline had given us a new reason for hope and optimism. Practitioners in the fields of psychiatry and psychotherapy defer to any findings coming from the highly specialized field of neuropsychology. We had gone right to the top for answers, and it felt right. Depression was a treatable condition! We breathed a huge sigh of relief before we began the search for a psychiatrist.

By October of that year, Elza's ability to form complex sentences had dramatically been reduced. The woman who had challenged some of the world's most prominent thinkers in open forum could now barely form a simple coherent sentence. This was one of the symptoms of her new diagnosis, we were told. The psychiatrist we had picked was a woman in her early sixties who had been in private practice for over three decades. Her office was a pleasant contrast to the dreariness of the cold concrete and crowded elevators of hospitals and clinics. There was an aura of hippie rebellion about her—from the way she dressed and spoke to the paintings and books that adorned the walls and shelves of her office. Elza had picked her from among other qualified doctors for her added experience as a couples' therapist. Maybe she emphasized *couples'* therapy to ensure my equal inclusion in the sessions in case she couldn't express herself and needed me to present her symptoms and relay to the psychiatrist the fullest quality of her identity.

Things went exceptionally well during our first session. As we told the psychiatrist about the important work Elza had done with Dr. Beck on the Israel-Palestine issue, she reached onto a shelf and held up a copy of the *Spiral Dynamics* book, announcing her familiarity with the concepts behind the work. She soon understood the issues that had fueled both Elza's and my passions for the previous fourteen years. And she understood the awesome responsibility of helping Elza return to the important work she loved. Overwhelmed by the serendipity and providence of what had just happened, I told the doctor of our greater plans to carry forward Dr. Beck's legacy and create the Spiral Dynamics Institute. We had put those plans on hold since Elza's symptoms first appeared in 2014. The universe could not have found a better vessel than this psychiatrist to help Elza's journey back to health and our return to our calling. Elza had brought a signed copy of her own book to the first session, and that set the stage for the doctor to understand Elza's spiritual and intellectual depth and the depth and breadth of her accomplishments in a short period of time.

Elza had spent years processing her past traumas through therapy and spiritual practices, but in 2016 therapists were convinced that she hadn't fully processed the loss of her son, Fawzi, and her daughter Nour and the guilt from her forced separation from her daughter Ghinwa. After the assurances we received that the cause of her cognitive decline was not neurological, Elza became newly committed to revisit these past traumas and engage in deeper therapies so that she could heal fully. For the remainder of the year, we attended therapy sessions twice a week. The deeper she got into past issues, the more vulnerable she became. She spent hours in tears talking to friends and to me about the guilt she felt from having left her daughter. Although her verbal abilities were compromised, her utterance of the words "I can't see my daughter" unleashed a tsunami of emotions. Maybe the therapist chose to process this issue first because Elza had dedicated her book *Emerge!* to her daughter in this way: "To my daughter Ghinwa, whom I haven't seen since her age of four, and to all Arab mothers and daughters—may you emerge!"

Weeks passed, and Elza's emotional state was getting worse. Her ability to speak had been reduced to just a few words. By early December she had been on three different medications, and none seemed to help. In the beginning, our joint sessions were held once a week, but as the psychiatrist got deeper into analysis, I found myself being excluded from most sessions. This puzzled me because I knew Elza couldn't communicate what was on her mind or the history that had led her here. The doctor became increasingly perturbed by my insistence on being part of the sessions. Every time I was left to read the outdated magazines in the reception area, I wondered about the doctor's decision to exclude me. Maybe she associated my frustration with a generalized perception she held about Arab men. With my help, Elza had previously described the verbal abuse she had endured with her ex-husband. Maybe the doctor had asked if she had suffered the same fate with me and mistook her inability to speak as confirmation of abuse. Maybe at six feet, two inches and two hundred and thirty pounds, a frustrated Arab man was a threat

143

to a five foot, four-inch therapist who was trying to help a female warrior fend off yet another ugly manifestation of Arab patriarchy.

As December drew to a close, the doctor finally called me in to a joint session. She had hit a wall and hadn't been able to get Elza to speak for weeks. She asked me about her behavior at home, and I said she had been frustrated with the lack of progress that was preventing her from resuming the work she loved.

Then, in a stereotypical way, the doctor turned to her and asked, "How does that make you feel?"

Elza's eyes roamed in silent frustration for over a minute. No answers came. Then the doctor asked a more general question, which only added to Elza's exasperation and impatience.

Then, relieved to be a part of the session after having been excluded for weeks, I chimed in with the simplest questions requiring one-word answers: "Did you feed the dog this morning? What did you have for dinner last night?"

Elza's frustration turned to relief as she heard me doing the questioning. With a deep sigh she leaned into me as a child would into the arms of her father, assured that the barrage of attacks was coming to an end. To the doctor this was a sign that Elza's depression was far worse than she had anticipated, and she proceeded to lay out a course of action with appointments well into the following year.

Prophets Shed Their Skin

It was very painful to watch the life we had once slipping helplessly through our fingers. Elza's mental condition and her ability to speak had been in free fall for three years, and no treatment or medication had helped to reverse it. At the beginning of 2017, we were determined to pursue more aggressive forms of treatment. Friends told us about advancements made in electric-shock therapy and urged us seriously to consider it. Because of its stigmatized history, though, Elza decided against it and searched for alternatives instead. Her intermittent ability to think critically and do research was puzzling, given her general cognitive decline. In lucid interludes she mined the Internet and found a similar, more modern treatment called transcranial magnetic stimulation, TMS for short. The Internet was full of comments by patients with similar symptoms who had seen great benefits from the treatment. Everything about this non-invasive, non-talk cure was being publicized as the next evolution in treating stubborn depressions.

This required the care of a new psychiatrist who was certified in the use of TMS technology. As much as we liked the previous doctor, her treatment hadn't worked. The new doctor we saw changed Elza's medications again as we waited for the sessions to begin. By now a pattern among healthcare professionals had begun to emerge. The word *incompetent* always lurked beneath the surface of how a new care provider described the previous one. It always felt like a sales pitch as we were told that "our school of thought" or "our level of care" was superior to everything else we as patients had experienced before. Yet when the new care provider failed to find a cure or a correct diagnosis in turn, *we* were the ones at fault. We were told that the condition required a lot more patience than what we had. At the rate Elza was deteriorating, patience was a rare commodity, but with every new start came a new sense of optimism.

The TMS treatment centered on the use of a piece of equipment placed over the head that sent targeted magnetic pulses to certain areas of the brain deemed by the doctor to be responsible for long-term depression. The protocols called for daily forty-five-minute sessions for a period of one month followed by less frequent visits, called maintenance sessions, depending on need. The facilities were an hour away, and a round trip during rush hour took up most of our day. This was a minor factor compared to the benefits this treatment promised. Elza's speech began to improve slightly, and by the end of the second week she showed noticeable progress. Her engagement in dialogue and her general mood were on the mend. That weekend, her depression lifted enough that she began to think optimistically about the future. For the first time in over a year, she began to read from the pile of new books stacked on her desk. Her longing to return to the work she loved was visible as she began to review her old training modules, looking for places to add what she was uncovering in the latest literature.

I was cautiously optimistic. The technology and the approach of this new therapy made logical sense. There was reason for us to put traditional forms of therapy in the rearview mirror and look forward to a return of the life we once knew. Week three showed further improvement, as the TMS technician and the doctor joined us in lighthearted banter celebrating this critical turning point. We met in the doctor's private office as we did every Friday. He confirmed that, along with TMS, the new course of medication was working and that much of the lingering depression should lift by the end of week four.

But alas, that weekend my optimism turned into despair. Elza slept late on Saturday, and when I went to check on her she was glued to a random television show, eyes glazed and expressionless. She had behaved this way sporadically throughout the previous year, and I had thought of it as a coping mechanism—her way of numbing all the emotions and unresolved issues she was processing in therapy. On this day, I gently lured her from bed, handed her a cup of coffee, and led her to the grandest room in the house, which was her office. I wanted her to talk to me about the book she had started reading.

Instead, I was met with that old blank stare mixed with confusion and resignation. The harder I tried, the more hopeless the situation became. Replaying in my head were those rhetorical patterns of blame shifting we had heard perpetrated by people in the most honorable of professions. TMS was yet another misguided prescription that had placed us again at the mercy of the unknown. Elza's decline continued through week four, and the optimism we had all experienced in the treatment room the week before had turned into a somber and dark silence. As we sat in the doctor's office, sadness and disappointment hung heavy in the air. I decided to break the silence and realistically asked about the next course of therapy.

"These things sometimes take a few weeks," the doctor said.

We had chosen this particular psychiatric clinic based on the extensive network it had with other mental-health practitioners. We knew that, in some cases, TMS alone might not be enough and that Elza might need follow-up therapy. That non-TMS follow-up care was available at one of the establishment's other clinics that was a few short miles from our house.

As I sat in the doctor's office, I was already planning our next steps and knew the nearby clinic had a long waiting list for new patients. "Can you get us into the Mission Valley office before August?"

My question must have translated into an accusation of failure in the doctor's mind. To my astonishment, with finger pointed at the door he asked me to leave. "You are not my patient. I need to talk to her alone!"

That was the last I saw of the doctor. We had desperately wanted for TMS to work and, as we drove home that Friday afternoon, feelings of emptiness and betrayal mixed with tears of hopelessness. Ten days passed, and the doctor did not return any of our calls. In a final voicemail I begged him to move the maintenance sessions up to a few weeks immediately following the last session. The technician scheduled four additional sessions over the month of March. No progress was made, and whatever improvement Elza saw over the entire course of treatment began to slip slowly through our helpless fingers. This was now the worst roller-coaster ride we'd been on, and the only memory I have of what was supposed to be the most promising treatment was the doctor's burst of anger ordering me to leave.

I was emotionally spent and had lost all faith in the psychiatric and therapeutic community. It was time to return to the drawing board. Is it possible that the neurologist had missed something? Based on his diagnosis of depression, the neuropsychologist had determined his, and every new therapist used the finding of major depressive disorder as their Bible, their Magna Carta, their unquestionable prescription for treatment.

I started to question the basis of all the previous diagnoses and decided that we should begin afresh. We would not wait for an appointment with yet another new psychiatrist at the Mission Valley office to lead us down a path we already knew. I requested an appointment with the best neurologist in our insurance network. We were told that he was a very popular doctor and the wait would be long. While waiting, we sought new therapy that our insurance didn't cover. Elza started a course of cognitive behavioral therapy, which ended after a few sessions due to her inability to communicate. We then started a three-month journey into natural remedies combined with cranial sacral therapy, acupuncture, and massage.

The long-awaited appointment with the new neurologist finally arrived. The expanse of his office spoke volumes about his accomplishments. This has to be the biggest corner office in the large, modern, five-story building, I thought to myself. Best Neurologist awards crowded the walls full of certificates and magazine covers.

"Do you wear glasses?" asked his nurse.

After hesitating, Elza answered "no"; then she slowly pulled her glasses from her purse and handed them to the nurse.

Visibly frustrated, the nurse said, "I just asked you if you wore glasses and you said no!"

"This is why we're here, Ma'am," I interjected.

Remarkably unfazed, the nurse continued clicking away on her keyboard.

I assumed that medicine is like all other professions: Physicians rise to prominence in their field by differentiating themselves from their peers. Maybe they master a procedure or invent a unique diagnostic tool that leads to their recognition. Maybe they rise to prominence through pioneering research. These were the thoughts swimming in my head as we waited for this new neurologist.

After asking the customary questions about medical history, the doctor directed Elza's attention to drawings on paper—one page, then another. These were the same drawings the previous neurologist had used. Then he turned and asked her some memory questions:

"When was World War II?"

She answered correctly.

"Where are we, what year were you born, who was the President in 1960?"

Elza took her time but answered all these questions correctly. As soon as this line of questioning ended, the doctor made his diagnosis:

"This is not a neurology problem; her memory is fine." I was taken aback at his quick dismissal of her symptoms.

"I'm sorry, we waited months for this appointment. Are you telling us that all neurology problems are memory problems? Shouldn't you order some tests?" I asked.

"I have her MRIs from last year," he answered. "This is a focus issue, which is resolved in therapy. She can't focus."

Elza's inability to focus was one of my primary concerns as a symptom that was being dismissed by both neurologists and therapists. We were told in therapy that it was one of the possible symptoms of major depressive disorder, but as her ability to speak got worse, so did her focus. I intuitively knew that the two were related and that therapy would do nothing to improve either condition. It was one of the primary reasons I wanted to have the best neurologist in San Diego offer his opinion, but instead of confirming my intuition or treating my concerns with care, he relied on past results and had us out of his office in less than fifteen minutes.

There was that punch-in-the-gut feeling again. Going "back to square one"—to determine a neurological basis for Elza's disease—wasn't possible for us anymore. In addition, the office of Elza's primary-care physician was visibly frustrated with us. They had fought with our insurance company on her behalf to approve the expensive TMS treatments that were not normally covered. Since the treatment didn't work, we were told that the insurance carrier had dropped the TMS office from their list of care providers. With every new referral came a new battle that her physician's office waged with our insurance carrier. We had tested the limits of their neurology and psychiatry networks, and the stress was beginning to show in their calls and emails. "Maybe it's time for you to go outside the network," one email said. Another chastised us for rocking the boat with the TMS group and for not accepting the August appointment they had made available for us. The ray of light, the glimmer of hope we had had while waiting to see this new neurologist was all we had left. But when he dismissed Elza's case as "not a neurology problem," just like the framed pictures that had been shattered on the floor a year earlier, our hopes were shattered into a million pieces by the continued incompetence of the American healthcare system.

Months passed, during which we had no further interactions with anyone in the medical community. We continued doing the things that calmed Elza's mood, even if just for a few hours a day. The daily routine alternated between walks on the beach or hikes in nature complemented by weekly acupuncture treatments and cranial sacral therapy. Daily meditation became increasingly difficult but a necessity that helped keep us sane. The aim of sending unconditional love and kindness to the world was slowly vanishing as the harsh physical environment, the despair made inner peace increasingly unreachable. Three years of battles against the unknown has rendered me exhausted physically and emotionally, and I began to lose faith. The warrior in me that had saved me from many unpleasant life events in the past had exceeded any reasonable level of protection and heroism. Yet, with every failed treatment, Elza became more helpless, and I became even more protective. We started to lose touch with people around us. I turned down speaking engagements in favor of staying home and writing an article or a blog.

As we became socially isolated, the warrior in me—my hero archetype—became the primary self that took over our lives. It fought with everyone who failed to rescue us. Just as the archetypal hero doesn't know how to accept loss or change, so I resisted change and fought the unknown. But the more we resisted, the more our world changed—and for the worse. Very little of our past lives remained. I all but stopped my running, and my visits to the gym became less frequent. I experienced physical pain that I had never experienced before. Every muscle in my body became tense. The tension in my shoulders, neck, and head became unbearable, so much so that at times I felt my neck muscles could not carry the weight of my head. The stress then spread to my lower back and on some days rendered me immobile. I sought physical therapy and deep tissue massage, but nothing seemed to help. Painkillers carried me through the days that became increasingly full of anger and resignation. The garden went unpicked for months and died from neglect. Fresh produce disappeared from our kitchen and from our diets. Meditation and deep reflection gave way to despair. Not only had the healthcare community failed to help Elza, I felt as if it had ensnared me in its tentacles of physical and emotional torture. This wasn't an ordinary stage or a small setback on an extraordinary journey. This was evil made manifest, I thought. Just as in the opening to this chapter Robertson Davies describes science, I considered our guides on this passage of trials to be the peddlers of false hope, tricksters, and shape shifters along a false path promising a return to a life of joy and happiness.

The High Priestess of False Hope

No one in the healthcare system had wavered from the initial diagnosis that Elza was suffering from a stubborn depression. With our options exhausted, we turned our attention to seeking treatment in Europe and specifically in Germany, where TMS protocols were more comprehensive and intense than those in the States. When we told Elza's primary-care physician about our plans, he asked to be given a few days while he talked to yet another psychiatrist about her condition. He offered no promises since this was a personal friend in private practice that had little room for new patients.

"Good news! She will take Elza as a new patient as a personal favor for me," he said in a call a few days later.

At that point, I wasn't sure whether he cared as much about Elza's condition as he did about exploiting the fact that we had the resources to consider treatment in Europe. The emotional roller coaster had taken its toll on us and turned me into a cynic. The window of hope was rapidly closing. My mind began to delve into conspiratorial thoughts. Maybe everyone in our healthcare network knew that Elza's condition had no cure but wanted to exhaust her insurance benefits down to the last penny. It was time to seek answers outside the network.

The appointment with the new psychiatrist came on an ominous day. It was August 21, 2017, the day of the solar eclipse, and the sun had just emerged victorious in her battle with the moon after leaving parts of the earth in complete darkness for a few hours. I wanted to ignore all the mythological signs and the nonscientific meaning of that day. There were no angry gods announcing the beginning of disasters and destruction. Nor did the sun leave the skies to begin her journey into the Underworld. We had done our research on this doctor, and we were filled with a new sense of hope and optimism. After all, who violates the established norms of medicine and places their genius skills in playing classical music above those in medicine and psychiatry? Yet this is exactly what this new doctor did on her website, a sign of more inclusive thinking. We were desperate for something different and fresh, and this young doctor did indeed deliver. After two-and-a-half hours of questions and tests—and in a move that could only be seen as a violation of the unspoken conventions of American medical practices—she threw out the neuropsychologist's diagnosis of major depressive disorder and diagnosed Elza with bipolar depression.

Was this finally the right diagnosis, or was this doctor yet another false prophet? Just as had happened on three previous occasions, Elza was taken off her medications and placed on new ones taken in increasing dosages. We attended therapy once a week for three months. Elza began to show marginal improvements in her mood and verbal abilities. Every time she plateaued on one drug, the doctor added a new one. This went on until she found the right combination of drugs that kept Elza stable and happy for weeks at a time. One bright day in November, the doctor told us that Elza's depression was finally lifting, as her ability to speak and focus held steady. The new diagnosis made by this rebel doctor was indeed the right one. We were in an ecstatic state and couldn't believe what was happening. As we left her office that day, the doctor followed us through the reception area.

"We finally found the right diagnosis and how to treat it," she said. "Elza should be back to her old self in a few short months."

Our descent into the abyss over the last few years was finally being reversed. Now, we could joyfully renew our journey into the life of the possible. We could forgive the healthcare system for its shortcomings and hope never to fall into its uncaring grip again. We celebrated our seventeenth wedding anniversary on a well-deserved vacation and returned to a home and a future full of hopes and of dreams yet to be fulfilled. The world that we had left behind three years earlier anxiously awaited our return. Planning the work on my next book, Elza's return to her work in the Middle East, and the legacy of Spiral Dynamics were the things that would occupy our merry days while Elza finished the needed time in therapy. For the first time in years, I was able to project myself into the future without the fear of greater forces driving our destiny.

I had surmised that Elza would be finished with her prescribed course of care by April 2018. So, I looked to plan an event to capture our newly revived commitment to serve humanity. Dr. Beck was turning eighty, and Elza and I wanted to honor his legacy and contributions for trying to make the world a better place. During our hiatus he had gathered a team of top Spiral Dynamics practitioners and heads of CHEs from around the world to contribute a chapter each in a sequel to the original Spiral Dynamics book that had changed the lives of countless people. Elza and I had each contributed a chapter from work we had completed before her symptoms appeared—which by now was over three years ago. Three years away from the things we loved had felt like an eternity, and we yearned for our return to them. I began to plan for a conference the likes of which our community had never seen. It would be a celebration for Dr. Beck like no other, honoring the man who had changed our lives while acting as the official launch of the new book. Most of all, it was intended to announce Elza's return to the community and the work she loved the most.

Through this winding road of life, we found ourselves on a new journey toward higher purpose and deeper inner growth. Our blind ambition was now being tempered by humility and a sense of unpretentiousness that reminded us of human imperfection. If the trials of the last four years had been part of our hero's journey, then allies and enemies alike had tested us, and we had become better warriors because of it. In the last four years, the tricksters had been many and the helpers but a few. We had been wounded and weakened by this ordeal, which had profoundly changed the trajectory of our lives. It would take us some time to heal and integrate the lessons the universe had thrown our way. If the old selves within us needed to die in order for more conscious selves to rise, then we needed a period of rest and peace. The new selves needed to emerge away from the slings and arrows of the dark part of our journey through which we had just passed. The lessons had to be processed in a nonreactive environment outside the tumultuous twists and turns. The powerful lessons from myth had spoken, and the gap between our old world and the new needed to narrow. The crucible of the material world and the spiritual world, the dying and the newly born, was being formed. As we lay beaten and exhausted, the twilight on the horizon was cautiously signaling a new dawn.

6
JOURNEY INTO THE DARK NIGHT

Your pain is the breaking of the shell that encloses your understanding.
Even as the stone of the fruit must break, that its heart
may stand in the sun, so must you know pain.
—Kahlil Gibran

The first time I heard the word *aphasia*, it sounded so innocuous. It was like hearing the name of a fragrant flower as the sound fell softly on my ears and soothed my heightened senses.

Then I innocently asked, "Would this explain why two years of psychotherapy haven't improved Elza's ability to speak?"

The answer was an immediate "Yes."

Then I followed with, "Would it also explain why the dozen different medications haven't helped?"

Again, the answer was an unqualified "Yes."

Then timidly I asked, "Could you repeat the full name of the condition?"

The voice on the other end of the phone said haltingly, "Primary progressive aphasia."

Suddenly, I felt the heavy weight of those words and pulled over to the side of the highway to continue the conversation.

Then I asked, "Is there a treatment for it?"

The answer came slowly: "Unfortunately, no. That's why it's called progressive. There is no known cure." This was followed by a period of silence that seemed to last for eternity. Then the voice on the other end said, "Call me anytime if you have more questions."

Elza's progress with the latest course of treatment came to a halt in late December 2017. Our heroine—the most recent psychiatrist who had defied the medical establishment a few months earlier and given us a new lease on life—had begun to doubt her own brave diagnosis of bipolar disorder. She had run out of new medications to give Elza. She had refined the diagnosis further from bipolar disorder type I to type II. Treating for either condition had proven futile. There was nothing left to give or to add. As Elza's other medications plateaued, there was no new medicine waiting in the wings to offer any hope.

When Elza began to experience negative side effects from the new treatments, the doctor became visibly upset at her failure. Strangely, there was a part of me that wanted to welcome the doctor to the darkness and the uncertainty of not knowing that we ourselves had been experiencing for almost four years. But that feeling didn't last long, as our new reality began to hit us hard and send us into a deeper layer of pain. The sun had indeed begun her journey into the Underworld on the day we had met this doctor.

I was dazed and stunned. A deeper sense of betrayal had overtaken me, and I blamed the medical community as the sole culprit, the deeds of a trickster God made manifest. It wasn't just our network; it was the entire healthcare system that was rotten to the core. The few months' respite we had experienced was over. I felt as if we were in a never-ending tragedy orchestrated by a horde of clowns playing on the stage of life and death. Had our newfound ally—this latest psychiatrist whom we saw as a helper along our journey—turned out to be just another trickster? Had she worn the same mask the others had that hid the darker side of mental health? Had she cleverly reached into her own bag of tricks to lure us into a false sense of hope and safety? In my frustration and grief, I thought she must be the biggest trickster of them all, the queen of deception masquerading as the wise guide, the false sage promising to lead us into a new world of transformation. She had taken over after all the other tricksters had failed. Destiny had placed us at her feet and begun to unveil to us the next part of our passage into darkness. This doctor was indeed the queen of all the tricksters and false prophets, and they were all making a mockery of our lives.

Although our struggles with the American healthcare system are not the focus of this book, it's important for me to highlight the role of the brave people who risk their professional reputation to take a stand against mediocrity and substandard practices in any profession, especially in the field of medicine. Those are the true heroes who facilitate the transformational nature of the human quest.

The person who gave us the alternative diagnosis of aphasia for Elza's condition was one of these heroes. He was a helper in the new direction our journey has taken and came from the most unlikely of places. He was not part of her professional care team. He was not her primary-care physician, her neurologist, or her psychiatrist. He was not one of the four different psychotherapists who had treated her until that time. Instead, he was a prominent neuropsychologist practicing in New York State. We would have never known him had it not been for our friend Manny Pearlman. Manny had known Elza for years because of her work with Dr. Beck on the Israeli-Palestinian issue, and this neuropsychologist had heard Dr. Beck speak about Elza's bravery in that part of the world in meetings with Manny. When I told Manny that she was suffering from depression and about all the failed treatments she had received, he insisted that we contact his friend no matter what day or how late the hour.

The neuropsychologist and we only spoke twice. The first conversation had taken place two years earlier when, after interviewing Elza for almost two hours on the phone, he determined that she had been diagnosed with the wrong type of depression. His opinion had been dismissed, however, by all Elza's healthcare providers for almost a year and a half, until all their other diagnosis had been exhausted and proven ineffective.

CHAPTER 6

My second conversation with the neuropsychologist took place on a day when Elza refused to take a new medication that had been added to her cocktail of pills. He agreed that this medication was in the wrong class of medicine to add to her existing treatment and explained why. It was then that he offered the diagnosis of aphasia. That opinion was to suffer the same fate as the first, though, until it was confirmed by accident the following January by an emergency-room physician who was not part of Elza's healthcare team. To us, Manny's friend is a modern-day David who brought down the Goliath of the American healthcare system and exposed its toxic underbelly.

Armed with the information the neuropsychologist had given me, I called Elza's treating psychiatrist. The response was stereotypical. Like many before her, she dismissed the validity of any advice from someone who was not a licensed healthcare professional in the state of California. After expressing our disappointment in the lack of progress after four months of treatment, I asked the singular question that had angered every doctor in the past, a question that had caused one psychiatrist to ban me from participating in joint therapy sessions and another to kick me out of his office. One would think that I was asking practitioners in this venerated field to do something illegal or immoral—but the question was this: "Why, after two years of neurological testing and psychiatric treatment, hasn't Elza shown any improvement in her ability to speak?"

The psychiatrist gave me the same standard and vague answer we'd heard so many times before: it was something about the severity of Elza's depression and the short time she had been in therapy.

Knowing that this doctor wasn't confined to the guidelines and restrictions of the insurance industry, I felt comfortable in asking questions freely without the fear of reprimand. During our next office visit, I repeatedly asked her about aphasia and why she and her colleagues had never provided us with this possible diagnosis before. Again, her answer was to dismiss the advice of Manny's friend and to focus on medication and therapy, in what amounted to a broken record that we'd heard over and over for more than two years.

On the following visit, the psychiatrist noticed that the little progress Elza had made since the last change in medication had been reversed and that Elza's ability to communicate had gotten worse. On that day, for the first time since Elza's symptoms had appeared in 2014, someone in the medical profession other than Manny's friend was finally asking about her family's history with neurological diseases. By the time the two-hour appointment was over, the psychiatrist had reluctantly reversed her initial diagnosis of bipolar disorder and acknowledged Elza's symptoms to be neurological in nature. In a voice full of humility and an acknowledgement of defeat, she said, "I'll send a referral to the UC San Diego neurological institute."

While waiting for the referral, I conducted my own research on primary progressive aphasia. The results showed no promise for a cure or an effective treatment. We decided that, since it was December, instead of worrying needlessly about a diagnosis given over the phone we should enjoy the holidays and wait patiently for the referral to come.

The Day the World Stood Still

Most of us remember where we were and what we were doing on the morning of September 11, 2001. There is something about a tragic event that imbeds the memory deep in our minds. Attacks like the ones on Pearl Harbor and the World Trade Center are the type of tragedies that are permanently etched in our collective psyche, making them difficult to forget.

Then there are the private tragedies, the ones that no one else knows about. To Elza and me, the most significant event that is forever etched into our memory was one most relevant just to the two of us. January 7, 2018 was a Sunday, and the sun was high in a cloudless San Diego sky. We were having our morning coffee when Elza began to experience a severe headache accompanied by numbness on the left side of her body. She had been having episodes like these every few days for a few weeks, and they were increasing in intensity with every passing day. The last time it had happened, I had convinced her to go to the emergency room, but by the time we were ready to leave the symptoms had disappeared. The numbness, we were told, could be a sign of a stroke, so we agreed that at the next occurrence we would seek immediate help. The minute the symptoms appeared on that Sunday morning, we were off to the nearest emergency room.

After describing Elza's symptoms to the emergency-room nurse, several CT scans were taken of her heart and brain. Three agonizing hours passed before a young resident physician walked into the room and asked to speak to me in the hallway.

"Did you say your wife was experiencing cognitive decline?"

"Yes" I said.

"Well, there is no evidence of a stroke, but the scan showed atrophy in the frontal and temporal lobes of the brain."

Suddenly, fear and horror set in about what this could mean. This was news that we had hoped never to hear. My rational mind immediately took over to remind me of the narrative that had been drilled into our heads for the last two years. I reminded myself that curable depression had been the right diagnosis rendered by those who adhered to the highest standards of medical care. It had been determined by seasoned medical professionals who were far more accomplished than this millennial resident was. This young doctor is clearly mistaken, I told myself. The official diagnosis was depression masquerading as dementia. They even had a clinical term for it: *pseudo dementia*. Elza's treatment for four years had been based on the diagnosis of depression, and I refused to accept the words of this uninformed resident.

But my curiosity got the best of me, and I wanted to dismiss the possibility that this was something incurable or hereditary. I promptly asked: "Is it Alzheimer's?"

He casually answered, "Well, it's one of the dementias called frontotemporal dementia. I'll send a referral to her primary-care physician for follow-up." He spoke as if he were speaking of the weather, coldly and casually, and then disappeared into the bustle of the emergency room.

Suddenly, everything around me became quiet. The clamor slowly subsided as the words of Manny's friend floated into my mind. The word *aphasia* joined with other words that had appeared in fine print in the footnotes section of Elza's radiology report two years earlier. They spelled frontotemporal dementia (FTD).

My optimistic mind began to battle my rational mind. Remember, I said to myself, the best doctors in San Diego dismissed that diagnosis and agreed that this was a depression masquerading as dementia. This was the refrain that had helped keep us strong for over four years. Every time a treatment had failed, the warrior in me arose to assure us that the next doctor would succeed. But this time was different. I had been the lone witness to my soul mate's deteriorating health, and I could no longer live the lie we'd been told. The false narrative had exhausted the warrior and the optimist in me alike, and I had finally reached the breaking point. Wishful thinking had turned into despair as my rational mind took over.

In an instant, it all made horrible sense. My feeling of betrayal was overwhelming, as if I had switched a light on the cockroach colony called the medical establishment that was peddling falsehoods and feasting on human misery. The images were crisp and archetypal, and like real bugs exposed by the light of truth the cockroach practitioners scurried to their underground holes in search of their next victim.

As these images slowly faded from my mind, I found myself all alone. Standing there in the hospital corridor, I felt a deep emptiness permeate every cell of my body, and my eyes welled with tears. I stood helplessly looking in Elza's direction. Although her room was less than twenty feet from me, it seemed like she was a world away. The time it took for me to get to her felt like an eternity. I could not form the words to tell her this life-altering news. In that moment, I felt so much shame and embarrassment for treating Elza the way I had for much of the last four years. I had blamed her for being weak and unwilling to work hard enough on conquering her depression. She had it in her hands to get better, I had thought, and she hadn't worked seriously enough to overcome past traumas. But now, all these assumptions were gone. If this diagnosis were true, then her cognitive decline was not her fault. It would not have been a condition that she could have willed away or had any control over. All I could do when I saw her anxious face was cry and say I was sorry while I held her tightly in my arms. Everything around us dissolved into tears as we both sobbed quietly and alone.

In his book *Grace and Grit,* Ken Wilber described what it was like the moment he discovered his wife Treya had cancer. It was something along the lines of the universe turning into a piece of paper tissue that was being ripped in half.[1] For me, all I had believed about the universe until that moment proved to be wrong. It was as if someone had pulled back the curtain on four million years of human drama to expose the dark and uncaring nature of something called *existence.* The world was no longer a loving and merciful place that sheltered those who helped humanity get to a better understanding of itself. The truth was revealed to me that the universe offered nothing but punishment for those who commit their lives to good deeds. It is strange how the human mind reacts in the face of a calamity of this magnitude. Maybe it was the shock that presented me with these dark thoughts, but they were accompanied with equally dark images that seemed otherworldly and for hours swarmed effortlessly in my mind.

I don't remember driving home that Sunday. I remember the car floating on air and all my senses being numb. Strangely, I had experienced this sensation once before, but that had been on an occasion filled with ecstatic emotions the opposite of what we were experiencing now. The earlier occasion had been the day when I had picked up my first-born daughter, Chloe, from the maternity ward to take her home for the first time. Indeed, it seemed to me that the universe had shown its utter indifference to the human condition and proven that joy and pain are the same; only the rational mind divides them into opposing emotions.

Life for the next twenty-four hours moved in very slow and painful frames. The agony was unbearable as we returned to our home in La Jolla and I began to research frontotemporal dementia. Everything about the disease was morbid. One website said that life expectancy was three to five years from time of diagnosis. I was determined to know as much about this disease as possible before we spoke to Elza's primary-care physician the next morning. It seemed to be related to primary progressive aphasia, a diagnosis no one had dared to confirm other than our friend from New York. Another website suggested checking for several behavioral changes:

- Has the person experienced loss of empathy? Yes.
- Is the person having difficulty with speech? Yes.
- Has the person developed apathy? Yes.
- Is the person experiencing loss of inhibitions? Yes.
- Is the person having problems with focus and concentration? Yes...

The list of questions went on, but I couldn't bear the pain. Every search added a layer of hurt, the new one more agonizing than the old, until I reached the point of exhaustion at 3:30 in the morning. Elza had slept most of the night. She could sleep because she knows me, and she knows that I don't give in until I find a solution to each and every challenge with which we are presented. I lay down but sleep never came. I reached over and hugged her warm body and began to cry. My mournful tears woke her up, and she knew I had nothing positive to report. We held each other tight, but I knew that no matter how tightly I held her I couldn't protect her from this awful and ravaging disease. I had never seen her so scared before in my life, and I had never felt so cowardly and powerless.

Within forty-eight hours of our emergency-room visit, Elza's primary care physician had examined her CT scans. This was the turning point in our relationship with his office, as he acknowledged for the first time that Elza's problem was neurological in nature. He frantically began to search for referrals within his network for doctors who specialize in addressing neurodegenerative diseases. I could tell he was sincere in his efforts when he personally called to inform me that he was able to get us an appointment with a new neurologist who specialized in neurodegenerative medicine. I felt vindicated for being right and for proving that all the other health-care providers had been wrong for the past four years. I had spent most of my energy fighting what amounted to collective incompetence, lost in the layers of bureaucracy of the health-care system. The problem was of a neurological nature, and now that we were on the same page with the healthcare providers my focus could shift fully into supporting Elza's treatment based on her new diagnosis. The appointment with the new neurologist was four weeks away, and I had thought we no longer needed to wait for the referral to the UC San Diego neurological institute.

The appointment came, and we sat anxiously waiting to hear about the new course of treatment or possible clinical trials in which Elza could participate. But our hopes turned to despair as this new neurologist—the third within this particular healthcare group—viewed the CT scans taken at the emergency room. As if reading from the same rehearsed script that her two previous colleagues had read from, she proceeded to tell us that the scans were inconclusive. She then reached into a filing cabinet and took out the same simple tests for Elza to point to the right shapes and forms, just as the first neurologist had done in the summer of 2016. By now, I had lost all hope for starting anew, and I intuitively knew what was coming next: the neurologist asked her a few memory questions to which she answered haltingly, but correctly. Then she repeated the same lines we had heard before, almost verbatim: "Her problem is not neurological. It's an issue with focus."

She ended our visit by making a referral for a neuropsychological assessment. This was the same five-hour battery of cognitive tests that had placed us on the wrong path from the beginning. I was furious, and I wasn't going to allow this to happen. The protector in me took over as I knew Elza couldn't possibly last through another few minutes of these tests. Not a word was said about the possibility of any progressive brain diseases that have no known treatment.

Four years into navigating the torturous landscape of American healthcare, we felt trapped in a system that only caters to patients as repeat customers who buy billable products with every doctor's visit. If I had agreed to have Elza take this neuropsychological assessment, it would have been the fourth of its kind. It would have placed us back in the vicious, unending cycle of psychotherapists and psychiatrists and at the mercy of a pharmaceuticals industry that still had a million anti-depressant drugs waiting to be experimented with.

That afternoon, we came home to find a referral in the mail from Elza's private psychiatrist—the one who had diagnosed her with bipolar disorder—indicating the name of a new neurologist at the UC San Diego neurological institute. He had agreed to take Elza as a new patient. I immediately switched our health-care services and our insurance carrier to accommodate the change.

On our first visit, and despite my frustration, the neurologist at the neurological institute also conducted simple tests by asking Elza to draw certain shapes and name certain objects. She did well in drawing the shapes but was halting in naming the objects. Before he could say anything, I voiced my objection to any lengthy cognitive evaluations, and to my surprise he agreed with me. He also acknowledged that the CT scans showed noticeable atrophy of brain tissue, but to ascertain whether it meant frontotemporal dementia or another form of dementia, he requested a more detailed scan called a PET Scan.

As we waited for the results, the uncertainly in not knowing had become worse than knowing the worst scenario possible. After the neurologist's evaluation of the new scan results, he summoned us into his office to give us the official diagnosis. It was now the middle of March 2018. Elza's official diagnosis was that she had logopenic progressive aphasia, which is a type of dementia characterized by language disturbance. This diagnosis included most of her symptoms of having difficulty producing and understanding speech. It was also a subset of primary progressive aphasia, which in itself is a syndrome of FTD. Additionally, the PET scan had revealed brain atrophy indicating an early onset of Alzheimer's disease.

In the strangest way possible, this news came as a welcome relief for the both of us. The storm of uncertainly that sent us to over twenty different specialists over the preceding four years had finally quieted down. As our appointment came to a close, Elza's new neurologist prescribed a 5-milligram pill no bigger than an eighth of an inch in diameter and took Elza off all her other medications. He also provided us with a list of clinical trials and support groups, but gave no leads on any promising treatments. I asked about the frequency with which we should have these scans done so we could better gauge the progress of the disease.

He smiled and provided an answer that I will never forget: "Brain science is medicine's final frontier. We know less than 7 percent about the brain and how it functions." After waiting for a reaction from us that didn't come, he continued, "I have a patient with terrible brain images that make us think he should be in a wheelchair, or bedridden, but he functions like any normal human being. And I have another patient with a brain scan that barely shows any abnormalities, yet he falls into the category of advanced stages of Alzheimer's."

With this revelation, I was led to the conviction that humanity was at the mercy of imprecise science and doctors who were flying blind with insufficient information. It seemed to be my proof that the Emperor of Modern Medicine indeed had no clothes. The wizard behind the curtain that had animated our every move over the last few years was indeed the fraudster, the high trickster who revealed his true self as the curtain was flung wide open.

The spectacular failure of modern science is that, realizing that we know only 7 percent of what there is to know about the brain, so many practitioners are arrogant enough to pretend certainty in their diagnoses and prescriptions. Their pretense of knowledge they don't really have is the rose-colored lens through which modern medicine dispenses false hope and plays with people's lives and emotions. This was the Stone Age disguised by the arrogant certainty of math and the pretense to know what was yet unknowable.

As we left the clinic, Elza reminded me of the words she had uttered repeatedly on that Sunday in the emergency room. "I want to be in nature. I want to hike with our dog, Buddha."

The Years of Anger and Self-Destruction

There it was, the green flash at sunset. What a rare sight to see, right before the sky turned to ruby and the sun disappeared into the deep waters of the Pacific. I could see the lighter orange hue on the waves as they crashed slowly onto the shore. The tall palm trees swayed in the gentle breeze until they were swallowed by the darkness. Another day in paradise came to a close. The sun kept her promise as she gave way to the stars, and soon I would have to turn off the flames in the fire pit and head in. Everything in the universe was in order except for our lives. Our days had become just like our nights, dark and full of pain. There was no therapy to go to, and no more medical mysteries waiting to be unraveled. Like the dark sky that swallowed the day, Elza's awful diagnosis was swallowing our lives.

The warrior in me—the hero—had nothing further to resist. He had been handed a resounding defeat, and the battleground on which we stood was left with nothing but burned hopes and shattered dreams. Whole health became whole misery. Caring for body mind and soul was buried deep in the bowels of a dark and uncaring world. With the exception of Dr. Beck and my family, communication with the outside world came to a stop. Social isolation had become permanent. Back pain and muscle tension had taken over my body, and I stopped running and going to the gym. Healthy eating was replaced by whatever was on the takeout menu, and weeds took over our garden. Meditation and mindfulness became a thing of the past, and I fell into a protracted depression.

Elza had not left my side for months. Like an insecure child fearing abandonment, she needed to keep me in her sights twenty-four hours a day. The only exception was when she watched TV, which gave me the respite I so desperately needed.

After the green flash at sunset, I came in through the sliding door as she was watching her favorite show, *The Crown*. She had eaten and poured herself a glass of scotch. With the exception of an occasional glass of wine, neither of us had been drinkers. But these were extraordinary times, and hard liquor provided the extraordinary measure that numbed the pain. We both had a low tolerance for alcohol. She got tipsy after the first drink, and I didn't last much beyond a second. Nevertheless, we had been drinking almost every night since that fateful visit to the emergency room. It was the only thing that helped us escape the dread and fall asleep.

But that night was going to be different. Earlier in the day, I had gathered all the pain pills into one bottle and placed them at the bar behind the Jack Daniels. There were about twenty. I figured that twelve for me, eight for her ought to do the trick. Like the character from the movie *Network*, we were mad as hell and weren't going to play by the rules of this cruel world anymore. No destiny was going to beat us on her terms—not even death.

Right before I approached the bar, my phone rang. It was my younger daughter, Quinn, who was in therapy. She always called after a therapy session to talk about the progress she was making. That night, her call was the hand of destiny that dragged us from the edge of hell and back into the inferno.

In the days that followed, darkness descended upon us, and it decided to stay for several months. Even with drinking, sleep became a rare commodity, and when it came it lasted for less than three hours. How could one sleep when everything that had defined one's world had been taken away? How could one rest when one's beloved was dying? The protector in me refused to give up. It appeared in my sleep only to shock me back into a new and waking nightmare. The voice screamed nightly as the guilt from my failure to protect my soul mate began to take its toll on me. For months, we both languished in obscurity, and I became suspended between exhaustion, depression, and anger.

A Godless World

On countless sleepless nights, I plunged into that darkness, searching for the merciless God who was behind all this cruelty. I wanted a fair trial. I implored him to explain himself and justify what was happening.

"How could you do this to us?" I ranted. "Is this one of your cruel, cosmic jokes? Haven't you appreciated our ideas to save this miserable world of yours? Which of our plans wasn't good enough for you? Or was it our rebellion against your religious doctrines that offended your godly sensibilities? Did you have a problem with the details about how Elza wanted to save the Middle East? Clearly, you sent your dark angels to stop her at the same time she published her manifesto for peace in that dark corner of your world. Maybe she meddled with forces that were far bigger than she had imagined. Did she interfere with your evil plans to keep that hellhole burning for eternity? Can no human soul intervene in your dark and vile visions of human suffering?

"What kind of god are you? You chuckle one day and you destroy lives and you think it's a joke? Is exposing human frailty a blood sport for you and those who roam the dark spaces around you? ... Do you understand how much work still needs to be done? Was it her ideas for Israeli-Palestinian peace that upset you? Or was it the way she was helping the Palestinians build their own state and institutions that unleashed your omnipotent wrath? What about her bigger plans to make the Middle East a more conscious and caring place? Was that what you didn't like, or was it something else entirely?

"Whatever it was, I can get her to back away. We can fix whatever might have disturbed your plans for this miserable planet. Whatever you want, she will do willingly. She will give it all up if you can alleviate this dreadful burden. If stories of your miracles are true, then have mercy on your angel Elza and spare her this awful fate that's cutting her down in the prime of her life."

Thus went my early-morning implorations to God. On other sleepless nights, I thought that perhaps God is a Western god, one who needs to be appeased by offerings to save the Western world in particular. With a renewed sense of purpose born out of utter desperation, and in the dark recesses of my soul, I cried out again:

"What about my feeble attempts to save Western Civilization from its own evils? I can't do it without Elza. What about our dreams to spread the good virtues of Spiral Dynamics to the world and help it become a more caring place? After all, this was the theory *that explained everything*. Was it because of that? Did it explain so much that it threatened to erode your powers? Maybe its ideas on conscious evolution threatened your invincible grip on a world of war and misery. Is this what unleashed your wrath at your angel? ... And what about me? Have you no mercy? I can't do it without her. How am I supposed to function without my Elza? How am I supposed to find purpose again?"

Months of such desperate appeals were met with nothing but silence. There was no bargain to be struck and no miracle to sooth our emotional state or comfort my ailing soul. Unlike in a Hollywood script or as described in an inspiring passage from a holy book, no beams of light shined down to comfort us, nor did the dark clouds part ways to show us a road forward. No miracles were performed, and no angelic music played. This indeed was a jealous god, full of envy, who wanted no mortal human messing with his grand design.

Busy Doing Nothing

During this long period of despair, one of my remaining connections to reality was the planning of the big conference scheduled to celebrate Dr. Beck in April 2018. After receiving Elza's grim news in March, I had thought of cancelling the event altogether, but deposits had been made, venues had been booked, and contracts signed. Our neighbor, a therapist who had become our confidante, told me that planning for the event would be a good way to help alleviate the symptoms of the deep depression that had permeated our lives. The conference became my muse. I decided that its title should be *The Spiral Dynamics Summit on the Future*. When I had decided on that title the previous December, the future had looked bright and the eternal optimist in me was standing tall. Then, by the second week of January, our hopes for that future had been dashed. Now, I saw that the conference topic was drawing inspiration from speakers and attendees alike. This event had to happen, I convinced myself. It was working. My preoccupation with its mundane tasks took my mind off our dark reality.

The conference was a smashing success. Attendees came from sixteen different countries. Colleagues were anxious for news about the future of Spiral Dynamics. Several executives from Elza's client's company in the Middle East came to witness her return to health and to the work she loved. None had known that her expected recovery had taken a turn for the worse. Except for our friend Dr. Beck, no one knew of the new diagnosis, and I tried my best to mask the truth. In my opening remarks I told everyone that Elza was suffering from social anxiety and requested that they be courteous in keeping their interactions with her to a minimum. This wasn't much of a lie, since this was what therapists had told us to say when Elza was in treatment. After the conference ended, we went back home to a world of emptiness. There were no menial tasks left to occupy my days as we began to confront the darkness ahead.

Dealing with the Unpleasant

The new and the unfamiliar had come to us in the form of an indistinct and unexpected fate. Nothing on this new journey was recognizable, and the protector in me began to lose hope. Nowhere in our new reality was there a ray of light that pointed to a way out of this dreadful dream. As we saw our old world vanish before our eyes, I decided to confront this new dread head on. We joined an Alzheimer's support group, hoping to form new friendships with people going through similar challenges. On our first visit, we met with the social worker, who turned to Elza and asked her the date I had been diagnosed with Alzheimer's. I could barely keep it together. Although Elza was fifty-two, she looked far younger. The social worker would not have been wrong in assuming that she was in her thirties and I was the one with Alzheimer's. In years past, Elza's youthful looks had been an easy target for jokes by friends and colleagues. Dr. Beck often teased her about finding something other than her high-school picture to put on announcements for press releases and joint events. When my brothers had met her for the first time, they jokingly asked if I had her mother's permission to date her. On that awful day when we met with the social worker, those memories came rushing back, only to add to the irony and the cruel punishment of that moment.

The Alzheimer's support group separated patients from caregivers so that the latter could share stories to help ease the pain of their fellow caregivers. Patients gathered in a different room and picked from a variety of activities that filled their time. At that first meeting, listening to others I became a witness to the dark turn our own lives had taken. Two weeks earlier I had been facilitating a global gathering of change agents and helping them formulate strategies for how to bring positive and lasting change to the world. That day at the Alzheimer's meeting, I was listening to a man my age describe his different approaches to handling soiled bed sheets. This was the world that awaited me, and I became very angry. Anger post-diagnosis took on a much darker form as more pieces of our new life began to appear. We were told this was the first stage of grief in our long process toward accepting our new reality. That first meeting was also our last, as our denial moved to center stage.

Elza was in a deeper state of denial than I was and refused to accept what amounted to an early death sentence. Out of desperation, she reached out to friends in her Evolutionary Leaders Circle for help. First it was Deepak Chopra, as she requested the support of his whole health team to assess her condition. No calls were ever retuned, and no answers to her numerous emails were ever received. A week passed, and I awoke to see her angrily shoving Deepak's books into a trash bag. Moments later she hauled them to the garage. A few days later, Jean Houston's books suffered the same fate. Then came the entire row of Ken Wilber's books. Elza's anger at the world was causing her to tear down everything she had built. All that had defined her psychospiritual depth and the intelligence that had brought her to prominence in the Middle East was being angrily dismantled. The sight was too much for me to bear, but my own sadness and exhaustion prevented me from stopping her. I hid all the books she had disposed of and replaced them later on shelves in my office.

The nights had grown darker as well. The protector in me who had haunted my every sleeping hour had transformed into my inner critic, and he refused to give up on finding someone to blame for our misery. The silence from the heavens wasn't enough, and the critic joined hands with my inner narcissist as we searched for outer answers. No inward exploration was needed, since this disaster could be blamed on a number of other people. Projection became the norm. Those who didn't offer emotional support became the enemy. Colleagues near and far fell by the wayside. They, too, became the enemy.

As for those in the medical community, they were still the recipients of most of my vitriol, but now that hatred had multiplied. If Elza had been diagnosed correctly in 2016, her test scores and verbal abilities would have enabled her to get into many promising clinical trials. But, due to the doctors' incompetence, by March 2018 she could barely focus or speak. Yes, the neurologists—and the whole lot of cockroaches in white coats—would remain the biggest enemy. The lines were drawn and allegiances were clear. On one side was an uncaring world and on the other was us. We had isolated ourselves in order to survive, and in that isolation we descended to a new dimension of the Underworld.

The Darkest Hour

The lack of sleep was taking its toll on me. Although I tried new sleeping arrangements on every couch and every bed in the house, meaningful rest remained illusive. My favorite spot to battle the night demons was on the soft, cloth couch in my office. I lay there one night as deafening silence filled the air. I turned to the powerful heroes who had guided our journey to the impossible heights of the past. Maybe it was they who had led her to the forbidden territory where her trespassing unleashed the wrath of the patriarchy. Myth at this point had become more reliable than science. The gods didn't speak, and so they became an easy target. Maybe the heroes we had so admired were also the false gods who were part of the conspiracy. Or, maybe what I was experiencing was a sympathetic resonance of sorts, a response to Elza's emotional cues. Maybe it was both that made me seethe with anger and blame everything on a new set of enemies for their betrayal and abandonment.

The broken rays of the moon shone upon a familiar image hanging on the wall. It was that of Dr. Clare Graves, the genius behind the academic research of Spiral Dynamics and the work to which Elza and I had devoted the last two decades of our lives. Like Dr. Beck, Elza and I had deep admiration for Dr. Graves. He had been a towering figure at six feet, six inches tall, his physical presence commanding respect as much as did his academic career. He was as much a psychologist as he was an existential philosopher, and because of that we had always reached out to his ageless wisdom. We had agreed ten years earlier that a portrait of him, along with one of his most famous sayings, should grace the largest wall in my office. The portrait was a collage of four identical images in four different colors in the artistic style of Andy Warhol. The quote was one intended to give us hope when all around us seem to fall apart: "Damn it all to hell. People have the right to be who they are."

On that night, when I was trying to sleep in my office, the moonlight had eliminated only the first part of the saying as Graves's face seemed to become animated and begin to mock my misery. This was the perfect trigger that unleashed my angry tirade that followed:

"Damn me? No, Damn you, Clare! Damn you and your whole bio, psycho, social theory of everything. Damn you and all your followers who don't have the first clue about how real life works. What value system do death and illness fall into? How can you claim to know everything when you can't answer that? Is there a hierarchy in death? What? No answer? Damn you and your theory of nothing! You and your followers can all go to hell, and the world would be a better place for it.

"Damn you, Don Beck, and your ego the size of Texas! Did you really think you could change six thousand years of hatred and bloodshed? You walk around with your Texas drawl and Texas swagger and you think the world will bend to your will? Ten years of your life spent on dismantling Apartheid, and look at that hellhole today! You think the Arabs and the Jews are going to fare any better? Damn you for making her believe that "yes" was the answer to that question! Damn you for unleashing the wrath of the patriarchy that made her sick and cut her down in the prime of her life. Damn the legacy of Spiral Dynamics and all those who believe in it. Damn it all to hell!

"And damn you, Ken Wilber, with your bald head and your four quadrants. Damn your whole consciousness movement and everyone in it. What a bunch of insecure, highbrowed weaklings hiding behind the intellectual façade of big words. Your pre – and post-fallacy bullshit, your interior subjectivity and subjective interiority, your lines and your states, and all the Buddhism and meditation don't amount to a hill of beans. Where on your spiritual line of development does our situation fall? Is it Buddhism or Hinduism that's supposed to make this all better? Put those questions on your quadrants and write a new six-hundred-page book about it. Do you really think the world cares about who you are? Damn you and all the followers of your Integral Theory to hell! That's where this bullshit belongs."

As I indulged myself in this tirade, the faces didn't stop coming. The images and the voices from every teacher and every discipline and school of thought crowded my head. My blind anger had delivered me into an altered state of mind where I'd never been. This had to be the inescapable belly of the whale or Dante's final circle of hell. The voices howled and screeched in increasing intensity before reaching a deafening crescendo.

Silence returned to the room as I lay there exhausted and spent. I slowly lifted my head and caught a glimpse of the man I'd become in the reflection of the sliding door. I was unrecognizable to myself, an ugly shadow of the man I used to be. A moment passed; then, just as Graves's face had seemed to move, my mind began to play another trick. My reflection took on a life of its own as it spoke in tones of an old abandoned self:

"No! Damn you, Said Elias Dawlabani! Damn you and your hypocrisy. All she did for eighteen years is prepare you for moments like these. You're an arrogant prick who refused to learn. Just how many more life lessons need to be wasted on you before you wake up? We all get sick. We're all going to die, Asshole!"

Slowly, everything turned dark and quiet. Something profound had happened, but I wasn't sure what. The powerful forces behind my anger had subsided. The voices of my inner critic and my narcissist became quiet as I collapsed into a peaceful slumber. I don't recall the last time I had slept with such reckless abandon.

Integrating the Conscious and the Unconscious

It was past 9 a.m. when I awoke the next morning. I sat straight up on the couch where I had battled my demons, recalling the vivid dream I had just had. It was Graves and I. The setting was academic, and we were colleagues. We were in his office as he sat in a reclined posture in my leather chair behind my antique banker's desk. His worn cowboy boots stretched across its entire width, the left boot resting on the top of the right. I was a few years younger, seated on the other side. My feet, too, were crossed, occupying the other corner of the desk. Nothing was said as we both sat in peaceful silence peppered by the occasional smile and a lazy glance out the window overlooking infinite green fairways and rolling hills. We were kindred souls.

If I had had this dream before 2014, Elza would have put it all in Jungian perspective for me. She would have told me that my psyche was using the unconscious to balance the dangerous direction my conscious mind and my ego had taken. She would have reminded me that everyone in the dream represented an aspect of me—that this was a needed dialogue the ego had to have with the self; that Graves in my dream was an unacknowledged aspect of my Higher Self. But today, my teacher, my lover, the gatekeeper to understanding my Higher Self, can longer speak those words and think those thoughts.

In years past, our Saturday mornings had been like Sunday school, with Elza my teacher and the subject, Jung. We could pick from any of his books that occupied an entire shelf in the hallway and, like children reading Dr. Seuss, we would sit together on the bed in our guest room. For the first few hours, I would feel resistance; then, with Elza's help, the breakthrough; and finally the peace that came with the deeper understanding of the self and the psyche. She always supplemented Jung's views with mysticism and spirituality. Life would go on with a renewed sense of meaning and purpose until the following Saturday, when we would do it all over again.

While my anger at Clare Graves was resolved in my dream, my anger at my friend and mentor Dr. Beck was processed in a different way. It happened in my waking hours on a warm June afternoon only a few days after the dream. Dr. Beck's wife, Pat, who had been ill, had just passed away that morning. Maybe it was my guilt from the angry tirade I had a few days earlier that drove me, but I needed to talk to him. We spent an hour on the phone, remembering the deep love he had for Pat and the love she had for Elza and me. To Elza, Pat was the mother she never had. They had been fond of each other since the day Pat had told her that she—Elza—had given Dr. Beck a new lease on life through the work they were doing together in the Middle East. Like Elza in my life, Pat was the stabilizing force in his life. We both lamented the loss of the most precious gifts life had given us. His was for a soul mate who had suffered physical death with her full faculties intact; mine was for the loss of my soul mate's faculties with only the physical body remaining.

I'm sure Jung covered the deeper source for processing emotions in such an awakened state, but all I wanted to do after the call was to remain still and be a witness to the love and the pain that had just unfolded. In a few days, Dr. Beck had returned to the hallowed space he had previously occupied in our lives and our hearts. He and I now shared a deeper more painful bond that will remain unbreakable for the rest our lives.

A few nights had passed, and sleep was becoming normal again. Archetypal dreams had become common occurrences, and in the days that followed I had the most profound dream of them all. I was waging an epic battle with all types of demons. As soon as I had killed one, three would take its place. The sky was dark and the earth was red. They were coming from everywhere, and I couldn't keep up. Death was imminent as I screamed in horror, waking Elza and Buddha from their deep sleep. For fifteen seconds, I stood terrified on the threshold between the conscious and the unconscious. Before fully transitioning into an awakened state, the hallucinations spoke: "Don't be afraid. Follow your bliss. Doors will open where you didn't think there will be doors." My conscious mind immediately identified the voice that had first spoken these words. I spent that day absorbed in Joseph Campbell's world. Myth and the archetypes had played their role again in giving me meaning and transitioning me out of one of the most difficult passages of my life.

The road ahead was still strewn with difficulties, but they had become less guttural in nature. The voices that had awakened me in the middle of the night for the past year had been transformed. Instead of anger and denial, they were bringing me to a place of deep sadness and solitude. The inner critic seemed to have subsided, and a different self was taking charge. It was helping me pick up the pieces of our broken lives and acknowledge our new reality. It held my hand as I began the long passage toward closure. The so-called good days began to outnumber the bad, knowing that the good would never be as good as it once was.

This was my new place of acceptance and quietude, where I could get in touch with my own needs and rediscover self-love. It was a premature but necessary stage of the journey of an extraordinary life that Elza and I had built together. Now, her own life was being cut short by destiny, karma, and disease. For the first time since we've been together, I began to see glimpses of the road ahead without my soul mate. It was a postapocalyptic wilderness full of charred memories and possibilities unfulfilled. This was the new normal that began to take hold. As otherworldly as it was, I began to accept it. I had to accept it. Without my Elza, I could see how ordinary and commonplace the road ahead was going to be. It was all unremarkable, lonely, and dull. But through it all, I decided to continue following my bliss. I continued to write.

7

GRIEVING AS ONE

Embrace your grief. For there, your soul will grow.
—C. G. Jung

"Hey, Said, the usual?"

"You know what, Elliot? I'm going to be a rebel today. I'll have a slice of the lemon poppy bread instead of the blueberry scone, and two large lattes instead of the usual medium."

"And water for Buddha?"

"Yes, indeed!"

The barista chuckled at my humorous take on rebellion. Even the quiet one, Kate, peered from behind the espresso machine and chimed in: "You're fifteen minutes late today, what's going on?"

We laughed as I waited, but my smile veiled my imprisoned ego bubbling with rage. Elza sat outside with our dog aimlessly staring into space. She had outgrown the clothes I had bought for her just four months earlier. The frontal-lobe disorder had completely wiped out the part of her brain that controls appetite, and she had put on at least fifty pounds since her latest diagnosis.

We couldn't go to fancy restaurants anymore. The last time we did, it had been with our neighbors. That night she finished her meal in seconds and began savagely to eat from everyone else's plate. Humor was a coping mechanism that stopped me from falling fully into the abyss. It appeared every time I experienced an emotional trigger that reminded me of how things used to be. No more rebellion against the current economic system, and no more revolt against all the injustices of the Middle East. Now it was all about the choice of pastry and drink. Could fate be any crueler than this? When was this nightmare going to end?

By the time June rolled around, our lives had settled into a predictable monotony. Along with the 5-mg. pink pill, we were told that familiarity and routine were the best medicine to keep an Alzheimer's patient in a stable mental state. It was the familiarity and the routine that were killing me. I could no longer differentiate the days. The sweetness of Saturday mornings was all but gone. The Sunday visits to the farmers' market had disappeared, and with them went the healthy lifestyle we once had. Monday looked like Thursday, and Thursday looked like all the other days. By now, I could perform the routine with my eyes closed. Coffee in bed at 8:00 a.m. while we watched the news for two hours—because, what the heck? There was nothing else to do. At 10:30 I fed Buddha, and then came the two hours of agony. I struggled to write but didn't give up: a blog here, an analysis there, a tirade at an imbecile posting stupid stuff to my Spiral Dynamics Facebook page. It was all routine, and it all made sense. Rage was now being directed at faceless readers whom I'll never meet. At 1:00 p.m. we had lunch, then watched television again. This was the only activity that stopped Elza from aimlessly wandering around the house. The show was *The Crown*, Elza's favorite, and by now I had memorized every line from its two seasons, especially those played by Winston Churchill's character. By 4:30 we hit the coffee shop, and by 5:30 we took our daily walk along the shores of the Pacific. Elza's weight gain had reduced our two-mile routine to a few blocks. We sat at our favorite bench hidden behind a bluff and waited for the sun to set. Dinner was take-out, and it was one of three choices: Thai, sushi, or chicken. Then it was more TV before bed until we woke up the next day and did it all over again. It was all ordinary, commonplace, and unremarkable. Yes, this was the other side of rebellion—the ugly indifference of the universe—and the tiny, laughable changes to the daily routine comprised the ultimate form of mutiny.

The Fourth of July came without the slightest celebration. In years past, the day had brought emotions and laughter to our lives. This was Ghinwa's birthday, and Elza would call her mom on the morning of every Fourth to reminisce about the four years of joy they had both spent with her daughter. She couldn't call Ghinwa herself to wish her a happy birthday, because Elza's ex-husband had threatened physical harm to Elza if she attempted contact. This was his way of dealing with his unresolved issues and expressing his wounded pride over her escaping his abuse and archaic beliefs.

The threat of harm was real. I had experienced it firsthand a year after we met when Elza tried to call her daughter on her birthday and her ex-husband answered the phone. I could hear the tirade of anger and belligerence as she pleaded to speak to her daughter. The next day, Elza received a call from a man named Frank who informed her that he knew where we lived, who I was, and the names of my two daughters. By the time she concluded the conversation, she was overcome by fear and dread. She told me the man was an ex-CIA agent who had become one of her ex-husband's henchmen.

Now, on this Fourth of July, 2018, except for my own misery, emotions were nowhere to be found—no joy and no fear. Apathy and indifference were Elza's constant expressions, and, for the first time, the date meant nothing to her. I reminded her of the significance of the day and said that it wasn't her fault she didn't remember. It was the disease that was making her forget.

I wasn't sure whether Elza was in denial over the morbidity of her multiple diagnoses or whether her apathy and indifference were shielding her from expressing how she felt. Maybe by now, she simply wasn't aware of her condition, but I couldn't tell. If the gods wanted to silence her, then the aphasia had done the job perfectly. If she could think, her tongue failed to utter the words and I had no way of knowing which was the culprit.

The mystery surrounding her state of mind came to an explosive end just a few weeks later. It opened my own healing wounds as we began the long road toward shared grief. It was preceded by the occasion of Elza's fifty-third birthday, July 17, 2018, when we celebrated by going to our favorite restaurant, Amardeen. It served authentic Lebanese food, and the owners, Camille and Eva, were from our hometown in Lebanon. Elza had attended Catholic school with Eva, and with every visit we felt the common bonds that tied us to Zahle. To the restaurant owners, we were the pride of the local American-Lebanese community. Camille always introduced us to his patrons, especially the professors from the nearby university. They had known that Elza was in therapy, but we hadn't been to the restaurant since her diagnosis. As soon as Eva saw us, she walked over and greeted us with a big hug. Elza showed no response, physically or emotionally. Apathy and indifference had become her standard reactions to every stimulus coming from her surroundings. The emotional traits that had made her who she was were disappearing as quickly as her ability to speak and focus.

The questions kept coming: "How is therapy? How's work? How's your friend Jean Houston? How's Dr. Beck? How's your project in the Middle East?" The more numerous the questions got the more distraught she became.

I broke the silence and told Eva about Elza's diagnosis. She immediately began to cry and put her arms around Elza. Minutes passed, and only sadness and tears filled our booth.

"God is taking all the good people and leaving us with nothing but evil," Eva said as she gathered herself and left to attend to her customers. In the face of all this sadness, I ordered an expensive bottle of Lebanese Syrah with dinner to preserve some semblance of the occasion. As we left, Eva followed us to the car and gave Elza another hug. I watched her in the rearview mirror, standing in sorrowful silence as we disappeared into the dark night. The only words on the drive home were spoken hesitantly and in a voice barely audible: "I'm fifty-three."

The Essence of Self

The next morning, July 18, Elza came to my office with a book in hand—Deepak Chopra's and Rudolph Tanzi's *Super Genes*. I had seen it a million times. The yellow tabs that protruded haphazardly from its edge were outnumbered only by the yellow highlights running through its pages. It was personally inscribed: "To my friend Elza—Love, Deepak." Many endorsers of the book were people who had been Elza's colleagues at the Evolutionary Leaders Circle.

Super Genes was published in 2015, and it was the last book that Elza would ever read and comprehend. The parts she had highlighted pointed to an abundance of new research in genetics. It provided scientific proof on how to escape the genetic destiny handed to us by our parents. For three years, this book had been Elza's primary source for optimism and hope. The field of epigenetics is the future of medicine, and she became convinced that our consciousness and our environment could alter our destiny. The book had become her Bible.

That morning, I could tell she was angry. No sooner had she handed me the book than she brought her laptop and wanted me to watch a TED talk by Dr. Tanzi, Deepak's coauthor of *Super Genes* and a renowned professor of neurology and a leading Alzheimer's researcher at Harvard Medical School. From Dr. Tanzi's first few words, it was clear that this wasn't the optimistic voice heard between the lines of his book. He began with this terrifying statement:

> I want to talk to you about a horrendous and devastating disease that slowly and steadily destroys the brain and erases the mind, and the entire time loved ones and the patient watch on helplessly as this horror unfolds.

I had thought I had moved on from being in denial about Elza's condition, but I found these words acting as a huge emotional trigger. I immediately hit the pause button to stop the onslaught of pain they brought on. Elza moved my hand and hit play again. This was one of those rare days when Elza's cognitive abilities seemed randomly to reappear. It was as if she wanted to confirm the biases

I had harbored about the entire medical community conspiring against us and that Dr. Tanzi was a part of that conspiracy.

> I'm talking about Alzheimer's disease. This is the quiet thief in the night. It robs the person from their sense of identity, personality, and, ultimately, the very essence of self.[1]

The lecture went on for another twenty-five minutes, and I watched myself feel the pain. Dr. Tanzi talked about the newest findings related to the disease, the different proteins that cause it, and the clinical trials and research that were taking place. I was familiar with most of what he talked about, and I had shared it all with Elza before. But today, she was intent on listening to the entire lecture again. Maybe the reason had something to do with my conversation with Eva the night before at dinner. That's when Elza had heard the word *Alzheimer's* for the first time. Maybe her resistance and her denial had reached their limit, and, with her diminished mental capacities, listening to this TED lecture was her way of acceptance.

Toward the end of the lecture, Dr. Tanzi spoke of his love for music and invited to the stage Chris Mann, a classically trained singer with whom he had written a song that had become the anthem to raise awareness for Alzheimer's. As Mann took to the stage, he shared how both his grandmothers had suffered with the disease and how his paternal grandmother, like Elza, had been diagnosed with an early onset of the disease in her late forties. The song he sang was a story being told from the perspective of the person with the disease. Although the written lyrics don't do justice to Mann's performance and the accompanying video, here are the words:

Remember Me

I need someone to hold, to hold on for me
To what I can't seem to hold on to
The life we used to live is slipping through my fingertips
Like a thread that's unraveling

I suppose that nothing lasts forever, and
everything is lost in its time.
When I can't find the words that I'm trying to speak
When I don't know the face in the mirror I see
When I feel I'm forgotten and lost in this world
Won't you please remember me
Remember me

I know there'll come a day, when I have gone away
And the memory of me will fade
But darling think of me, and who I used to be
And I'll be right there with you again

I hope I'm one thing worth not forgetting
Tell me that you'll never let me go

When I can't find the words that I'm trying to speak
When I don't know the face in the mirror I see
When I feel I'm forgotten and lost in this world
Won't you please remember me
Remember me

I hope I'm one thing worth not forgetting
Tell me that you'll never let me go

When I can't find the words that I trying to speak
When I don't know the face in the mirror I see
When I feel like I'm lost and alone in this world
Won't you please remember me
Remember me[2]

If Elza could speak, then Mann's lyrics would have been the desperate pleading of what remained of the person who was once the
strongest woman I had ever known. All she needed now was to be
loved, protected, and remembered. The emotions were guttural

and despairing. The poignancy of it all cut right to my heart like nothing before ever had. It tore at every ounce of my being. It steered a Herculean storm of emotions that silenced every voice that had kept me from falling further into the abyss. There I was, in a new free fall, holding her hand as we both descended into a new and unknown darkness. It thrashed us into a new state of shared grief the depth of which I had never experienced. I cried and she pleaded, mumbling and struggling to form the words every time Chris Mann sang the line, "Remember me." I held her tight, like a mother would a frightened child, as we both collapsed in tears.

This is what she had been trying to tell me for months. She had finally found the words and the most heartbreaking, agonizing method to deliver them to me. The aphasia had completely taken away her ability to communicate. Her thoughts, her fears, and her desires had been muted and were forever being kept behind a wall of stubborn silence. The other diseases in her brain had dulled all her other natural gifts. Even the fury that had driven her to break things two years earlier had disappeared behind a veil of apathy and indifference. Over the preceding four years, I had witnessed her become weaker and increasingly helpless, but this was different. Her presence carried a sense of resignation. It looked like the final phase in a valiant battle, the stage of honorable surrender. I held her tenderly in my arms, hoping against all hope to stop this thief in the night from robbing us of what little remained of our lives. Hours passed, and with the exception of the occasional "I love you," nothing was said.

In weeks that followed, an uneasy calm befell the both of us. Elza's stress subsided, and her odd behaviors all but disappeared. The anxious nights she had spent aimlessly walking around the house gave way to deep and restful sleep. The emotional experience of that day we had listened to Chris Mann's song had also delivered me to a new phase in my life and in my grief. I can only guess that it was the power of the unconscious that thrust us into the eye of the hurricane and shielded us both from further turbulence. For four-and-a-half years and against all odds, I had fought against the forces of this relentless storm; yet, in one act of courage, Elza had provided the protective wall that sheltered us from its furious wrath and howling winds. This was a new layer of the self that tore away another manifestation of the ego and placed us both at the center of a simple truth. In the eye of the storm, I began to find new inner peace. The outside world began to fall away, and I was left only with the love for my wife. Nothing else mattered anymore and, for the first time in my life, I was okay with it.

Playing the Blame Game

The next few months were defined by a relative sense of emotional stability. I returned to writing and could sit and write for hours at a time. Elza slept on the couch in my office while I wrote. This was her way to show her unconditional support for my telling our story on paper, of manifesting the voice of Chris Mann. In my writings, she knew I was going to remember her and never let her go, and that made all her phantoms disappear. It turned all her despair into hope and in the process made me find new purpose. In remembering her, I wanted to know how she would have interpreted the deeper forces that made July 18, 2018 such a transformative day. For weeks I meditated on that question, trying to tap into the psychospiritual realms that had defined our lives before 2014. All the selves that had fought along my side on this journey began to reappear. They were the archetypes of strength born out of desperation and anger. The deeper the meditations became, the more I became a witness to that anger. That which had saved me had also led me to a place of self-contraction. It had closed the door to pure awareness and true conscious thought. But now, I was in a place of love where I could reexamine the journey from higher realms and return to a sense of oneness with truth.

In this new state of bliss, I came to realize that I had been addressing our challenges from the outside. The chosen self-prescribed therapy had been that of blame. It had been an unconscious attempt to mitigate the collateral damage caused by Elza's condition that had destroyed our careers and our social life. I had been blaming it all on the "other." Blame, as the mystic poet Hafez said, is what keeps the sad game going. It had stolen my empathy and higher consciousness and given them to my lower selves, who had no coping skills or capacity for inward reflection. I became Hafez's imbecile out of my need to cope with my harsh reality, and blame is what I used to make my world safe. Blame was an easy dish to serve, and I had served it everywhere and to everyone who couldn't deliver us from the hands of disease and put us back on the right path.

As profound as these insights were, I reminded myself to search for deeper answers for why that TED talk on July 18 was such an emotional and transformative event. I know Elza would have scolded me for allowing such a profound experience to pass without uncovering its deeper psychospiritual basis.

Then it came to me like an awakening. For the past four years, I had consciously and unconsciously included Elza in my tirades and fits of anger. Of all the "others" whom I blamed, I blamed her the most. I blamed her for my having abandoned my career and set aside all those years to help her. I blamed her for the aphasia. I blamed her for my losing my passion for writing. I blamed her for having chosen parents who gave her such horrible diseases. I blamed her for ruining my love for solitude. The list was endless and it kept coming. I blamed her for the loss of marital intimacy. I blamed her for the Alzheimer's. I blamed her for the embarrassment we suffered in public and for the loss of our friends. I blamed her for the FTD, but most of all I blamed her for her complete dependence on me. On that day, the fog had lifted and it all became clear. The imbecile who had run the sad game of blame had played his last hand, and he would not blame others for his misery anymore. Most importantly, he would not blame the victim.

This was a profound breakthrough that put yet another aspect of my past behavior into perspective. It removed my focus on the "other"—all of it—and widened the gateway for me to be delivered into higher realms of the Self. It opened the door for my acceptance of my own heroic selves who had appeared out of the urgent necessity to survive. It removed the masks I had worn interchange-ably and exposed my face to the sun, the place of truth and self-love. It reminded me of the importance of continuing my inner growth through meditation and inward reflection. Playing the blame game was truly sad and had been the primary cause of my own misery. In my meditations, I came to realize that July 18, 2018 was the day that had brought a swift end to the blame game. In the days that followed, I began to contemplate other factors that had made the experience of that day so profound.

Tau, Amyloid, and the Wall of Safety

In addition to playing the blame game, I realized that I had also built a wall of safety between Elza's different diseases and me. This wall was made up of the multiple layers of rational analysis that had shielded me from a sure meltdown. After all, what was the purpose of a rational mind other than to create filters through which we interpret and compartmentalize the deluge of endless stimuli? It was the working of the pragmatic self that had kept the oxygen flowing and prevented the hand of destiny from pulling me fur-ther into the abyss. Now, in my new state of bliss, I became a wit-ness to my inner pragmatist. I had understood Elza's multitude of diagnoses not from the subjective place of emotions but through the lens of science. This is how I had kept my world together. I had become well versed in knowing everything that causes diseases in the brain. I understood the different functions of proteins and amino acids, the amyloid beta peptides and the amyloid plaques, the tau protein and the tau tangles—the accumulation of the pro-tein in Alzheimer's disease that interferes with brain signaling and communication. Of the twenty-three pairs of chromosomes, it was gene mutations in chromosomes number 1, 4, 19, and 21 that were responsible for Alzheimer's. For FTD and aphasia, it was the muta-tion on the MAPT gene on chromosome 17.

No doctor, not even the last neurologist, had gone as far as identifying any of these culprits. This was all my own doing. The detective work that had propelled me into action in other areas had also led me to discover the main perpetrator of our misery: It was the MAPT gene, the one-stop shop for all the known variants of FTD, and it began to manifest increasingly in Elza's behavior as her condition progressed. It lent its horrific destruction to an alphabet soup of the different subtypes of the disease. There was the behavioral variant, the semantic, the non-fluent, and the logopenic. Elza was exhibiting all these symptoms, and they were getting worse.

Each time a new and odd symptom appeared, I turned to MAPT and found the answer. The gene is present everywhere in the nervous system, and its mutation causes cells to release too much of the tau protein that causes the tangles to form and kill the brain tissue. I wanted to understand the killer from the perspective of science. I tapped into what little knowledge I still had of organic chemistry and genetics from my two years of pre-med. I wanted to understand MAPT's molecular structure and its position on the chromosome. I thoroughly familiarized myself with everything I could, aware that such knowledge would prevent me from being caught off guard when the remaining list of possible subtypes began to manifest. As heartbreaking as it was to witness the life we had once slowly slipping away, something about having this knowledge kept me from total emotional and physical collapse. It represented the triumph of the scientific mind.

I had also mastered the names of the different parts of the brain, along with their function and the diseases for which they are responsible once neurodegeneration sets in. To help the common person understand the complexity of the brain, science has labeled it all by color. There is the peach-colored hippocampus that looks like a horseshoe sitting in the inner part of the brain, sharing the limbic system with a number of other parts. That peach-colored horseshoe is the main culprit in FTD. In the upper-right part of the brain is the purple-colored parietal lobe. It is responsible for language and the main culprit in logopenic progressive aphasia. In the lower right, wearing a beautiful color of green, is the temporal lobe, which is responsible for memory. That fact remains mysterious to me because, on those rare occasions when Elza has spoken, she has showed a remarkable grasp on her memory. That was what steered several neurologists away from classifying her symptoms as neurological. Green is my friend. In the upper-left part of the brain is the pink-colored frontal lobe, responsible for intelligence, judgment, and behavior. These are the aspects of Elza that began to disappear in a systematic and abrupt way in late 2017. The pink-colored frontal lobe was the main culprit in her sudden and painful decline.

There it all was! My own brain had arranged all that data in logical, non-threatening patterns. I dared anyone to ask me about the function of the different parts of the brain or the details of Elza's disease. Like the doctors who held on to the certainty of the 7 percent of all that's currently knowable about this organ, I held on to the certainty of all that I had uncovered. This knowledge was innocuous and objective. I had successfully built a wall of safety through reason and made myself immune from subjective emotions.

Wild Fire and Terminal Diseases

November came, and I had been adjusting well to our new reality. My meditations became peaceful, and there was nothing compelling me to seek deeper meaning for how I had transitioned into such a serene state of acceptance. The mind works in mysterious ways, and I wasn't about to overanalyze my current state of emotional stability.

Then came the day of November 17, 2018. It was the Santa Ana that woke me at 6:45 in the morning—meaning not the saint but the hot, dry winds that descended from California's Great Basin through the Sierra Nevada Mountains, drying and burning everything in their path. As they reached the coast, they carried with them the unmistakable smell of charred embers before they made their way to the Pacific. It was California's fire season, and this paradise on Earth was burning.

There's something about California's wild fires that is monstrous and unruly. I had worked to understand the science behind it just as I had Elza's diseases. I had even drawn parallels between the idiopathic and spontaneous nature of the two phenomena. Tau tangles and Amyloid plaques devour brain tissue just as flames devour brush property and lives, viciously and indiscriminately. These ravenous beasts don't stop until everything and everyone around them lies helpless or dead. In these epic battles, it is always the fires, the tangles, and the plaques that emerge victorious, leaving nothing but death and destruction in their wake.

I can't claim to know what it's like to lose your home, your community, or your loved ones to these devil winds, but the threat of fire surrounded us constantly, and it wasn't confined to the fall months anymore. Back in May of 2014, I had been on a highway heading home when fire forced the closure of the road. I found myself helpless as the flames kept creeping closer from every direction. The scene was otherworldly. Awestricken, I had never been in the middle of something so horrific and powerful as the walls of fire crept closer and the black smoke carrying the red ashes of destruction rolled across ten lanes of gridlocked traffic. The Gods were angry. I could see Prometheus, the Greek God of fire, smiting humanity for its insolence and its mistreatment of the earth.

That entire week in November 2018, scenes were haunting me from the fires burning in the town of Paradise in Northern California. The headline "Paradise Lost" had crammed the airways and filled the front pages of every newspaper in the country. The media had cleverly compared the devastation to John Milton's epic poem about the fall from grace of Adam and Eve and their ultimate expulsion from the Garden of Eden. I turned on the news to see if Mother Nature's wrath had subsided from the night before.

"A hundred-and-fifty-thousand acres burned, ninety-thousand structures destroyed, and seventy-six lives lost," said the voice of one reporter as he turned to a weary man for questioning: "Why has this fire been so destructive? Why is the loss of life so high? Couldn't you get people out of harm's way any faster?"

The reporter's frustrations reminded me of my desperate search for answers every time one of Elza's treatments failed. My mind picked up on the syntax in some of phrases uttered by the exhausted voice of the fire chief. They were almost identical to what Dr. Tanzi said in the TED Talk we had watched in July. "We're dealing with a completely unpredictable force." Then, "Fire is like the quiet thief in the night"; and then the warnings and the desperation: "We prepare residents the best way we can, but if you're not careful, you can lose everything—your property, your pets, and your loved ones. You have to understand this monster for what it is."

The image of an unruly monster began to disturb my peaceful scientific understanding of fire and disease. I now wanted to revisit the TED talk in search of my deeper understanding of Alzheimer's and neurodegeneration. I knew I was in a different place emotionally and so might understand better why the talk and Chris Mann's accompanying song had had such a profound effect on me.

The Other Side of Complexity

In the applications of Spiral Dynamics, we often use the concept of "simplicity beyond complexity" to remind us of how important it is to explain complex concepts in simple terms. American jurist Oliver Wendell Holmes Jr. initially coined the phrase: "I would not give a fig for the simplicity on this side of complexity, but I would give my life for the simplicity on the other side of complexity."

For all the complexity that Spiral Dynamics is, if we couldn't explain it in simple terms then all would be lost. The more complex anything is, the higher the need for it to be explained in simple terms without eroding much of the meaning. Few are the people who can do that, and fewer still are the ones who can successfully communicate a complex concept simply to the masses in a masterful way.

The day the town of Paradise was burning, Dr. Tanzi helped me eliminate some of the few lingering blockades on my journey toward our new reality. Hearing the thief-in-the-night metaphor a second time cut through my thick wall of safe medical understanding like a hot knife cuts through butter. He was the master communicator who put the scientific complexity of Alzheimer's into simple terms—terms that tore away the last façade that had kept us from full acceptance of this devastating disease. He was no longer the researcher but the town crier, sounding the alarm about the horror that was unfolding and the misery that was yet to come. He was the social worker, the neighbor, the parent, and the caring friend. He was the prosecutor in the court of life, pleading the case of millions like us in agonizing detail to whichever higher authority was listening. He was the healer, holding the hand of millions and sharing our pain and sorrow. For the first time, someone in the medical community was discussing this disease from the perspective of the patient and their loved ones. Suddenly all the ugliness had a face. It was horrific. I saw its thieving hands robbing millions of us of all the precious things we held so dear, and, so far, no one has been able to do anything to stop it. It is a ravenous and unruly monster that follows no rules and obeys no laws; it answers to no one. It deserves all the fear and respect accorded to it.

This was the powerful simplicity hiding behind the cold and unemotional complexity of science. It was naked and disarming. I felt its searing hand forging a bond with millions of others like us. We were not alone anymore.

Maybe it was this new realization that caused me to listen to the rest of Dr. Tanzi's lecture again through different ears. The first time around, it had all been about confirming the science I had already known about the disease. I had hidden behind the safety of the pragmatic mind. But this time, something completely new was happening. For the first time since that dreadful day in the emergency room, I was hearing the words of hope. Simplicity had opened me up to believe that there will be a cure for this devastating disease during my lifetime. In months past, my anger and my blame had prevented me from hearing these words—perhaps because none of them could help Elza now at this stage of her disease. Dr. Tanzi's message was all about stopping the disease decades before its symptoms appeared. It was about early awareness, early prediction, early detection, and early prevention. This second time I listened to his lecture, the witness in me showed me how much I have transcended the most limiting parts of my ego. The conscious work I have done on myself had delivered me to the other side, the side that cares and loves unconditionally. I found myself caring about those who are suffering and are brought together through common grief and misery. I found a new love for Ghinwa, who had a 40 percent chance of suffering the same fate as her mother. She and the millions like her will be the ones who will be saved by science.

In my meditations, I became the witness to Dr. Tanzi's quiet thief in the night that is Alzheimer's disease. I saw its indiscriminate hand scorch away identities and selves, just like wildfires scorch the wilderness. The amyloid plaques slash and burn brain tissue capriciously. They don't discriminate based on one's race, skin color, or religion. They don't care if you are black, white, or Middle Eastern. It doesn't matter if you are male or female, gay or straight. The tau tangles don't spear you specifically if you have a high IQ or possess any other of the highly desirable intelligences. It doesn't matter if you are sexual or spiritual, conscious or unwitting. Neither protein cares whether you have been saving the world or living an obscure life. Neurodegeneration doesn't spare you even if you are the embodiment of the Buddha or the Christ reincarnate.

Chris Mann's anthem to Alzheimer's was now a large part of my newly found hope. It became a coping mechanism whenever the face of despair reappeared. It directed my conscious mind to pursue all the things within my reach to remember Elza for what she was and who she is. It provided me with a new purpose to keep pursuing my bliss, my passion for writing. I will write for those who want to be remembered when they can't remember themselves. I will write so that the millions suffering from this disease will not be quickly forgotten. I will cry and plead my case to whomever reads these lines about the frailty of the human condition and the need for a deeper love.

This new awareness came to me as a knowing, not a passing thought or a learning opportunity. It parsed the darkest night into which I had been thrashed and beaten violently and unwillingly. It put me in the witness state beyond subjective emotion and hard cold fact. I began to feel the common bonds that tie us together as humanity.

I began to care about generations yet unborn and the millions who are yet to be diagnosed. My life, with all its past accomplishments, had yielded to a new unbound life of stillness and solitude, driven by transcendent love. All the selves and the helpers along my way were standing in reverence of my new state of being. I had willingly walked into the river of life again, letting the torrents of destiny run through me—again. I was again at the mercy of fate, written by the hand of time and driven by the big wheel of karma.

My new awareness carried me beyond Alzheimer's and all other forms of disease. They were nothing more than a karmic imprint, a marker on the path of destiny that prompts the ocean to call back the rain drop to its eternal home. This awareness moved me from being a reluctant caregiver to being a loving husband again. It placed me on the harsh grounds of a new state of consciousness where I could no longer see separateness. Beyond the mind, I saw the universal soul. I saw us all as one.

8

GODS, KARMA, AND THE GARDEN BY THE SEA

Karma is the supreme principle superior both to gods and men. The various gods and goddesses in different realms of Nature take a much longer time to serve in their respective heavenly spheres than human beings, but all the same they have to reincarnate in flesh before they can aspire to, and win final emancipation from, the Karmic round of births.
—Kirpal Singh, *The Wheel of Life*

A friend recently asked me if I had processed my grief, and I answered sarcastically, "I'll let you know when I get there."

What was there to process, and what milestones would I need to reach in order to complete the task? What visible marker had the world of psychotherapy given us that indicated recovery and a return to happiness and hope? And when would all the triggers that threw me back into anger and heartbreak come to an end? I had asked myself a thousand times: How do other people measure loss, and why was I grieving so deeply? How could the grief I was experiencing be processed, when the experience itself violated the loosest clinical definition of *grief*? Isn't grief a process that is supposed to help those who have experienced the *death* of a close person? Well, this wasn't that. Was it fair to call it grief when the loss was that of essence and of mind and spirit while the physical body

199

remained? Were there parts of my soul that grieved differently than other people, and did that prolong my state of sadness?

Grieving is for people who experience the death of someone close to them and when physical death comes, it is complete. It's final. It's the death of the body, the mind, and the soul in one spectacular event that continues the cycle of life and death and allows for the efficient processing of the loss. People plan their grief around that singular event, and sooner or later they move on and find inner peace.

But in a world defined by the meritocracy of the mind, I was grieving the death of the world that Elza and I had created. That world had been taken away from us too soon, and I was struggling to process it all. The body and the soul of my lover had remained, and I was grieving the absence of her brilliant mind. This was my new reality, and it was indeed my new teacher. My soul needed to learn this psychospiritual lesson slowly and over the span of many years.

More than six years have passed since Elza began to show signs of cognitive decline. 2014 marked the beginning of a journey into the darkest night of our lives. That was when the early stages of Alzheimer's disease and frontotemporal dementia began to manifest. We were lulled into a state of denial as the medical community failed to detect either disease until the neurodegeneration entered its middle stages. That's when her diagnosis was made by accident by an emergency room doctor looking for signs of a stroke. Today, according to the guidelines of the Alzheimer's Association, about half of Elza's symptoms fall into the middle stages of the disease's advancement, while the other half falls into the late stages. Her focus has vanished, and her angelic voice has all but disappeared. Managing difficulties with toileting and issues with incontinence have become part of the daily routine. Sleep disturbance has become a nightly occurrence, coupled with strange, obsessive behaviors such as moving cell phones and keys up and down the stairs from our living room to our bedroom. The routine lasts for a few hours, and I have learned to sleep through it. All the symptoms of the behavioral variant of FTD—such as disinhibitions, loss of executive functioning, and binge eating—have all manifested fully. The only bright spot that remains is Elza's ability to walk. Even that has become a source of concern, as she wanders off on occasions and becomes lost in a crowd.

One of the most heartbreaking things to observe is her waking up from a dream. It begins with loud, unintelligible proclamations that build up for a few seconds. They are carried on the familiar intonations she was known for when she admonished those responsible for some unjust act somewhere around the world. The babbling then crescendos into a stream of uncontrollable laughter that awakens her. She sits up only to realize that it was just a dream and then falls back to sleep under the heavy weight of her reality.

We are now more than two years past the time when the verdict of the gods was made official by the peddlers of false hope. If Elza's speculation about her mythical journey to empower the feminine was right, then the patriarchy has spoken, and in the spaces between their words, our universe lies in ruin, shattered into a million pieces. The unexpected intrusion that came into our lives has shredded them into unrecognizable slivers of what were once joyous and purposeful existences. It has brought us into the deepest recesses of the psyche where everything defies explanation, nothing has meaning, and actions have no purpose. This has been no ordinary journey, and there are no heroes to be crowned. There are no gods or eternal salvation waiting on the other side. This has not been a second calling to adventure, and no Holy Grail has appeared. This hasn't been a new quest to seek balance between the material world and the spiritual world. There is no Hollywood ending and living happily ever after.

Individuation and the Ever-Changing Self

On this solemn journey, the belly of the whale was reserved just for me. It was mine and mine alone. It had become my own personal hell from which there was no easy escape. Formerly, Elza had been the warrior who led the way on our journey together toward the highest possibility; but, with her illness, I found myself without ambition. In her absence, peace in the Middle East disappeared from my awareness, and so did the calling for evolved economic practices. Invitations to lucrative speaking engagements went unanswered. Teachers and helpers disappeared, and two decades of conscious pursuits were shelved away, never to see the light of the day again. Like the cells in Elza's brain, I myself was dying a slow death. We seemed to share one soul, and I never thought of myself apart from her. This was a free fall that had plummeted me to the darkest recesses of the psyche— Dante's seventh hell and Ishtar's seventh gate.

As I have related, once I was swallowed by this darkness, a deep state of denial engulfed me and I cast the widest net of blame on all those whom I felt were behind this malicious plot. I spared no one—the gods, the universe, karma, and destiny. And when that reality didn't yield to a mere mortal like me, I cast a smaller net. I blamed everybody I knew, from our guides and helpers all the way down to my two brothers, who, like their counterparts in medicine, failed to save us with the miracle of science. Finally, when there was no one else left to blame, I blamed the person who had started it all: Elza. I became the champion of projection as I withdrew into the angry recesses of my ego, waiting for it all to go away. I was waiting for someone—anyone—to say it was all going to be okay. The downshift from caring for all humanity to categorically hating and holding it culpable had never happened so quickly.

The gods, destiny, and the archetypes had their work cut out for them. If I needed to be reborn, then the universe needed to tear me away from my known world and scatter me into a million pieces. I wasn't having any of it. I resisted all the change until destiny plucked my resistance out by its roots. I watched it all burn— the whole conceptual framework that had given my life richness and meaning. This was a baptism by fire that left me with nothing but the dust and ashes of the world I had so cherished.

I was in my mid-fifties and facing the biggest existential crisis of my life. The deep, dark night had veiled all the good things Elza and I had done in our lives and left me with nothing but punishment. This state of meaninglessness spared nothing with which I had identified. It destroyed whatever remained of my ego and any perception of Self. It thrashed me into the space of no return until I reached the point where there was nothing left for me to lose.

Just as Ishtar was painfully stripped from her worldly possessions on her descent to the Underworld, destiny had stripped me from mine. Just as she had to die to be reborn, I had to die to everything I had known to begin the long journey toward my own rebirth.

In that space of surrender, I saw my soul in the darkness, bare and naked. I saw myself letting it all go. And just as I did, a rare sense of calmness enveloped me. It was a strange stillness that placed me in the position of a witness where I saw my ego shriveling in shame. I decided to engage the night and parse through the darkness. The universe had swallowed me again and brought me into my inner temple a second time, where I alone would endure the new and unfamiliar trials of my journey. I began to see glimpses of the future, a tattered picture that included Elza only in her present diminished state. This was as good as it was ever going to get. With that acknowledgement, I began the long bumpy road to acceptance.

My journey to this new state of consciousness had no map and no timetable—maybe because it looked nothing like anything I had expected. There was no conscious embrace, only the fear of what the future might bring. But with that fear, blame and projection started to disappear. They began to fade in the exact reverse order from that in which I had cast them: from the smallest to the largest. It wasn't the universe and the gods whom I had first blamed who had started all this, it was I myself.. Acceptance started in the stillness of knowing myself again. I rediscovered my meditations. I embraced the Middle Way again, and this time it was different. Finding the balance between the ordinary and the extraordinary, the conscious and the unconscious, was no longer what represented the nondual world. Rather, balance was now in the absence of meaning between life and death, between the mind and the soul. It was in the vast emptiness of being.

I rediscovered the teachings of the saints who lived the life of the soul beyond the cycles of birth and death. I learned to love myself again and recognized that living a life of selfless service, truthfulness, and love for humanity all starts with me. Practicing nonviolence in thought and in action are virtues I had to reclaim for myself.

As I began to emerge from my journey into my inner temple, the truth about life and soul, permanence and mortality, took center stage. I began to remember what it means to be a drop in the divine ocean of love and how my presence in physical form is a microcosm of the heavenly universe beyond. Above and below, pain and joy became one and the same. Just as the widest net of blame I had cast ended with me, my rebirth cast the smallest net of responsibility that began with me and projected outward. Among the remembrances that returned to me was the importance of caring for the vessel—the physical body the soul inhabits on its brief journey in life—while it does the work of the universal Soul. This was the other temple I needed to care for as I began to reclaim my own healing.

With this awareness, the physical tension that had strained my body for the last few years began to disappear. The back pain started to subside as physical exercise and regular trips to the gym came back into my life. For the first time in two decades, I went to the gym without Elza, and that became okay. I rediscovered the importance of eating healthily and took ownership for our nutrition. The joy of cooking and knowing what entered our bodies gradually replaced the thoughtlessness of takeout. After years of neglect, I decided to bring our garden back to life. I took long walks on the beach and rediscovered the importance of my solitude. I found a loving caregiver to be with Elza during those hours of self-care I so desperately needed. The more accepting I became of our new reality, the more love I had for Elza as I began to project that acceptance on to the road ahead.

Healing the Jealous Self and the Wounded Warrior

As my new awareness expanded, it began to encompass a larger circle of healing. During my journey into the dark night, not only had I made enemies of those who couldn't help us, I had become jealous of other people whose lives weren't affected by our tragedy. The smallest observation of the things that destiny had denied us triggered a tsunami of pent-up emotions. I was jealous of our maid, Gladiz, and her gardener husband, Alfredo, as they walked away holding hands after a day's hard work. That simple expression of intimacy had disappeared from our lives. I was also jealous of the old couple in their eighties that we observed on our daily walks. A few minutes before sunset, the frail wife would help her husband wheel his walker to the sandy cliffs across the street to witness the sunset. I was jealous because I will never get to experience old age with Elza. Destiny has forever denied me what that would feel like. But when I considered such instances from the nondual side of existence, they became just another of a million expressions of universal love. Gladiz, Alfredo, the old couple, and the universe beyond had remained the same. It was I who needed to change, accept my new reality, and see the world through more evolved lenses.

During the early stages of my denial, I also adopted an unrealistic sense of expectations about friends and family. The first were the expectations I had of my brothers, whom I knew weren't part of the conspiracy being perpetrated on us by the rest of the medical community. They both came and spent time with us and promised to do whatever was in their power to help. It felt good to be around family and to have two people who were practicing medicine be unconditionally on our side.

Nickolas, my younger brother, is a researcher, and if anyone was going to get Elza into clinical trials that she couldn't get into on the West Coast, he was the one to do it on the East Coast. Armed with Elza's entire medical history, her MRIs and PETs, and her list of medications he convened a group of researchers and neurologists at his hospital. I was full of anticipation when he called, but it turned into despair when he related the findings of his team confirming the severity of Elza's condition. After comforting me for what seemed to be hours, he invited us to spend Christmas with his family. It was at that moment that I saw the first glimpse of the road beyond our state of isolation and denial. Christmas still takes place, and the world still moves forward regardless of one's personal tragedy or emotional state.

The friends of whom we had unrealistic expectations were both therapists. Tom and Christine are a husband and wife team who apply the integral approach to couple's therapy. Tom had invited both of us to speak at the Center for Integrative Psychology in San Diego, and when Elza declined the invitation, he knew something was wrong. He had seen her speak at conferences before, but, during her last few appearances, he had noticed she wasn't the old courageous Elza he knew. She was still in therapy at the time, and I told them both about our ordeal and asked for their help. After reviewing Elza's history and the types of therapy she had been through, they suggested a non-talk form of therapy and sent us the name of a specialist. Shortly afterward, Elza's diagnosis of frontotemporal dementia was made, and we cut ourselves off from Tom and Christine and the rest of world. A few months later, as I was going through my darkest hour, I decided to share Elza's diagnosis with them. I reached out to Tom in the hopes that he could ease my pain with his professional skills and that he could guide me through it all. Those were my unrealistic expectations. After initially showing empathy for what I was going through, Tom defaulted to treating me like one of the guys. He invited me to play a game of pick-up basketball with him and some random men on Wednesdays and to join him with some friends at an arbitrary bar for beers on the second Thursday of every month. I wasn't sure whether this was an indication of the end of his empathy or his way of coaxing me back into leading my own life.

As I looked back at the anger and bitterness I had harbored against all those whose world was unbothered by our tragedy, I gained a deeper understanding of myself. My journey into the dark night showed me my own emotional, psychological, and spiritual weaknesses. The incidences that triggered anger and depression were many, and I learned to live in the spaces between the triggers.

I became obsessed with understanding the greater meaning of the emotional cascades that plunged me into the abyss. In my meditations and the nondual world, they became my teachers. I learned to embrace them for my own growth. I gradually expanded the spaces between one trigger and another, until the space around me became one. As above, so below; the ecstasy of recovery and the laundry of examining the darkness became one.

The Mad Man Yields to the Good Man

"You're a good man, Said. She's lucky to have you." Those were the words of our friends Jasmine and her husband, Sam, who we ran into at the local coffee shop. We hadn't seen them in over a year, and they were shocked to hear about Elza's diagnosis. The pattern by now had become familiar. Jasmine cried as she experienced Elza's apathy and silence firsthand. Then came the shock and disbelief as I told them of her grim prognosis. We shared a few mournful minutes at an outdoor table. Jasmine asked if our phone numbers were still the same, praised me for my patience, and promised to stay in touch. That was over two years ago, and no calls from either of them ever came.

"You're a good man, Said. She's lucky to have you." By now the statement was becoming familiar, and I could guess what would come next. But this time it was Elza's youngest brother, Ghassan, who was talking, as I shared with him the details of her diagnosis. He would surely be supportive, I thought. But then the strangest thing happened: he stopped communicating with us altogether. At first, I surmised that maybe he wasn't ready to repeat the same emotional rollercoaster ride the whole family had experienced when Elza's dad had been diagnosed with Alzheimer's. Ghassan adored Elza, but he hadn't moved past the anger and the emotional and financial burden their dad's illness had inflicted on the whole family.

After I told Ghassan about Elza's diagnosis, almost two years passed before I spoke with him again. He had remained in Lebanon, and I wanted to share with him the idea of our living there part of the year so that Elza could be close to her extended family and childhood friends.

"No one knows about Elza's illness, and we want to keep it that way," was his sudden and stern answer to me. As hurtful as this was, by then it wasn't unexpected.

I got to experience the isolation of the good man one last time from a source I had never thought possible. It started on Christmas Eve, 2018, when I received a friend request on Facebook from Elza's daughter, Ghinwa. A flood of emotions overtook me, and I wasn't sure what to do. A few days later, I helped Elza log into her Facebook account and noticed that Ghinwa had requested to be friends with her mother a month earlier.

I began to deliberate the nature of this occurrence and wondered if Elza's ex-husband was plotting something cynical. After much thought, I decided that I should accept the friend request on Elza's account. Within twenty-four hours, Ghinwa responded with an image of the dedication page of Elza's book, *Emerge!*, thanking her for dedicating it to her. For weeks I was torn about what to do. It had been twenty-four years since the two of them had spoken, and now that Ghinwa was the one initiating contact, her intention might be genuine. A thousand thoughts went through my mind. Maybe she had parsed through the smoke and mirrors of her dad's narrative and begun to form her own conclusions about her mother's absence from her life. Maybe she was dealing with an existential crisis of her own. Maybe she was getting married and wanted her mother to be part of her life again. At first contact, what would I possibly say to her? Should there even *be* any further contact? For better or for worse, I decided to ask for her phone number and requested a convenient time for us to speak.

Ghinwa found it odd that I was the one calling her instead of Elza, and the first thing she asked was whether her mother was okay. I proceeded to tell her about Elza's condition, and the conversation quickly turned melancholic. It transformed Ghinwa from the child dealing with the wounds of abandonment to the caring daughter full of love for her ill mother.

For the next few months, we spoke daily. They spent hours on a video camera, Ghinwa laughing and crying and Elza smiling at the sight of her daughter. Ghinwa wanted to visit us, and I wanted to prepare her as much as possible. I sent her passages from Elza's unpublished book and poems she had written about the love she had for her and the sorrow she had experienced because of their separation. Through tears, Ghinwa would read what I sent her back to her mother. Months passed, and July 4 came. It was Ghinwa's birthday, and a friend helped Elza record a birthday-celebration video and send it to Ghinwa. At the end, Elza said the words, "I love you." This is the most she had spoken in over a year, and it was the first time Ghinwa had heard her voice. She decided to visit for two weeks and bring along her stepmother, Caroline. Although Ghinwa was twenty-eight by now, her family still subscribed to the archaic values that a single Arab girl should not travel alone. Ideally, she would have been accompanied by a male family member, but her father couldn't do it for obvious reasons, and her two brothers from her father's new wife were too young to accompany her. Ghinwa and Caroline stayed at a nearby hotel.

Figure 8.1. Mother and daughter reunite, August, 2019.

The first encounter between mother and daughter was very emotional, and we all cried. On the first day we spent together, I wanted to be Elza's mouthpiece for all the things she wanted to say but couldn't. I spoke about how Ghinwa's presence had been a constant part of our lives and about the emotional rollercoaster ride Elza had experienced in trying to deal with their painful separation. I was being mindful not to speak ill of Ghinwa's father. On occasion, I couldn't tell whether it was emotions that prevented the daughter and the stepmom from responding or the conflicting narratives about who Elza was in their lives—abandoning parent or wronged and sorrowful mother.

Ghinwa spent the next day with us at our home. She told her mother about all the things she had missed—the proms, the boyfriends, the heartbreaks, the college years, and the love Ghinwa had for her younger siblings.

"Like you, I'm very successful in my field of work," she said. Hours went by like minutes, and when I suggested lunch at our favorite seaside café, she insisted on preparing lunch for us herself. She reached into the cupboards and prepared an extravagant meal, and we celebrated the long-awaited reunion with a bottle of white wine.

Figure 8.2. Elza with Ghinwa, August 2019.

The next day we met for coffee, and Ghinwa was agitated. I wasn't sure whether she was struggling to reconcile the new things she had discovered about her mom with the only narrative she had ever known or whether she was dealing with something entirely different. Maybe she didn't trust my version of how her mom had felt about her for the last twenty-four years. Maybe she had thought that if she could somehow get her mother to speak, Elza would tell the version she wanted to hear.

From her first sip of cappuccino, Ghinwa began to question her mom: "How could you not care about me? It's been twenty-four years; why didn't you contact me? Did you even love me? Do you know how much I struggled, thinking that there was something wrong with me and that that was why you left?"

I tried politely to remind Ghinwa of her mother's condition as Elza looked on and smiled throughout the barrage. But the questions kept coming, and I felt the need to defend my wife while remaining mindful not to tear down the image Ghinwa had of her father.

"Maybe you should consider a different perspective," I interjected.

But the questions kept coming.

"This is not fair to your mom. She can't defend herself. Please, let's not do this," I said as we walked back to the car and headed home.

The ride back was quiet, and I decided that they should spend the afternoon alone together so that Ghinwa would have sole access to her mother and the chance to begin healing some long-open wounds. I dropped them off at our home and left for the afternoon. As I returned, Ghinwa met me in the driveway. She was visibly upset at the length of time I had left them together. I wanted to inquire about their time together, but she wanted to leave. She walked to the curb and announced that she was going back to her hotel. When I offered to give her a ride, she told me that she had called an Uber. I surmised that the afternoon was full of emotion and didn't give much thought to her behavior toward me.

The next day went by, and all my calls and text messages to Ghinwa went unanswered. It was dinnertime, and I suggested in a text that I drop Elza off so the two of them could have dinner alone. She agreed, but the dinner was brief and she called me within an hour to pick Elza up.

The next few days passed, and a million calls and texts went unanswered. Then a message came at 2:30 a.m., exactly a week after we had first met: "I had to return for a work emergency." This was followed by, "Said, you are a good man. She's so lucky to have you. Thank you for taking care of my mom."

I knew exactly what that meant. Any hopes of having Ghinwa in our lives disappeared with that message.

By now the pattern was clear, and the words *good man* became synonyms with the declaration, *You're on your own.* The burden of dealing with what destiny had thrust upon us would be mine and mine alone. Social isolation didn't just end with neighbors, friends, and casual acquaintances; it included close family members as well. The mad man who had bravely torn off the masks of identity in search of the Holy Grail had become the good man who was caring for his ill wife. To remain without masks became the way to end all internal struggles and to accept all the selves, the shadows, and the greater reality and be in the presence of the divine will. Even on the two sides of this odd spectrum, chopping wood and carrying water were one and the same. The care for one human was not smaller or larger than the care for all humanity. The microcosm and the macrocosm were one, and, for me, the nondual nature of existence had become an observable state of being.

Karma and Deliverance

After becoming aware of the grief Elza and I shared with all humanity and of my own internal changes, I was also conscious of the need to return to the real world and navigate its torturous passages. As my acceptance of our new reality grew, I sought to embrace that return. I decided to accept an invitation from Elza's brother Michel to visit him and their mother in Quebec City. The trip would be the first time Elza had traveled internationally in over three years. By now, her ability to focus or form simple words had all but disappeared. In stressful situations, neither focus nor words would come to her, only inappropriate laughter. It looked very strange to the outside world, but I had gotten used to it. I had surmised that, with the full onset of aphasia, laughter was what her brain substituted for words to defend against any form of questioning. The darkness needed to be parsed further, and I needed to lead us out of it in a return to community that went beyond social embarrassment. The trip to Quebec was the first test of our acceptance of our new reality outside the confines of our self-imposed isolation.

During her former globe-trotting days, Elza had had a high-level clearance on her passport, called Global Entry, and I had had a lower-level clearance that enabled us both to proceed to a much shorter line at the security desk. But by now, Elza's weight gain had rendered her unrecognizable regarding all the identification documents she carried. On our way to Quebec City, trouble began at the airport gate as the TSA officer looked at her passport photo, trying to match it to her face. Elza couldn't hold eye contact, and the officer became suspicious. Questioning began, and I was stopped immediately from saying anything on her behalf. Soon both of us were taken to separate areas for questioning. I could see the TSA agents interrogate her through the glass as I frantically searched for the documents that explained her condition. It was stressful and she laughed, and the more she laughed the angrier and the more belligerent the agents became. Bewildered passengers looked on while we waited for a supervisor to assess the papers holding the proof to her condition. An hour had passed before everything was verified and we were allowed to board our flight.

Similar challenges tested my new state of being upon our arrival in Quebec. Elza was lost in the garage at the airport for over twenty minutes searching for me while I went to pick up our rental car. She had wandered off several times before, but this was an unfamiliar place and I began to panic. Then an automatic sense of calmness overtook me, and I was able to observe myself being fearful for her safety from a calm space within me as the airport police and I searched for her.

If this had happened two years earlier, I would have not been able to process the emotions and the humiliation. I would have either exploded in anger or dissolved into a pool of my own tears cursing the gods for sending us the worst form of punishment possible. But by then, I was walking the streets of destiny without a mask. My mind and soul had played these types of scenarios a hundred times over. It all happened in slow motion, and I was witnessing myself watch this drama unfold outside my conscious awareness as if it were happening to someone else. Even if this was a new low on our new journey, the emotions tasted the same as those that had come when we had been at the height of our highest possibilities.

Elza's mother, May, became emotionally distraught at the very first sight of her daughter. She had been very supportive since the diagnosis, and I had arranged for them to be in dialogue on a video screen whenever May wished to spend time with Elza. As Elza's ability to speak began to wane, May would use the time to sing to her. It was a miracle to hear Elza sing with her mother, as if the part of her brain that stored music was exempt from the ravages of disease and the wrath of the gods. A few days after our arrival, May remained in an emotionally fragile state and suggested that our family gatherings should take place at Michel's apartment.

"It's all karma," Michel declared. "Elza has done enough good work in the world to last many lifetimes. Maybe she has burned up all her karmic debt and her soul will now escape the cycle of life and death."

A year earlier, these words would have only added to my misery and isolation. I had concluded that there was no merciful God and there was no good karma. The new journey into the dark night that had befallen us was that not of the soul but of the dark forces that ruled over human misfortune. At our worst hour, I had abandoned the knowledge of the soul and the teachings of the saints. But by the time we went to Quebec, my soul was craving a return to that knowledge. So, I found Michel's words to be uplifting. They enriched my spirit and gave me a deeper understanding of the pain and agony we had gone through and began to remind me of the deeper mystery of being.

"Our family has a shared karmic destiny," he continued. "The master told me a long time ago that the gods who rule over the Middle East don't want it to change, but Elza and I were stubborn. We didn't listen."

Michel has a deep inner wisdom and a reservoir of knowledge about the soul and the role of karma in the universe. This man, whom the heavens have sent to be Elza's guardian angel, has been confined to a wheelchair since the spring of 2005. He has multiple sclerosis, and, with the exception of the use of his right arm, all muscle function in his body has atrophied. His brilliant mind has remained intact, though, and to make sense of the disease that ravaged him physically, Michel has become fully immersed in the teachings of the masters he has admired from a young age. To him, it all makes sense: destiny, the soul, the oversoul, and karma.

On my own road to acceptance, I, too, began to think of the teachings of the masters. It all began to make sense to me through Michel's words. "It is all predestined," he said. "The only thing we can do is to try to transcend the limitations of our minds to see the eternal light of our souls."

Elza, May, and I sat and listened to Michel speak about his illness: "I first felt it in Tunis when the master and I were thrown in jail. My left leg felt weak, and I could barely move it."

The story Michel was telling was very familiar to us. The master he was speaking of was Thakar Singh, the successor of Kirpal Singh, who had brought the spiritual teachings of Surat Shabd Yoga to the world. According to the teachings, this is a meditative practice that unites the soul with the essence of the Supreme Being. The new master was invited to tour Tunisia to give lectures on the spiritual benefits of these meditations and offer meditation retreats. He had received assurances that, unlike in other Muslim countries, the Tunisian authorities showed tolerance to other religions and would not consider his teachings blasphemous. Michel served as the official Arabic translator for the trip. He was also the official translator for the French – and Spanish-speaking parts of the world that the teacher visited.

After only three days In Tunisia, the authorities brought a quick end to Michel's venture with his teacher. Their books and pamphlets were confiscated, and, after a night in jail, Michel and the guru were kicked out of the country.

"I should have listened to the master back then, and I should have given you the same advice," said Michel. "I traveled with him all over the world, and, when we came to the Middle East, the gods decided to punish me with physical confinement. They spared my mind so I could learn the lesson over many years."

Then he continued, "Elza has been vocal about injustice in the Middle East from the time she was born, so the gods silenced her by taking away her voice and her mind, leaving her body and her soul to prolong her pain and agony. It's all karma."

Elza, May, and I got to hear Michel tell stories of his adventures with the master and the humilities they endured as part of their calling to make the world a better place. During our two-week stay in Quebec, I meditated on these lessons and reconnected with the deeper awareness of our shared destiny and that of the souls of all humanity. Michel's wisdom helped me rediscover the source of existence. It reconnected me with my knowledge of my own soul and the power of karma. It provided me with another piece of the puzzle that made the picture of healing and acceptance more complete. This was the wider net I had cast on my journey to heal, and the wider I cast it, the more awareness I had that humility and the work of the noble hero are one and the same.

The Garden by the Sea

After returning from Quebec, the healing process took on a wider dimension. Michel's strong spiritual convictions allowed me the freedom to engage in the exploration of the power of myth and of gods and goddesses again. If the teaching of the great masters such as Kirpal Singh were true, then karma was the greater power behind all godly powers. Its supreme influence was the beginning and the end, the alpha and the omega, and to exclude those teachings from my journey would not serve my soul and that of the universe. If it were karma that was determining Elza's destiny and that of all souls, then I wanted to dive into it all again and try to understand where my soul was on its brief journey to this world. I, a drop of confused elements, was yearning for my true home again, the ocean of boundless love. I wanted to know where the wheel of karma had placed me after painfully tearing away half of my soul and thrashing me onto the solemn and trying path of my own return.

As I further considered the idea that Elza's soul has won final emancipation from the karmic wheel of life and death, the images of the goddess Ishtar reappeared in my mind. Ishtar withstood a trying journey that transcended physical death; she reemerged from the Underworld to become immortal. If Elza is like Ishtar, then I am her Gilgamesh, her Tammuz, her Adonis—frantically searching for her and for immortality and being denied entry at the eternal gate. Outside the gate, Gilgamesh emerges into a beautiful garden by the sea after his harrowing passage through the darkness. He returns empty-handed and is resigned to his own mortality. It is here, in this garden, that he begins to see his achievements in a whole new light. They will be the closest things to immortality to which a mortal like him can aspire.

Life mimics myth. My own garden by the sea had been neglected for years while I fought on my passage through the darkness. After returning from Quebec, I decided with the help of Alfredo to make the soil of our garden fertile again. Just like the darkness had taken hold of me, wild weeds had taken hold of our garden. Just like me, the garden needed rehabilitation and healing, and I began to take extra care in bringing it back to life. I wanted to plant it with all the things that Elza loved. The strawberries and the peppermint had survived my absence, and Elza and I rescued them from the choking assault of invasive weeds. Beefsteak tomatoes would fill one bed, while another would have the cherry variety in it. Two beds were reserved for the heirloom kind that she always ate right off the vine. One bed was marked for Mediterranean cucumber; and the last, the one closest to the sea, was planted half with basil and half with Italian parsley. A special order had to be placed for the heirloom tomatoes, and we planted them the day they arrived, two weeks after the other beds had been planted.

Before leaving the backyard that afternoon, I took a long and deliberate look at our new garden, taking it all in. The wounded healer in me had risen again and given life to other forms of life. The garden soil became the source of earthly existence, Mother Nature's womb and the ecology from which all life sprang and to where it all returned. I had neglected that relationship for three years, and with my return I became part of nature's ceaseless breath again. The worms, the microorganisms, and all the organic matter that lay dormant came back to life, a reminder that nothing ever dies. I felt the magnificence of being one with the earth again. To plant a garden is to be reminded of the cycles of the seasons, of the life and youth that come after a long, harsh winter. I watched as the gentle ocean breeze seduced the newly planted stocks in a soulful, intimate dance. It reminded me of my first dance with Elza. Soon the colors of green, yellow, and red would fill our garden again. Soon the hummingbirds would return. Soon the bees would start building their honeycombs behind my toolshed. Soon, balance would be restored.

It was on a Saturday when the heirlooms tomatoes were planted, and that was the day I checked emails. For the preceding three years, nothing in the form of electronic communication had been urgent enough to deserve an immediate response. Nothing other than the existential crisis I was dealing with had ever brought greater clarity to my priorities in life. Care for the Self, the soul, and for Elza and our dog Buddha took center stage, and very little else mattered. A year earlier, I had gone for weeks without checking emails. But now my journey was bringing me back to the world, and I began to engage with it from my new perspective of nondual existence.

One of those emails that Saturday was an invitation to partici- pate in a conference in Bretton Woods, New Hampshire, on the design of the next global monetary system. It was to be held in July, 2019, a month before Elza's daughter, Ghinwa, came to visit us that August. The event was to mark the seventy-fifth anniversary of the creation of the Bretton Woods financial architecture, the post-war global monetary system that remains in place today. The same invitation was extended to Dr. Beck. The organizers wanted to have the models of Spiral Dynamics and Memenomics serve as the showcase for the conference. They wanted participants to start thinking about the entire field of economics from the whole-systems perspective that I had put forth six years earlier in my book.

I wanted to take my time to respond, as I wasn't sure if my return to the world included a return to a dismal science that measured humanity's worth by the size of its balance sheet. I had surmised that the field of economics is where human conscious goes to die and that a response to express my regrets for not attending could wait.

A few days passed, and I received a call from Dr. Beck. After asking about Elza and reminding me of how much of a void he feels in her absence, he asked if I had picked a title for my keynote speech.

"Did you see the list of speakers? The guy you criticized in your book, Clinton's Treasury Secretary, will be on stage with us," he said.

After waiting for a response and only hearing regrets and excuses, he started again: "This is the highlight of both our careers."

He kept nudging me gently and reminding me of the significance of my work and our years of collaboration. "You can do the same presentation you did at the Integral European Conference. Six hundred people gave you a standing ovation. It was brilliant."

The helper who guided me on my journey to the possible was now pulling me out of my own gloom and back to the world. We agreed to a time the following week to discuss possible topics and a visit to Dallas where I could be with my mentor and friend who I hadn't seen in over a year.

After my long absence, the return to the work I had once loved looked sterile and commonplace. While I have gone through personal transformation, the field of economics itself had remained cold and uncaring, incapable of implementing meaningful change. My personal journey had brought me to a more conscious and spiritual state of being, and I knew my work needed to become an extension of that new awareness. I reached out to the organizers of the event to better understand the circumstances that had led them to plan the conference around the themes of Spiral Dynamics and Memenomics. The answer came swiftly: "At the recommendation of our late friend Bernard Lietaer, we've been studying your book and Dr. Beck's book for over year."

I was taken aback at the sad news of Bernard's passing, and that email removed any lingering doubt about wanting to take part in the conference. Bernard had been quietly fighting a battle with cancer that he lost in early 2019. As fate would have it, he and I had only crossed paths once after the 2004 Spiral Dynamics weekend training in Boulder: In the summer of 2013, destiny had brought us together again at the office of a book publicist in Westport, Connecticut. We were both using her services to promote our respective books—his being *Rethinking Money: How New Currencies Turn Scarcity into Prosperity* and mine being *MEMEnomics*. I reminded him of how our conversation in 2004 was one of the catalysts that had led me to write the book. We exchanged signed copies of our respective titles. As we parted ways, he looked at my book's outline, saying, "I can't wait to read it."

When the invitation to speak at the Bretton Woods conference came, the effects of climate change had been weighing heavily on my mind, and I decided that my new work, which would inform my presentation, would be about the economics of the *Anthropocene*, geologists' name for the new epoch in history we are entering in which the survival of our planet depends entirely on the collective actions of humanity.

Just as I had previously pioneered the use of the Graves/Spiral Dynamics model to the field of economics, I was now pioneering its use to address climate change. I became excited about my work again. I read several books on the subject and began to sketch an outline for my next book and to refine the keynote presentation that would mark my professional return.

The time for the conference came, and the speaker presenting the opening remarks stood on the same stage where seventy-five years earlier John Maynard Keynes had announced the new economic and financial world order. Keynes was the genius economist who gave us the postwar financial architecture that has shaped the world as we know it. The presenter then proceeded to describe the keynote speakers as some of the world's boldest thought leaders: There was the former secretary of the US Treasury and the head of the White House Council of Economic Advisers. There were past directors of the International Monetary Fund and the World Bank. There were a number of prominent economists, change agents, and spiritual thought leaders, as well.

Figure 8.3. Speaking at the Bretton Woods 75th Anniversary Conference, New Hampshire, July 2019, on the same stage where John Maynard Keynes had announced the new economic world order in 1944.

At the time of the conference, Dr. Beck was too ill to travel, but he was able to make some introductory remarks by live video from his home. I was allotted the remainder of his time as I introduced my new framework that put in perspective the economic activities of the human race for the last five hundred years. It all fell into the values of subsistence, the lowest six levels of human consciousness on the spiral of values. I explained how, due to the limits of their psychosocial awareness, those six lower levels of human existence offered little care for the planet. Then I presented the case for the adoption of the highest levels of values, the evolutionary consciousness to which we as humanity must ascribe in order to save the only home we have ever known.

That night the band that played under the starry skies of Bretton Woods, New Hampshire, dedicated the last set of songs to Spiral Dynamics. During their final number, a falling star screeched across the heavens. I saw John Maynard Keynes riding Phaethon's chariot in the shape of a spiral, scattering the sparks of a new form of alchemy on those who had gathered. I smiled in contentment as I returned to my suite to prepare for my return home.

Elza's caregiver, Tamar, had stayed with her while I traveled; on the night I came back, her sleep disturbance and obsessive behaviors were worse than usual. Her wanderings up and down the stairs lasted for hours. She gathered everything of value from jewelry to currency and placed it in the drawers of the nightstand on my side of the bed. This was one of those nights when I couldn't sleep through the commotion. After three hours, I walked downstairs to find Buddha, who by now was eleven years old and had become arthritic. I carried him back upstairs and put him in his old sleeping spot in the middle of our bed. His presence calmed Elza and, soon after, she fell asleep and we all rested soundly till the morning.

After coffee the next day, I began the daily routine and attended to Elza. I bathed her. She could no longer bathe on her own, since she had lost sensation a few months earlier and scalded herself with hot water. As it is for a child, bath time is her favorite activity, the first in a day full of routines that bring her joy. While I was drying her hair, she pulled down the towel and looked at me, giggling like a child emerging from her hiding place in a game of hide-and-seek.

Then, as if in a hurry to go play with her friends, she raised her arms one at a time for me to dry them. I then dressed her, since she can longer dress herself. First came the adult diapers, then the yoga pants and top. After putting on her socks and sneakers, there was just one last task left. This one she can still do on her own. She reached into a shelf for one of her expensive handbags. Her favorite was one I had given her for her fiftieth birthday. She had chosen it over a trip I had planned for us to Assisi, Italy. She had wrapped an elegant scarf around its handle. The bag and the scarf had become the only two accessories she carried that reminded the world of the elegant woman Elza used to be.

I looked at our garden from the bedroom window, and I found it festive. In my absence, Mother Nature had orchestrated an elaborate celebration. There he was, the airborne mystery, the hummingbird sipping on blooms of blue and yellow wet with ocean dew. He sang in gratitude with every rapid movement as he mingled with the bees in an ecstatic dance.

We had a bumper crop that year and had shared the bounty with neighbors and friends. But the bounty of that day was reserved just for two old lovers. We walked to our hideaway overlooking the sea and sat on the worn-out bench that held all our secrets. The tomatoes and the basil, and even the unruly peppermint, bowed in silence as my lover made her way through the garden. The heirlooms offered their abundant fruit still on the vine. The green basil leaves knew our secret snack. I went to the kitchen and fetched the mozzarella, the olive oil, and the sea salt. We snacked without a care in the world.

Time passed in our garden, and I could tell Elza had missed me. Her obsessive behavior had given way to an unusual calmness, and we became one with our garden. She leaned her head into my chest, and I heard Rumi's tambourines. We danced. There were no global bankers, no John Maynard Keynes, and no new world order. There were only the unspoken secrets of two souls navigating the mystery of life in a world that had forgotten the transcendent and the Divine.

Hours went by as I contemplated the nondual nature of existence, above and below, the macrocosm and microcosm. They were one and the same. My provocative speech to save the planet days earlier did not preempt my care for my garden and for Elza. The patriarchal gods of myth who stopped Athena and Ishtar from resurrecting Gaia and the powers of the feminine were no different than the patriarchy of men who were destroying our planet. After much contemplation, the sounds of the tambourines faded and the sky turned dark. And somewhere in a place beyond space and time, on heavenly planes where gods and goddesses roam, Anu, the Supreme God, the source of all authority, looked upon the earth and wept.

Figure 8.4. Elza, 2019

EPILOGUE

It was on the day of my fifty-eighth birthday in January of 2020 that I wrote my final lines of this book. Right before sending the first draft to our friend Jean Houston and to my editor, Elza and I partook in a celebration reserved for occasions just such as these. Seven years earlier, we had been in Santa Barbara with Dr. Beck delivering the spring Spiral Dynamics training when I had completed the first draft of my first book, *MEMEnomics*. That evening, he had insisted on making a *big deal* of the event. Back then, hubris ran hand in hand with the highest possibility. We had thought then that among the three of us, there would be many more books to be written and celebrated. After having dinner with our closest colleagues at Zeitoun, a popular Lebanese restaurant in Santa Barbara, Elza had requested dessert to go and then made an unscheduled stop to pick up an expensive bottle of champagne and a single candle in the shape of the number one. As we toasted the completion of *MEMEnomics*, Dr. Beck, knowing that Elza's book, *Emerge*, was a few months from completion, had joked about soon needing a bigger piece of *kneffe* (Lebanese cheesecake) and a fire extinguisher if we were going to keep up the frantic pace at which we were producing books.

That was then. By the time I had completed the first draft of *this* book, time and destiny had muted the passion and enthusiasm of my two closest cheerleaders. Throughout this writing process, I had been sending Dr. Beck the first draft of every chapter I had completed; but by early 2020, contact with him had become quite difficult as he was living alone and dealing with chronic health issues.

We could speak only when he was feeling well enough to initiate a call. Even then, he would tire after just a few minutes into our conversation. I could no longer engage him in intellectual discourse on big world issues as the three of us had done on our weekly calls in years past. Just as Elza's illness had removed her from the crucial debate on the future of humanity, Father Time was now slowly removing Dr. Beck's voice from the same debate.

On the night of January 20, 2020, the birthday dinner was delivered from Camille's and Eva's restaurant, Amardeen, accompanied by a generous slice of kneffe. A candle in the shape of the number three sat atop the tasty delicacy as our dog, Buddha, sat in his high chair at our dining table next to Elza, both waiting to partake in the celebration. I lit the candle and then popped open the bottle of Dom Perignon. It was a 2008 vintage—the best the winemaker had produced in decades—and the same vintage as the bottle we had opened on that balmy April evening in 2013. We celebrated. It was a deliberate act, as if I were defying the universe that had taken so much away from me. With this current book, I had cast forth a new die into a future full of uncertainty and in a style of writing I had never thought was within me. That night, after the fog from the champagne had lifted and Elza and Buddha had gone to bed, I meditated on the journey that had led me to write this book—from the first journal entry that began with the words "Not in a million years…" to the place of humility and sweet surrender that define my life today. This indeed had been a journey like no other in my life. As I approached my laptop to send out the first draft, a voice within me spoke. I wasn't sure whether it was the champagne or my Higher Self that whispered the words, "Release it to the universe." I did. The next day, the first case of the coronavirus (COVID-19) was confirmed in the United States, and shortly thereafter the world began to grapple with the worse global pandemic in modern history.

My solemn journey into the dark night of the soul has now become that of all of humanity. Just as Elza's illness had plunged me into the abyss years earlier, the coronavirus has plunged the world into the dark bowels of the collective psyche, suggesting again that the macrocosm and the microcosm are one and the same. Ironically, though, my own return to the world through acceptance of Elza's condition was now being met by the world itself being swallowed into the metaphorical belly of the whale and the collective unconscious. But in spite of the stresses that came with the necessary personal confinement, I decided to redirect myself inwardly again in an attempt to understand the collective meaning of what was happening to humanity.

Through it all, I was able to write a few critical pieces on what the virus meant to the world through the evolutionary lenses of Spiral Dynamics and Integral Theory and about the economic devastation that was to follow: The first piece was entitled "What Can Evolution and Spiral Dynamics Tell us about the Coronavirus?"[1] It was shared widely and became a "must read" piece for our community worldwide and for those who were searching for evolutionary change. The second was a three-part series of articles entitled "Castles in the Sand: Socioeconomics in the Aftermath of the Coronavirus."[2]

These new writings were different as they reflected the deeper psychospiritual understanding to which my journey with Elza had brought me as well as an understanding of time and space and of the life of viruses that had existed billions of years before humans ever roamed the earth. I was reminded of how fragile the most conscious human constructs can become in the face of such an existential threat. The theories that had explained everything that had defined Elza's life and mine for two decades suddenly had nothing further to explain.

During that time of confinement, I had a rare lucid conversation with Dr. Beck. I wanted to tap into his reservoir of knowledge to see if I had missed anything in my writings about the virus. We discussed its meaning and the limitations of our models. He reminded me of one of our graphics that I have long forgotten. It depicts a top view of the spiral, which had an undifferentiated black mass and a simple coil at its center.

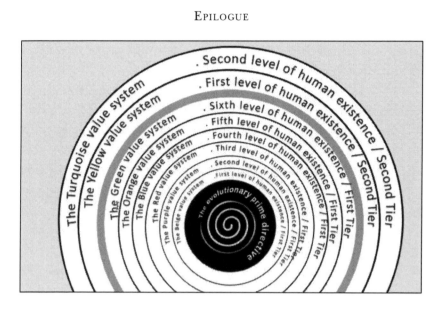

Fig. E.1. The Evolutionary Prime Directive. Copyright 2003 by
Dr. Don E. Beck. Used by permission from Dr. Beck.

He had labeled it "The Evolutionary Prime Directive" specifically to capture the unacknowledged complexity of the evolutionary process that existed before humans differentiated themselves
from it and evolved into the beige stage, the first level of existence
in our model.

At the beige stage, which is still characteristic of some third-
world societies today, people are preoccupied with sheer survival
and the immediate gratification of needs with only minimal control
over their surroundings. (For the characteristics of the higher levels
in the model, see chapter 4, pp. 99-100.) Dr. Beck and I speculated
about how quickly the virus can bring us back to this beige level if
we continue to ignore the warnings coming to us from our environment as well as from manmade threats. Together, we revisited findings of the research of CHEs from around the world that indicate
humanity is still struggling to emerge from every level in the first
tier due to the pervasive effects of the values of the Industrial Age—
whether it's our preoccupation with economic prosperity at the cost
of our planetary ecosystems, our ongoing issues with globalization

and world security, or the absence of a coordinated and sustainable global response to climate change.

Revisiting the research put our vulnerabilities in greater perspective. It showed that even the most advanced cultures in our model—Northern European countries—are struggling to exit the Green humanitarian level due to the high cost of social programs. China is attempting to enter the Orange level out of normal evolutionary sequence as it ignores human-rights abuses that place its 1.4 billion citizens at the mercy of leadership that is at the Red level. The United States and the United Kingdom seem similar in their inability to extract themselves from the corrosive values of the Orange level of financial capitalism. Findings also pointed to the struggles on the lowest levels of the spiral, which are the most concerning since they affect the least developed parts of the world: issues such as the unaddressed droughts that are keeping much of Africa and parts of the Middle East and South America at the beige and purple levels.

After that sobering reacquaintance with reality, Dr. Beck reminded me of a simple metaphor we had used at training events that depicted the mechanics of evolutionary change. It was a demonstration done on staircases with trainees in which each step represented an evolutionary stage or level of existence on the spiral. The point was that when we want to climb to the next evolutionary stage with both feet, to do it successfully we must bend our knees. The climb is made more difficult if the person or culture making it has been in an arrested or closed psychosocial state of existence.

Dr. Beck and I speculated that if the coronavirus were the existential threat that would move humanity to a higher level of consciousness, then all six value systems that humanity had experienced to this point in its history were simultaneously bending their knees with a great degree of difficulty and against the collective will to accomplish this monumental task. The death toll, the economic devastation, and the global chaos ensuing from the coronavirus were nothing more than the byproduct of a subsistent humanity being forced to bend its knees out of the necessity to survive.

That conversation sent me on a search for some of Clare Graves's original research. It reminded me of his "six-upon-six" hypothesis and of how each of the six levels of human development represent one tier of values, or one flight of stairs. Furthermore, the hypothesis says that as we move up the developmental staircase to the next tier—or the next six levels—we experience a monumental upshift in human behavior from the preceding tier.[3] The first tier, or the first flight of stairs, contains the first six value systems, and they all identify with the *values of subsistence* that still define most of human behavior today. The second tier, or the second flight of stairs, Graves often referred to as the *values of magnificence*, what Spiral Dynamics practitioners refer to as the *emerging values of humanity*. He had also uncovered that the theme of each value system repeats as we enter each new tier, but at an exponentially higher level of psychosocial development. So, while the beige theme, comprising the first value system in the first tier, deals with the survival of the *individual*, the same beige theme of the *seventh* value system, which is the first level in the second tier—or the first step on the second flight of stairs—remains that of survival, but now as the survival of *all life on the planet*. To understand fully what is needed to save our planet, our psychosocial capacities need to recalibrate at an exponentially higher level from where the leading edge of evolution is today—somewhere between the fifth and sixth levels of the first tier.

In theory, unless all six value systems in the first tier remain in an open psychosocial state—meaning that they openly assimilate higher-level values—then the transition into the second tier will be mired with difficulty and unpredictability, subject to many wildcards that could destabilize life on the earth. Dr. Beck and I speculated that, due to humanity's arrested state in the first tier, wildcards seem to be appearing in increasing intensity, the virus being the most intense so far. The result is a humanity spread on an entire first flight of stairs painfully bending its knees.

Also, Dr. Beck reminded me of the danger that Dr. Graves saw on the horizon if we were to continue to ignore the damage we're causing to our planetary ecosystems. Dr. Graves had speculated that if humanity fails consciously to take the necessary momentous leap into the second tier of values, Mother Nature will do it for us at the cost of the earth's population being cut by as much as half. Dr. Beck and I theorized that, due to humanity's failure to think and act from the more inclusive values of the second tier, where we, individually and collectively, uphold the wholeness of existence over material possessions, our ascendence to them will come to us as a painful and unexpected fate. Mother Nature will do it for us as a way for her to regenerate, evolve, and adapt to the damage we have caused.

That conversation was the last meaningful interaction I had with the man who has always given me a glimpse of the simplicity beyond complexity, which remains the rarified realm where exceptional genius dwells. In weeks that followed I found myself having a renewed appreciation for Dr. Graves's work and remembering the closeness he had to Dr. Beck. Elza and I have been as close to Dr. Beck as he had been to Dr. Graves. I reminded myself that at the height of our possibility, I was the one who founded the Third Generation Gravesians movement. Its members were a constellation of Spiral Dynamics practitioners and heads of CHEs who will carry forth the Gravesian legacy beyond Dr. Beck. This was an origins story of a unique nature that continues to inspire new generations and must not be forgotten. Just as Dr. Tanzi three years earlier had put a face to all the ugliness that is Alzheimer's disease, Dr. Graves's unheeded warnings about the psychosocial limitations of the first tier of values suddenly gave the coronavirus a face. The illness is a wildcard that comes from the collective unconscious that has remained in an unprocessed state due to humanity's prolonged entrenchment in the values of subsistence. It reminded me of something Elza used to say about C. G. Jung's observation of the danger of things in the unconscious that we ignore; they come to us as fate.

Reflecting on this material, I became animated again about the work that has defined our lives for the last two decades. I revisited Graves's old writings, looking for findings that can tie his research to the challenges humanity is facing today. In a flash, all the knowledge I had accumulated came rushing back. It reminded me of the uniqueness of the evolutionary mechanisms that decades earlier had led Dr. Graves to call his life-long work *The Never-Ending Quest*. His writings felt as fresh and up to date as if they had been just written.

I decided to write a major piece for an academic publication that made the Gravesian conception current. The piece was entitled "Clare W. Graves Revisited" and was published by *Integral Leadership Review*, the most widely read publication for the followers of Integral Theory and Spiral Dynamics.[4] It dealt primarily with the coevolutionary nature of things and reconfirmed, in scientific terms, what William Shakespeare and other poets and philosophers knew about human nature. Dr. Beck had rephrased the well-known idiom, "cometh the hour, cometh the man," in these terms: "cometh the time, cometh the thinking." The Gravesian simplicity beyond the complexity is this: Humans are equipped with the neuropsychological faculties (Dr. Beck's *thinking*, and the idiom's *man*) to solve our existential problems as they appear (Dr. Beck's *time* and the idiom's *hour*). Dr. Graves called this feature of his model the *double-helix pairing*. He had hypothesized that this relationship between humans and their environment in time is a delicate dance that is coevolutionary in nature; in our quest to solve higher-order existential problems, we trigger the higher circuitry in our neuropsychology that remains dormant until new, higher-order existential problems appear. In the piece, I associate Dr. Grave's evolutionary mechanisms to the challenges we are currently facing and how we have ignored the intricate coupling that defines the coevolutionary process. I call it the *misalignment* and identify two major existential threats we face: The first addresses the insufficient triggering of the collective neuropsychological faculties needed to address the looming threat posed by the Digital Age, and the second is the insufficient triggering of the intelligence needed to address climate change effectively. These two challenges can only be addressed from the value systems of the second tier. The threat posed by the

Digital Age must be addressed from the Yellow level of existence, which is tasked with placing all the lower six systems into an open psychosocial state, integrating their best and healthiest capability into to a trajectory of sustainable, long-term practices. The latter threat of climate change must be addressed from the Turquoise and highest-known level of existence in our model, which places the survival of the planet as its priority and connects everything through ecological alignment.

The pieces I wrote during the quarantine showed me the passion I still have for this work. It is indeed my calling and my bliss, and now I was coming back to it from the nondual place of surrender. But, as months went by, I found myself searching for a deeper spiritual meaning of what was ailing the world. If humanity was indeed bending its knees, then I was feeling its every ache and pain, and I wanted to know why. In years past, Dr. Beck's insights on chronic problems had always been augmented by Elza's psychospiritual wisdom and further deepened by my own meditations that defined balance and wholeness. But now, I profoundly feel Elza's absence from my life as I again find that the nondual quality of my own state of consciousness gets tested repeatedly. Time is cruel, and with every passing day memories of who Elza was and what she represented fade slowly, just as the faces of people in old pictures do over time. The rate at which her condition is deteriorating seems to have slowed down, but I increasingly find less solace and comfort in that knowledge. Our new reality is in constant battle with my memories of her, and it is always the memories that end up losing in this long and cruel war. I have relived them all, from my first sight of her in Miami to the heights of possibility and then to the dreadful day when we discovered her disease. I have listened to every recording of her voice and played every video of her, desperately enticing my other senses to activate their memory cells so that I can continue to remember her and never let her go.

I did it all. I revisited every crevice of our lives together that held each of our memories until there was nothing left that could be forgotten. Or so I thought—until one long-disregarded memory reappeared: On a day when the death toll from the coronavirus set new records, I sat at my desk with a heavy heart, listening to music in an attempt to forget our collective misery. That's when iTunes randomly started to play a recording of Elza that I hadn't heard in over a decade. It was as if the gods had conspired to remind me of the nature of human suffering through words that my soulmate had written long ago. It was poetry rendered against the backdrop of classical Arabic music, and it reminded me of the transcendent realms where poets and saints reside and of the fleeting nature of time, space, and the physical world. The recording immediately transported me to 2003 and the Iraqi war. It reminded me of Elza's divine nature and her transcendent presence that existed before Jean Houston, Ken Wilber and Don Beck, in a realm where mystic poetry and meditation define the eternal nature of her soul and her essence.

Back in 2003, Elza had been deeply affected by images of the battlefields of the Iraqi war. The cries of orphaned children and the starving elderly were being carried daily by Al-Jazeera television into our living room. There is something about stories of horror being told in one's native tongue that carves deeply into one's soul. Elza decided to capture the essence and the pain of Iraqi suffering the only way she knew how—through the universal language of poetry. After a month of deep reflection and meditation, she emerged with an anthology of six poems that chronicle humanity's journey from suffering to oneness. She called it, *You Are the One: Thoughts and Meditations for the World Soul.*[5] The poetry was put to music by Lebanese American composer Paul Hage, whose father, Antione, is a master oud player and performed with one of the Lebanese singer Fairuz's earliest bands. After reading Elza's poems, Antione decided to play all the oud arrangements for the songs.

Below are three of the poems that capture the essence of the soul's spiritual transformation. The first, "Pain and Joy," encourages us to realize the unity of all life and to act on this awareness in whatever way we can. The second, "The Rapture," guides us through the awareness needed to enter our inner temple, where we lose our identity and begin to identify with the Higher Self. The third, "You Are the One," defines that inner temple where we transcend identity and embrace that which is the highest spiritual calling, the universal soul.

Pain and Joy

Now, explore your sensations.
They're like the different colors of the rainbow,
Like the different people and beings in the world.
Reduce your sensation to the one sense,
The white color behind all colors.
Suspend your belief of separateness;
Reduce it to the one in all,
The One Soul, One Spirit.

Lose the boundaries, trust your heart.
Care, love, connect, breathe.
Breathe deeply into unity;
Become this unity.

Building bridges starts with you, in you.
Tolerance of others is nothing
But self-love and acceptance of your limitations.
Caring for the world is caring for the energy
That envelopes you.
Embracing differences and diversity
Is really embracing your beauty,
And your darkness.

Realize that every breath you take
You share with every creature and every living being.
Every child crying in Africa is *your* child.
Every girl raped in Ecuador is *your* daughter.
Every elder starving in Iraq is *your* grandfather.
Every Israeli and Palestinian mother is *your* mother.

Feel the heart of the sea beating in you
And the joy of the bird elating you.
Radiate the calmness of the desert
And the wisdom of the mountains.

Exude generously what God has given you—
Compassion, love, kindness, and forgiveness.
Act in thoughts sleeping within you;
Awaken them; shape them; send them out.
They will come back and replenish you.

The Rapture

You are the music.
Listen and share your symphony.
You are the light; shine upon the world
From the depth of your being
To the mountains of Everest.
Fly, embrace, love, understand,
For your sake, you … you … you.

If you're starving for love, give love.
When you're in pain and looking for kind arms
To wrap around you,
Wrap your soul around the pain in the world.
Let your pain take you to unlimited spaces,
To complete openness and liberation,
Total freedom.
And repeat with the poet. Say:
The deeper pain carves into my soul,
The more joy I can contain.[6]

Then this joy, *your* joy,
Spreads over the lands and into the oceans,
Radiates like the rays of the sun, soars with the eagle,
Dives into the hearts of children,

Heals the wounds of rape and revenge,
Soothes the agony of despair,
Brings hope and trust to a world of
Constant confusion and change.

Take a glimpse at eternity
Lose your name,
Lose your label.
Are you John? Ahmed? Fatima? Or Mary?
Are you a Christian, a Muslim, a Buddhist, or a Jew?
White, or black?
From the East or from the West?
China? India? Jordan? Ghana? Or New York City?

You, my friend, are the Spirit,
You are a universe holding this universe.
Claim your greatness,
Lose your smallness,
Take a leap into your vastness.
Explore yourself.
Get to know you—
All your faces,
All your languages,
All your colors,
All your creeds.
Drop your name;
Carry your wholeness.

You Are the One

You are now reborn in the silence of the spheres,
In the sublime darkness of nature's womb,
And the magnificent rapture of morning light;
In the echo of the song of God,
The divine sounds of angels and deities,
The humble prayer of monks and nuns.

Shine like the light you are,
Smile and rejoice.
You have met the universe,
And it is you, you, you.

You are now the boundless breath,
The soaring spirit that knows no barriers.
You are bewitched! It's too late.
The kiss of love had birthed you
Giving you the ultimate gift of life.
Be the ultimate love.
Be the One.
Be the harmony between the universe,
Nature, and all the people in the world.

The world's soul is now awakened in you.
Say, I am the world's Spirit.
I am all the continents and all the faces,
I *am* the creative intelligence,
The drop in the vast ocean of eternity.
I am the rising of the mightier love,
The enchantment of endless freedom,
The blissful child of the sacred family.

I am him … her … you … me … them.
Him, her, you, me, I.
I am the One, the One.
I am the world's Soul.

Fifteen years have passed since the last time I listened to Elza's poetry. Now I listen to it repeatedly, always finding new meaning between the lines. Oh, how I miss her sweet voice! Strange how the universe works. As disease took away her ability to speak, her poetry pierces through the years to remind me of how fleeting life is and to heal my wounds. As I listen to the melodies in her voice, emotions overtake me as I marvel again at how the enormity of my loss is diminished only by my memory of the riches I have known.

La Jolla, California
Valentine's Day
February 14, 2021

NOTES

Foreword
1. Joseph Campbell, *The Masks of God: Creative Mythology* (New York: Viking, 1964), 4–6 passim.

Chapter One
Epigraph: Jalal ad-Din Rumi, "Rumi Quotes on Love," *Quotes of Islam.* Retrieved November 7, 2019; http://quotesofislam.com/rumi-quotes/.
1. Hal Stone, PhD, and Sidra L. Stone, PhD. *Embracing Our Selves; The Voice Dialog Manual* (Novato, CA: New World Library, 1989), 131-137.
2. Joseph Campbell, *Joseph Campbell and the Power of Myth with Bill Moyers*, ed. Betty Sue Flowers (New York: Doubleday and Co., 1988), 113.

Chapter Two
Epigraph: Samuel Noah Kramer, *From the Poetry of Sumer, Creation, Glorification, Adoration* (London: University of California Press, 1979), 92.
1. See the *Center for Human Emergence, Middle East* (2006–13). Retrieved September 9, 2020; http://www.humanemergencemiddleeast.org.
2. Joseph Campbell, *The Hero with a Thousand Faces* (Princeton: Princeton University Press, 1968), 3.
3. Joseph Campbell, *Joseph Campbell, The Hero's Journey* (Novato: New World Library, 2003), 221.

Chapter Three
Epigraph: Kahlil Gibran, *A Treasury of Kahlil Gibran*, ed. Martin L. Wolf, trans. Anthony Rizcallah Ferris (Secaucus, NJ: The Citadel Press, 1951), 274.

1. Kahlil Gibran, *The Madman: His Parables and Poems* (New York: Alfred A. Knopf, 1918), 7–8.
2. Coleman Barks, *The Essential Rumi* (New York: Harper Collins Publishers, 1995), 281.
3. For a listing of several of Bishop Dawlabani's titles, see https://www.librarycat.org/lib/Beth_Mardutho/search/author/16875421/Hanna+Dolabani.
4. George A. Kiraz, "Sebastian Paul Brock: Haddaya of Syriac Studies," *Journal of Assyrian Academic Studies* 18, no. 1 (2004). Retrieved October 11, 2020; http://jaas.org/edocs/v18n1/Sebastian%20Brcok-Kiraz-Final.pdf.

Chapter Four

Epigraph. Jean Houston, *Jump Time: Shaping Your Future in a World of Radical Change* (Boulder, CO, Sentient Publications, 2004), 290.
1. Elza S. Maalouf, *Emerge! The Rise of Functional Democracy and the Future of the Middle* East (New York: Select Books, 2014), 6-7.
2. Don E. Beck and Said E. Dawlabani, "MEMEnomics through the Framework of Spiral Dynamic: The Eight Stage Spiral of Development," *The MEMEnomics Group* (February, 12, 2013). Retrieved April 18, 2020; http://www.memenomics.com/what-is-memenomics.
3. See "Advisory Board," *Integral Insights*. Retrieved March 12, 2020; http://www.integralinsights.net/advisoryBoard.htm.
4. See "Bernard Lietaer," *Wikipedia* (last updated August 24, 2020). Retrieved September 9, 2020; https://en.wikipedia.org/wiki/Bernard_Lietaer.
5. Don E. Beck, "Six Games to Glory," *Spiral Dynamics Global* (December 15, 2017). Retrieved April 16, 2020; https://www.spiraldynamicsglobal.com/single-post/SixGamestoGlory.
6. Don E. Beck, "Windmills, Tulips, and Fundamentalism," *Center for Human Emergence—The Netherlands* (April 12, 2005). Retrieved April 16, 2020; http://spiraldynamicsintegral.nl/wp-content/uploads/2013/09/Beck-Don-Windmills-Tulips-and-Fundamentalism-Kosmos-2005.pdf.

Chapter Five

Epigraph: Robertson Davies, *The Merry Heart: Reflections on Reading, Writing, and the World of Books* (New York: Viking Press, 1997), 98.
1. Paul Mattick, "Hotfoots of the Gods," *New York Times* (February 15, 1998). Retrieved April 18, 2020; https://www.nytimes.com/books/98/02/15/reviews/980215.15mattict.html.

Chapter Six

Epigraph: Kahlil Gibran, *The Prophet* (New York, Alfred A. Knopf, 1923), 52.

1. Ken Wilber, *Grace and Grit: Spirituality and Healing in the Life and Death of Treya Killam Wilber,* 2nd ed. (Boston: Shambhala Publications, 2000), 35.

Chapter Seven

Epigraph: C. Screechinth, *Musings of Carl Jung* (N.P.: Creative Space Independent Publishing Platform, 2018), 117.

1. Rudy Tanzi and Chris Mann, "Curing Alzheimer's with Science and Song," *TEDxNatick* (March 3, 2017). Retrieved November 23, 2019; https://www.youtube.com/watch?v=iuel1AFKSDo.
2. Ibid.

Chapter Eight

Epigraph: Kirpal Singh, *The Wheel of Life* (Anaheim: Ruhani Satsang-Divine Science of the Soul, 1980), 7–8.

Epilogue

1. Said E. Dawlabani, "What Can Evolution and Spiral Dynamics Tell Us about the Coronavirus?" *Medium* (March 29, 2020). Retrieved February 11, 2021; https://s-dawlabani.medium.com/what-does-evolution-and-spiral-dynamics-tell-us-about-the-coronavirus-1d6d244656ba.
2. Said E. Dawlabani, "Castles in the Sand: Socioeconomics in the Aftermath of the Coronavirus," *Medium* (June 29, 2020). Retrieved February 11, 2021; https://s-dawlabani.medium.com/castles-in-the-sand-socioeconomics-in-the-aftermath-of-the-coronavirus-68d50213cf19.
3. Clare W. Graves, *The Never Ending Quest: Dr. Clare W. Graves Explores Human Nature; A Treatise on an Emergent Cyclical Conception of Adult Behavioral Systems and Their Developemnt.* ed. Christopher Cowan and Natasha Todorovic (Santa Barbara: ECLET Publishing, 2005), 396-400.
4. Said E. Dawlabani, "Clare W. Graves Revisited: Beyond Value Systems; Biocultural Coevolution and the Double Helix Nature of Existence," *Integral Leadership Review* (December 21, 2020). Retrieved February 13, 2021; http://integralleadershipreview.com/17759-12-21-clare-w-graves-revisited-beyond-value-systems-biocultural-co-evolution-and-the-double-helix-nature-of-existence/.

5. Elza Maalouf, *You Are the One: Thoughts and Music for the World Soul,* with music performed and composed by Paul Hage (La Jolla: Selfwork Productions, 2003), compact disc.

6. Derived from the poet Kahlil Gibran: "The deeper that sorrow carves into your being, the more joy you can contain," *Goodreads.* Retrieved February 19, 2021; https://www.goodreads.com/quotes/1175.

SELECTED READINGS

Barks, Coleman. *The Soul of Rumi, A Collection of Ecstatic Poems*. New York: Harper Collins Publishing, 2001.

Beck, Don E. and Christopher C. Cowan. *Spiral Dynamics: Mastering Values, Leadership, and Change*. Malden, MA: Blackwell Publishing, 2005.

Beck, Dr. Don and Graham Linscott. *The Crucible: Forging South Africa's Future*. Johannesburg, South Africa: New Paradigm Press, 1991.

Bredesen, Dale, E., MD. *The End of Alzheimer's: The First Program to Prevent and Reverse Cognitive Decline*. New York: Avery, 2017.

Campbell, Joseph. *The Hero's Journey: Joseph Campbell on His Life and Work*. Edited by Phil Cousineau. Novato: New World Library, 2003.

_____. *The Hero with a Thousand Faces*. New York: Princeton University Press, 1973.

_____. *The Masks of God*. 4 vols. New York: Viking Press, 1959, 1962, 1964, 1968.

Campbell, Joseph and Bill Moyers. *The Power of Myth*. New York: Knopf Doubleday Publishing Group, 2011.

Chopra, Deepak. *How to Know God: The Soul's Journey into the Mystery of Mysteries*. New York: Harmony Books, 2000.

Chopra, Deepak and Rudolph E. Tanzi. *Super Genes: Unlock the Astonishing Power of Your DNA for Optimum Health and Well-Being*. New York: Harmony Books, 2015.

Dance, Richard. *The Education of Adam Speaker, a Philosophical Adventure*. Self-published, 2015.

Dawlabani, Said Elias, *MEMEnomics: The Next Generation Economic System*. New York: Select Books, Inc., 2013.

Frankl, Victor. *Man's Search for Meaning*. Boston: Beacon Press, 1963.

Gibran, Kahlil. *The Madman, His Parables and Poems*. New York: Alfred A. Knopf, 1918.

_____. *The Prophet*. New York: Alfred A. Knopf, 1998.

_____. *A Treasury of Kahlil Gibran*. Edited by Martin L. Wolf. Translated by Anthony Rizcallah Ferris. Secaucus, NJ: The Citadel Press, 1951.

Hafiz, *The Gift*. Translated by Daniel Ladnisky. New York: The Penguin Group, 1999.

Hillman, James. *The Soul's Code: In Search of Character and Calling*. New York: Warner Books, 1997.

Houston, Jean. *Jump Time: Shaping Your Future in a World of Radical Change*. 2nd ed. Boulder: Sentient Publications, 2004.

_____. *A Mythic Life: Learning to Live Our Greater Story*. New York: Harper Collins, 1996.

_____. *The Possible Human: A Course in Enhancing Your Physical, Mental and Creative Abilities*. New York: G.P. Putman's Sons, 1982.

John of the Cross. *The Dark Night of the Soul*. Translated by E. Allison Peers. New York: Doubleday, 1990.

Jung, C. G. *The Archetypes and the Collective Unconscious*. Translated by R. F. C. Hull. New York: Princeton University Press, 1990.

_____. *The Essential Jung*. Edited by Anthony Storr. New York: MJF Books, 1983.

_____. *The Undiscovered Self*. Translated by R. F. C. Hull. New York: New American Library, 1958.

Kornfield, Jack. *After the Ecstasy, the Laundry: How the Heart Grows Wise on the Spiritual Path*. New York: Banton Books, 2000.

Kramer, Samuel Noah. *From the Poetry of Sumer: Creation, Glorification, Adoration*. London: University of California Press, 1979.

Kushner, Harold S. *When Bad Things Happen to Good People*. New York: Schoken Books, 1981.

Lietaer, Bernard and Jacqui Dunne. *Rethinking Money: How New Currencies Turn Scarcity into Prosperity*. San Francisco: Berrett Koehler Publishers, 2013.

Lipton, Bruce H. *The Biology of Belief: Unleashing the Power of Consciousness, Matter, and Miracles*. New York: Hay House, 2016.

_____. *The Honeymoon Effect: The Science of Creating Heaven on Earth*. New York: Hay House, 2013.

Maalouf, Elza S. *Emerge! The Rise of Functional Democracy and the Future of the Middle East*. New York: Select Books, 2014.

Moyne, John and Coleman Barks. *Say I am You, Rumi*. Athens, GA: Maypop, 1994.

Munro, Alice. *Away from Her*. Toronto: Penguin Canada, 2007.

Perera, Sylvia Brinton. *Descent to the Goddess: A Way of Initiation for Women*. Toronto: Inner City Books, 1981.

Reynolds, Marilyn. *'Till Death or Dementia Do Us Part*. Sacramento: River Rock Books, 2017.

Screechinth, C. *Musings of Carl Jung*. N.P.: Creative Space Independent Publishing Platform, 2018.

Singh, Kirpal. *The Way of the Saints*. Tilton, New Hampshire: The Sant Bani Press, 1989.

————. *The Wheel of Life*, Anaheim: Ruhani Satsang-Divine Science of the Soul, 1980.

Stone, Hal, PhD, and Sidra L. Stone, PhD. *Embracing Our Selves: The Voice Dialog Manual*. Novato, CA: New World Library, 1989.

Watts, Alan. *The Way of Zen*. New York: Vintage Books, 1957.

Wilber, Ken. *Grace and Grit: Spirituality and Healing in the Life and Death of Treya Killam Wilber*. 2nd ed. Boston: Shambhala, 2000.

————. *A Theory of Everything: An Integral Vision for Business, Politics, Science, and Spirituality*. Boston: Shambhala, 2001.

Wright, J. Kim. *Lawyers as Changemakers, a Global Integrative Law Movement*. Chicago: ABA Book Publishing, 2016.

INDEX

* Illustrations are indicated with *italics.*

C

Beck, Don, and, 17, 98, 100, 102–103, 109, *115*, *116*, 216, 219
bipolar depression in, 152–153, 156, 165
birthday dinner of, 226
birth of, 20–23
blame and, 189–191
brain cells of, 202
Campbell, Joseph, and, 25–26
certification as personal coach, 91
as certified practitioner in Voice Dialogue, 91
changes in behavior of, 130–131
as Christian, 31, 37
closing of meditation center by, 79–80
coaching work of, in the Middle East, 97
cognitive behavioral therapy for, 148
cognitive decline in, 2, 130, 133, 134–135, 140–141, 155, 159–160, 185–186, 200
combination of rebellion and intelligence in, 18
consultancy work of, 107, 136
CT scans in diagnosing, 163, 164, 165
as cult hero, 37–38
on dark history of traditional Arab marriage, 37
Dawlabani, Said, as caregiver of, 222–223
Dawlabani, Said's courtship of, 63–69, 72–75, 77, 80
decision to leave daughter, Ghinwa, 84
denial over morbidity of multiple diagnoses, 172, 183
depression in, 130–131, 132, 133, 140, 141, 144, 151
descent into the Underworld and, 40
description of, 16
desire to leave Lebanon, 53, 54
desire to return to work, 145–146
desolation and hopelessness in, 28
destruction of books by, 172
divine nature of, 234
double life of, 39
dreams of, 33–34

About the Author

SAID E. DAWLABANI is a leading authority on the application of values systems to large-scale change and the author of the 2013 book, *MEMEnomics: The Next Generation Economic System*. After a career in the real-estate industry, he turned his attention to applying the value-systems framework and its evolutionary consciousness to the dismal field of economics. With his wife, Elza Maalouf, and Dr. Don E. Beck, he is the cofounder of the Center for Human Emergence Middle East. He is a public speaker and academic lecturer on transformational leadership. He lives in La Jolla, California, with Elza and their dog, Lil Buddha.

Elza and Lil Buddha, 2014